P9-DDI-737

PRAISE FOR *THE DECLARATION OF INDEPENDENTS*

"*The Declaration of Independents* is a refreshing political book in that it kind of, well, hates politics, and it's worth reading on this issue alone. . . . An important read with solid insight into today's political mess. . . . Gillespie and Welch are full of optimism for the future."
—RealClearPolitics.com

"An enthusiastic, entertaining libertarian critique of American politics, brimming with derision for the status quo and optimism for the future."
—*Kirkus*

"One of the best written books on this subject and one of the most insightful. . . . Provocative and substantive . . . a book worth reading that can shake up some core assumptions that many Americans maintain."
—Michael Medved, nationally syndicated
talk show host and columnist

"A fun and ultimately positive look at how anti-authoritarianism, entrepreneurship, and independence have led to one revolution after another in the way we think about the world, the products we buy, and the jobs we end up getting (or creating for ourselves). . . . It's a good book, a well-written, easily accessible manifesto on how libertarian ideas and anti-authoritarianism can help change the world, and how they will one way or another, whether we like it or not. Just as importantly, the book is uplifting, optimistic and full of energy."
—Forbes.com

"Refreshingly optimistic. . . . The book succeeds, not least because it gives life to the animating ideas behind this often-misunderstood approach to politics. But, perhaps more importantly, because it reminds those Americans who have grown despondent watching political elites continually jockey for control over the lives of others, recklessly spend taxpayer money, and write, enact and enforce laws that have very little to recommend them, that it doesn't have to be this way."

—*The Daily*

THE DECLARATION OF INDEPENDENTS

THE

DECLARATION *OF* INDEPENDENTS

HOW LIBERTARIAN POLITICS CAN FIX WHAT'S WRONG WITH AMERICA

NICK GILLESPIE & MATT WELCH

PUBLICAFFAIRS
New York

Copyright © 2011 by Nick Gillespie and Matt Welch.

Foreword to the paperback edition copyright © 2012 Nick Gillespie and Matt Welch.

Hardcover first published in the United States in 2011 by PublicAffairs™,
a Member of the Perseus Books Group

Paperback first published in the United States in 2012 by PublicAffairs

All rights reserved.

No part of this book may be reproduced in any manner whatsoever without written
permission except in the case of brief quotations embodied in critical articles and reviews.
For information, address PublicAffairs, 250 West 57th Street, Suite 1321, New York,
NY 10107.

PublicAffairs books are available at special discounts for bulk purchases in the U.S. by
corporations, institutions, and other organizations. For more information, please contact
the Special Markets Department at the Perseus Books Group, 2300 Chestnut Street, Suite
200, Philadelphia, PA 19103, call (800) 810-4145, ext. 5000, or e-mail special.markets
@perseusbooks.com.

Set in Goudy Old Style

The Library of Congress has catalogued the hardcover as follows:

Gillespie, Nick.
The declaration of independents : how libertarian politics can fix what's wrong
with America / Nick Gillespie and Matt Welch.
p.   cm.
Includes bibliographical references and index.
ISBN 978-1-58648-938-0 (hardcover)—ISBN 978-1-58648-939-7 (electronic
book) 1. Libertarianism—United States. I. Welch, Matt, 1968–   II. Title.
JC599.U5G528 2011
320.51'2—dc22   2011008600

ISBN (paperback): 978-1-61039-100-9
ISBN (paperback e-book): 978-1-61039-200-6

To Izidóra—Matt Welch
To Jack and Neal—Nick Gillespie

CONTENTS

PART III
OPERATIONALIZE IT, BABY!

FOREWORD TO THE PAPERBACK EDITION

We're writing this foreword to the paperback edition in spring 2012, months after the presidential primary season got under way in places such as Iowa and New Hampshire, those mythical Brigadoons of the American political process that appear just once every four years and momentarily assume an archetypal representativeness of the nation that's directly inverse to their small population and actual influence. As an incumbent president, Barack Obama is sitting pretty (and on top of hundreds of millions of campaign dollars that he has not yet begun to spend). On the Republican side, the battle for the nomination has been longer and more drawn-out than expected.

As Herman Cain could tell you—if anyone could find him these days—predicting partisan politics is a mug's game. Just last fall, the former Godfather's Pizza magnate and talk-radio personality was barreling full-speed ahead toward becoming the second consecutive African American president of these United States. There was no stopping the "Cain Train," and a country weary of recession and bailouts and partisan gridlock was jumping aboard the irresistible bandwagon of a man given to quoting lines from the cartoon series *Pokémon.*

Cain's mighty campaign was derailed first by what even his supporters knew all along but refused to acknowledge: other than a winning personality, he had no qualifications for the job he was seeking. His "9-9-9" tax plan seemed more like a pizza-delivery deal than a serious revenue program, and YouTube proved too cruel a mirror, showing Cain blanking on just whose *side* President Obama favored in Libya. Multiple policy-related brain burps combined quickly with revelations of past legal settlements for sexually inappropriate behavior (and a former mistress going public) to send the social conservative packing not just from the 2012 election but from public view altogether.

Other Republican candidates—Texas governor Rick Perry, Minnesota representative Michele Bachmann, among others—experienced poll-topping boomlets that popped as quickly and decisively as Charlie Sheen's promotional tour for tiger blood. Such is partisan politics, more transitory than a shooting star, less substantive than a butterfly's wings. Remember this the next time you catch the onetime darling of the 2008 election cycle, actor and former Tennessee senator Fred Thompson, pitching reverse mortgages at 2 AM on the least-watched channels in your cable or satellite package.

Yet if partisan politics are as volatile as the future of the euro on any given Monday, the longer-term trends described in *The Declaration of Independents* have only become clearer since the hardcover was published in the summer of 2011.

The essential starting point of our analysis is that—for perfectly rational reasons, and mirroring what's happening in the broader culture—fewer of us want to define ourselves as Democrats or Republicans. According to Gallup and based on 20,000 interviews during 20 polls in 2011, "a record-high 40 percent of Americans identify as Independent." The decline in party loyalty has been continuing since the early 1970s and, unlike the Cain Train, it's not getting derailed. "Voters bolt top political parties," announced *USA Today* on the front page of its December 23–26, 2011, weekend edition. "More than 2.5 million voters have left the Democratic and Republican parties since the 2008 election, while the number of independent voters continues to grow," wrote Richard Wolf, further noting that the trend toward disaffiliation from Team Red and Team Blue is most "acute in states that are key to the [2012] presidential race." This "decades-long trend" means that, like every other recent national election, the winner will be, in the words of North Carolina elections director Gary Bartlett, "whoever is attractive to the unaffiliated voter."

Without making a huge fuss about it, voters have been declaring their independence for a very long time. As they slough off conventional political identities, they continue to embrace the seemingly endless shift toward increasingly personalized lifestyle options and choices available to them in their nonpolitical lives. Down the street from our offices in Washington, DC's Dupont Circle is a burger joint that recently installed a soda machine that allows diners to customize whatever they're drinking. You can start with caffeine-free Coke, say, and add a shot of vanilla and raspberry, then top it off with orange soda or even, God forbid, Mr. Pibb. Such indiscriminate mixing and mongrelizing is totally up to you.

That proliferation of relatively banal choices extends to far more important ones: survey after survey, poll after poll show increasing margins of Americans becoming more tolerant and pluralistic about their neighbors' choices in sexual partners, religious preference, and use of marijuana (a majority of the country, for the first time, now believes that pot prohibition, like liquor prohibition before it, is bad policy). Last fall, Gallup found that fewer than half of Americans believe "the government should promote traditional values in society," a finding that is consistent with a steady decline in public support since October 2001 for the government playing this role. Where once there was a single way of living respectably (or peacefully) among your neighbors, there are now as many choices as you can imagine, whether we're talking about varieties of Pop-Tarts or varieties of people.

In other words, the sour economy has not soured our libertarian impulses toward an ethos of live and let live. The purpose of this book is to marry that thoroughgoing embrace of individualization, personalization, and experimentation to the policies that govern too many of our most important decisions: where our kids go to school, how we find (and pay for) health care, how we plan our retirements, and more. Since publication of the hardcover edition of this book, the country's mood has turned darker toward politicians and politics. Last fall, Gallup found that 56 percent of Americans felt the federal government had "too much power" versus just 8 percent saying it had "too little" (35 percent thought it had "about the right amount"). At the same time, levels of support for bailouts, stimulus spending, and President Obama's health-care reform have all been sliding.

That general and growing discontent with government undergirds at least to some extent the Occupy Wall Street movement, which didn't exist when *The Declaration of Independents* was first published. Although smaller in number and more confrontational in tactics than the Tea Party (discussed at length in Chapter 11, "The Permanent Nongoverning Minority"), the left-leaning protesters in New York, DC, Oakland, and other cities around the country share with their right-leaning counterparts the same outrage at preferential treatment for politically connected businesses, industries, and constituencies. You might think that savvy politicians of whatever stripe would pick up on what has long been evident to everyone outside the Boston–New York–Washington corridor: the Troubled Asset Relief Program (TARP) and related bailouts to particular parts of the economy (ranging from automakers to green-energy outfits) don't play well with the great unwashed for the simple reason that they offend our sense of basic fairness. That the bailouts have not helped the economy is surely another reason for opposition. With the exception of lonely pols such as Ron Paul, astonishingly few top-level officeholders get that basic point.

Where the Occupy movement splits from the Tea Party—probably fatally, as a long-term political and cultural movement—is that its attacks on bailouts for "the 1 percent," or Wall Street, or whomever, have typically been followed by me-too demands. Protests against funneling taxpayer dollars to "banksters" are immediately drowned out by calls for student-loan forgiveness, free health care, jobs for life, or, in the most extreme cases, the abolition of money altogether and a return to a barter economy.

As we discuss, the new technologies that have powered up protest politics from the antiwar movement in the early 2000s to today's marijuana legalization movement to the Tea Party work best when tightly organized around a single issue, not a bundle of overlapping and often mutually exclusive positions that define traditional coalitional politics. Once Howard Dean shifted from being an antiwar candidate to being an antiwar, antibusiness, anti-whatever candidate, his insurgency lost its animating force and unique selling proposition. And when, again like Dean, the protest bloc ends up in a mutual love fest with one of the two major political parties (as happened with Occupy LA and the highly progressive Los Angeles City Council), that's when radical movements disappear and legacy political apparatuses lumber on into our increasingly broke future.

Groups such as the Tea Party or Occupy can only remain viable to the extent they remain independent from establishment parties. In effect, they must hold the parties hostage to votes that would not merely not be cast but thrown in the direction of unelectable candidates who hold unorthodox views on the issues that are most mangled by both parties when in power. Given the ways that traditional Democratic special interests, especially organized labor in the form of the Service Employees International Union (SEIU), are working to influence the Occupy movement, it seems highly unlikely that the group will play a decisive role in 2012 or beyond. The Tea Party, which clearly tipped the 2010 midterm elections toward small-government candidates in dozens of congressional races, faces a similar challenge. If it is to remain potent, the small-government uprising on the right must continue to stiff-arm the GOP unless and until Republicans finally begin to spend less at all levels of government.

Which brings us to a final reflection on developments since *The Declaration of Independents* was first published. For us, the most surprising response to the book was what readers and reviewers universally characterized as our unbridled optimism, a sense that the world, for all its problems, was getting better and better. The *Washington Post*'s George Will cheered us on as "incurably upbeat journalists," while former George H. W. Bush adviser James Pinkerton, writing in *The American Conservative*, largely dismissed *Declaration* as an out-of-touch "survey of human history inexorably chugging toward Liberty Station." At every one of our speaking engagements, readers would either thank us for offering a reprieve from doom-and-gloom scenarios or upbraid us for our unrealistic enthusiasm.

When we sat down to write this book, we didn't realize just how rare it was to have generally positive thoughts both about the recent past (especially the 1970s) and the future (*despite* politics, not because of them, of course). In our epilogue, we unironically entertain the hope that the "future's so bright, I gotta wear shades," especially if the concrete policy steps we lay out in these pages are taken seriously. If that marks us as odd ducks in a realm of discourse where the body politic is treated to routine warnings of Apocalypse Forever should the other guys win the latest midterm, then so be it. Part of escaping the pit beneath the two-party pendulum is not just to deny but to actively laugh at a hyperventilating political world in which national weatherization programs and banning the construction of mosques are treated like urgent national priorities. At the same time, we want to emphasize that public policy dead-ends can in fact be escaped, often more quickly and easily than we dare to hope. As Václav Havel, whose funeral in December 2011 included a stirring set by the once-banned rock group Plastic People of the Universe, put it at the end of his famous 1978 essay "The Power of the Powerless," "The real question is whether the brighter future is really always so distant. What if, on the contrary, it has been here for a long time already, and only our own blindness and weakness has prevented us from seeing it around us and within us, and kept us from developing it?"

Still, on one major issue, we do plead guilty to excessive optimism. We thought that more Americans, especially the earnest ones who fill our city halls, statehouses, and federal legislature, more fully grokked the unsustainability of the twenty-first century's endless spending increases. Consider just the federal level. In constant 2005 dollars, the government spent about $1.85 trillion in 1991, an amount that rose slightly to $2.1 trillion in 2001. In 2010, the total was $3.1 trillion. Although the federal government has not (and will not) pass a budget for the third straight year in 2012, the two main plans currently on the table envision spending either $4.9 trillion or $5.8 trillion (in current dollars) in 2022. The feds are already borrowing about 40 cents of each dollar they spend and there is simply no credible way to generate the revenue for even the lower of those two numbers (which represents the dreams of the supposedly small-government Republican party). Financing government spending through massive borrowing, inflation, or anything other than raising the necessary revenue to pay for it in the here and now is not just bad economic policy but a form of theft from our children and grandchildren, who will be stuck with the tab for meals they never ate and toys they never played with.

When we first started thinking about writing *The Declaration of Independents*, we thought the conversation about reducing the size and scope of government—about getting the government out of the bedroom and the boardroom, about spending less but doing more for the truly needy, about ending failed nation-building abroad and domestically—was much further along than it is. The recognition that we're only at the start of that vital and necessary discussion, rather than in the middle of it or, heaven forbid, near its conclusion, gives us serious cause for pause—though never for pessimism or resignation.

Nick Gillespie
Matt Welch
March 2012

PURSUING HAPPINESS, NOT POLITICS

When was the last time you read the Declaration of Independence? Go ahead and call it up; give it a quick scan—we'll wait. Focus less on the detailed bill of particulars against King George ("He has called together legislative bodies at places unusual, uncomfortable, and distant"!), disregard completely the bit about "the merciless Indian savages," and concentrate instead on the two majestic, throat-clearing paragraphs at the top. Particularly this, the most influential English-language formulation of liberty, written during the 1700s: "We hold these truths to be self-evident, that all men are created equal, that they are endowed by their Creator with certain unalienable rights, that among these are life, liberty and the pursuit of happiness."

You don't have to be one of those guys who dresses up in knee breeches and tricornered hats on the Fourth of July to feel, lo these many years later, the refreshing blast of radical Enlightenment thought contained within those three dozen words. Here is the source code not just for the revolutionary moment being heralded but for the very notion that individual rights precede—and therefore should be explicitly protected from—government. Jefferson and the other signers based their righteous complaints of injustice on the foundational insight that we are all born not just naked but equal and free, laying more than the groundwork for the bloody business at hand. They created a self-replicating sequence that led to the assertion in 1848 by the radicals at Seneca Falls that women were part of the deal and the deliverance, as well as to what Martin Luther King called, nearly two centuries later, the "promissory note" of full civil rights for the descendants of Jefferson's slaves. The world would never be the same. And by enumerating three specific unalienables at the top of the don't-tread-on-me list, these eighteenth-century hotheads laid out some intellectual bread crumbs for those of us looking for a fresh way out of the desultory state of American affairs in this to-date-disappointing twenty-first century.

Note what Button Gwinnett, Caesar Rodney, Richard Stockton, and all the other signers did not include on the short list of worthy endeavors no government should thwart. The document says nothing about pursuing politics. It does not read, "Life, liberty, and the watching of *Meet the Press*." No, the men chafing and gnawing at the crown's leash elevated above all other pursuits the quest for *happiness*, as defined by each individual, by his own lights. It was a declaration-within-the-Declaration that existential meaning derives neither from the whims of a sovereign nor from enlistment in some grand national project or even humble civic initiative but rather from the most atomized level of being: the personal, private, idiosyncratic human heart. Liberty was both a means and a destination—a process and a goal worthier than specific policy results. Happiness was aspirational; it was all about the journey, the pursuit.

In 2011, we do not equate happiness with politics; the mere juxtaposition of the words feels obscene. And for good reason: Politics, as John Adams's great-grandson Henry famously observed, "has always been the systematic organization of hatreds." Every election cycle—and we are always in an election cycle—we are urged to remember that deep down inside we really despise the opposing gang of crooks. We hate their elite (or Podunk) ways, their socialist (or fascist) economics, their reliance on shadowy billionaires with suspect agendas. In a world where mutual gains from trade have lifted a half billion people out of poverty in just the past half decade, politics is one of the last remaining zero-sum games of I win, you lose, where the victor gets to spend everyone else's money in ways that appall the vanquished, until they switch places again after the next election. We instinctively know that our tax dollars aren't being spent efficiently; the proof is in the post office, or the permitting offices at city hall, or the neighborhood school. We roll our eyes when President Barack Obama announces a new national competitiveness initiative in his State of the Union address just five years after George W. Bush announced a new American Competitiveness Initiative in his, or when each and every president since Richard Milhous Nixon swears that this time we're gonna kick that foreign-oil habit once and for all. And yet, the political status quo keeps steering the Winnebago of state further and further into the ditch.

A growing majority of us have responded to the stale theatrics of Republican and Democratic misgovernance by making a rational choice. We ignore politics most of the time and instead pursue happiness by falling in love, starting a home business, making mashups on YouTube, going back to school, bumming around Europe for a year or three, playing fantasy baseball, or tricking out our El Caminos. Through these pursuits we eventually find almost everything that is wonderful and transformative about our modern lives: the Internet, travel, popular (and unpopular) music, the spread of freedom and prosperity around the globe. The Declaration's most famous pursuit has delivered specific outcomes that eighteenth-century minds could not have divined, though the insight was there all along: People acting peacefully, mostly left to their own devices and not empowered by the state to force others into servitude, will create riches far more meaningful and vast than the cramped business of tax-collecting, regulation-spewing, do-as-I-say-or-else governments.

As robust and infinitely varied as our private universes may be, however, they no longer provide a reliable refuge from the destructive force of politics. Today, there is only one real policy issue facing the country, and unfortunately it threatens each and every one of us, even (especially?) those of us not yet born: We are out of money. At least forty-eight of the fifty states are running shortfalls, many of them staggering. Cities, counties, and states are on the hook for an estimated half trillion dollars' worth of pension promises for which they haven't socked away any money. New Jersey can't build tunnels, California pays more in debt service than it does in funding its once-enviable universities, and the president's home state of Illinois is in receivership. The U.S. budget situation is much worse than that of Greece, a country that has been wracked with violence and instability after bondholders refused to keep propping up its fiscal fantasyland. We are one sharp turn in international market sentiment away from a crisis none of us has ever lived through.

The president himself says we're confronting "an untenable fiscal situation"; yet, in the face of a $1.5 trillion deficit and a decade-long spending binge that hiked federal outlays by 62 percent in real terms, he cannot screw up the courage to suggest more than $400 billion worth of spending cuts—over the next ten years. Meanwhile, the allegedly limited-government Republicans refuse to get anywhere near a "radical" plan from Rep. Paul Ryan to balance the budget by 2063. It is a bizarre snapshot in time, in which sizable majorities think the government is doing too much and spending too much, where bailout-supporting Democrats and Republicans alike were bounced out of office in 2010 by a new Tea Party movement centered on cutting the size and scope of government, and where even Federal Reserve Chairman Ben Bernanke, nicknamed "Helicopter Ben" for his belief that showering down fiat currency will solve all economic woes, is saying, "If current policy settings are maintained . . . the federal budget will be on an unsustainable path." Yet, *still* the prospect of imminent fiscal catastrophe is not focusing minds in Washington or in the fifty state capitals or in countless town halls on the need to change politics-as-usual. It is a turbulent moment, one that cannot, by definition, last much longer as is. Something has got to give.

This is another reason to reread your Declaration, especially the first ten words: "When, in the course of human events, it becomes necessary . . ." Sadly, it has become necessary to become political. We didn't want to get into politics, but politics got into us. The country is flat broke, the economy is in miserable shape, we're still fighting two wars, the Social Security "trust fund" is now in permanent deficit, and all this debt-financed bounty will get even more expensive as foreign and domestic investors lose their appetite to lend us more money. The normal course of human events may be to pursue our private happiness as we see fit, but in 2011 we are in urgent need of course correction.

The moment does not call for dumping tea into Boston Harbor, or taking up arms against the Redcoats (the Red Sox are another matter altogether), or, God forbid, canvassing your neighborhood to elect the next Christine O'Donnell or Alvin Greene. The moment calls for political engagement, to be sure, but not traditional partisan activity.

That original American source code contains something worth pondering today. What if the private pursuit of happiness is the way to address the problems that have become necessary to solve? What if we were to foist the lessons, creativity, openness, and fun of our fantabulous nongovernmental modern world onto the unwilling and unaffordable bureaucracies keeping us down? What if we were to declare independence, not from a country or government but from the two political parties that have been dividing up the spoils for far too long?

Welcome to *The Declaration of Independents*. We've been expecting you. Maybe you are now, or will soon be, a member of what has become over the past forty years the largest bloc of American voters: independents. You have an unfavorable opinion of Congress, and you don't think too kindly about bailing out Wall Street and car companies, letting Big Pharma write the new health-care law, or having the Federal Communications Commission regulate the Internet. Yet, this sort of thing keeps on happening. Why?

This book intends, in part, to document the fact that the two major parties are not what they say and that you are right to be angry with their false claims about core beliefs. It is a shock to tender ears, we realize, but by any meaningful yardstick, Democrats do not care about free speech, and Republicans do not care about free enterprise. They are much more concerned with convincing you that the other guy is a Nazi than they are about relaxing government's control over activities it has no business meddling in. Political independence in and of itself is a private and public virtue, with potency that only grows with each passing year. Thinking for yourself is much more work than setting your compass by the direction of the tribe, but, oh, the liberation. Suddenly the world looks a good deal more ridiculous, tawdry, and intellectually beatable. And the same technologies that have jazzed up the rest of our lives and roiled every American industry you can name have made it exponentially easier for like-minded single-issue coalitions to swarm together and wreak holy havoc on a political establishment that hates, above all else, uncertainty.

The Declaration of Independents aims to let you know that you're not crazy, that there are people out there who might not agree with you on everything but who share your distaste for twenty-first-century politics and your fear about the fiscal guillotine careening toward our necks. In fact, these people—some Democrats, some Republicans, some independents, and some part of an increasingly familiar subspecies known as libertarians—have been among us all along, laying down their own source code for life, liberty, and the pursuit. Because history is written mostly by people who love politics, we know far less than we should about the trailblazers who have made life richer and more democratic for all Americans over the past forty years, in part by prying apart the clenched fist of government.

Yet, the revolutionary actions of these cultural, technological, and business innovators—the folks who created everything from the Pill, to venti macchiatos, to Wikipedia, to you name it—suggest a bold way out of our current mess, one that embraces rather than rejects the fact that Americans are the most culturally diverse people in the world and that we have an abiding faith that the pursuit of happiness will create a world that is richer, more interesting, and goddamned breathtaking in its particulars. Eventually, those same forces and insights that democratized our lives by decentralizing power to the individual will come knocking at the front door of a seemingly immovable political status quo. First, though, we have to realize that even the most permanent-looking bureaucracy isn't remotely permanent at all.

THE DECLARATION OF INDEPENDENTS

PART I

THE END OF THE WORLD AS YOU KNOW IT

CHAPTER 1

BEYOND DUOPOLY

The human brain is capable of memorizing 67,890 digits of pi, composing side two of *Exile on Main Street*, and inventing a dog-to-human translation device called the Bowlingual. Yet, we often brilliant, always innovating bipeds find it impossible to imagine changing the trajectory of the world we think we live in by more than a few degrees at any given moment. Whatever dominates today we assume will dominate tomorrow. This is true for our private lives, this is true for commerce, and this is especially true for politics.

Tectonic shifts in the course of human events are almost never predicted ahead of time, even by the very terra changers who stomp on the cracks. When asked in August 1989, only a few months after the electrifying demonstrations in Tiananmen Square, whether the communist East Bloc would ever be democratic and free in his lifetime, Czech economist Vàclav Klaus said no. Less than five months later, he was the first finance minister of a free Czechoslovakia. Morgan Stanley trader Howie Hubler lost $9 billion on a single stock market bet in 2007, not because he didn't think the bubble of mortgage-backed derivative securities would pop but because he couldn't conceive of the price reduction exceeding 8 percent. For all but the last ten days of 2007, the famed Iowa Electronic Markets (IEM) trading system for predicting major-party presidential nominees established as its clear Republican favorite famous ex-mayor of New York Rudy Giuliani. Yet, when it came time for people to actually vote in the primaries and caucuses, Giuliani lost in more than forty states to Ron Paul, a mostly obscure obstetrician-congressman whose name never even showed up on IEM's 2008 election trading board despite his ending up with the fourth greatest number of delegates. Massive, fast-paced change, whether liberational, destructive, or just plain weird, is always and everywhere underpriced.

You may have heard of *confirmation bias*, whereby people choose to notice and believe whatever rumors, news stories, and quasi-academic studies confirm their basic worldview. Well, get your mind around *existence bias*, where the mere fact of a person's, business's, political party's, or country's existence is taken as unspoken and unchallenged proof that the same entity will exist in largely the same form tomorrow, the next day, the next month, the next decade, forever and ever, amen—this despite the fact that the Western world, and the United States in particular, stands out in the history of *Homo sapiens* as the most vigorous producer of constant, dynamic change. Dig up the time capsules for every decade preceding us, and you'll find retrospectively laughable anxieties about seemingly intractable threats that no longer exist.

At the dawn of the new millennium, for example, the overwhelming majority of media observers agonized over how mere mortals could cope with the advent of the new Big Brother–style corporate behemoth called AOL Time Warner. As it turned out, the company set new records for financial losses before disbanding altogether. A decade before that, the question wasn't whether the Japanese would own and operate the U.S. economy but whether the American workplace would be free of insidious group calisthenics led by Toshiro Mifune types. The graduating class of 1980 could not imagine a world without inflation and the growing communist threat, and its 1970 counterpart forecasted constant Southeast Asian war fed by an endless military draft.

In 2011, it's tempting to give in to the pessimism and existence bias of the moment. Unemployment has reached levels not seen since the 1978–1982 recession, and unlike in that era of Federal Reserve Bank–imposed austerity via heightened interest rates, the economy has not been dosed with any medicine that hints at a better tomorrow. Debts and deficits are reaching levels not seen since World War II, when, as you might recall, we were fighting a world war—against Hitler. And as bad as the current fiscal picture looks, there is rare unanimity across the discipline of economics—as well as inside the administration, from President Barack Obama on down—about one singularly unhappy fact: As the first wave of the baby boomers born between 1946 and 1964 start to retire and go on the public dole, things will only get much, much worse.

Yet there is a glowing ember of real hope in this gloomy picture, and it lies, paradoxically, right alongside our inability to detect it. The same revolutionary forces that have already upended much of American commerce and society over the past forty years, delivering us not just from yesterday's bogeymen but into a futuretastic world of nearly infinite individual choice, specialization, and autonomy, are at long last beginning to buckle the cement under the most ossified chunk of American life: politics and government. A close if idiosyncratic reading of recent U.S. history gives us a blueprint for how to speed up that process of creative destruction in the realm of public policy. Because it's not true that nobody predicted such history-altering innovations as the Internet, successful and nonviolent resistance to totalitarianism, and the home-brewing renaissance, among a thousand other happy developments in the modern world. If we listen carefully to the theoreticians and practitioners who helped midwife these giant leaps toward the decentralization of power and the democratization of mankind, they have some surprisingly consistent things to say about changing or working around restrictive regimes and—above all—altering the mind-set that tolerates and perpetuates them. As any revolutionary will testify, there are structural impediments galore to our personal and global pursuit of happiness. Before we can sweep those roadblocks away, we have to declare our independence from the forces that conspire to keep us less than free and recognize that the status quo has no inalienable right to keep on keeping on.

Nothing in twenty-first-century life seems as archaic, ubiquitous, and immovable as the Republican and Democratic parties, two nineteenth-century political groupings that divide up the spoils of a combined $6.4 trillion annually in forcibly extracted taxpayer money at the federal, state, county, and municipal levels. While rhetorically and theoretically at odds with one another at any micromoment in time, the two parties manage to create a mostly unbroken set of policies and governance structures that benefit well-connected groups at the expense of the individual. Americans have watched, with a growing sense of alarm and alienation, as first a Republican, then a Democratic, administration has flouted public opinion by bailing out banks, nationalizing the auto industry, expanding war in Central Asia, throwing yet more good money after bad to keep housing prices artificially high, and prosecuting a drug war no one outside federal government pretends is comprehensible, let alone winnable. It is easy to look upon this well-worn rut of political affairs and despair.

But what if that is existence bias talking? What if the same elements that extend the incumbents' advantage threaten to hasten their demise? Luckily, economists have a particular fondness for studying what Democrats and Republicans have become: the longest-lived duopoly in American history. Remember *A Beautiful Mind*, the story of the madly brilliant Nobel Prize–winning economist John Forbes Nash? Nash was all about duopolies, coming up with an "equilibrium" theory explaining that two powerful competitors frequently end up locked in a stable, mutually beneficial dance of tit-for-tat strategy. Experimental economists, who love crafting duopoly simulations, tend to be less conclusive, finding that duopolists' behavior largely depends on unique circumstances. But while the Nash equilibrium and its descendants are useful in explaining how duopolies collude with one another to carve up captive markets, such formulas generally fail to address the most interesting moment of all: how customer-unfriendly collusion produces an inevitable consumer revolt and technology sweeps one or more of the dominant players into the dustbin of history.

In a widely circulated 2009 paper surveying the vast economic literature on the topic, the late Larry F. Darby presented a list of classic duopolies for discussion. Tellingly, several no longer existed, including MCI and AT&T (MCI, then known as WorldCom, became history's largest bankruptcy in 2003) and Macy's and Gimbels (Gimbels was the country's—and the world's—dominant department store chain in the 1930s; it ceased to exist in 1987). As such examples illustrate, there is nothing inherently stable about two organizations dominating a particular market in the hurly-burly of modern American life. In fact, there is plenty of reason to suspect that such arrangements are, if anything, unstable—particularly if and when technology allows captive consumers to flee.

It's worth taking a closer look at a single such case, one of the duopolies on Darby's list: Kodak and Fujifilm. Like the Democratic Party with the House of Representatives, Kodak was, for much of the twentieth century, synonymous with color photography. We even dreamed in company terms: Memories captured on film were "Kodak moments," and the Dow Jones Industrial Average listed

Eastman Kodak for more than seven decades. At one point the company enjoyed an amazing 96 percent share of the U.S. market for photographic film. Such was its dominance that the federal government sued Kodak for antitrust violations not once but twice, producing out-of-court settlements in 1921 and 1954. As recently as 1994, long after Japan's Fujifilm had entered the scene, the Justice Department argued that the antitrust settlements should remain in force, since Kodak had "long dominated" the industry, still enjoyed a U.S. market share of around 75 percent, and could "greatly outsell its rivals despite charging a higher price" (careful observers and participants of capitalism may notice in that latter claim a wonderful market opportunity).

Fujifilm began competing with Kodak globally in the 1970s and seriously in the United States after the 1984 Olympics. Though always the junior partner on Kodak's home turf, the conglomerate held its own enough that the duopoly soon attracted academic studies such as "Entry, Its Deterrence, and Its Accommodation," "Vertical Restraints and Market Access," and "Advertising Collusion in Retail Markets." The underlying assumption was that you could assume the duopoly's equilibrium for the foreseeable future. Even those who noticed Kodak faltering in the late 1990s at the dawn of the digital age were still apt to say, as *Fortune* magazine did, "The Kodak brand remains solid gold, and its quality is not in dispute." No one could conceive of a photography world without Kodak playing its customary leading role.

This, stunningly, is no longer true. Eastman Kodak share prices tumbled from $60 in 2000 to $40 in 2001, then to $10 in 2008; by 2011, they were below the $4 mark. The Dow Jones kicked the stock off its bedrock industrial average in 2004. Kodachrome—subject not just of a hit Paul Simon song but of the 1954 antitrust settlement that the federal government was trying to maintain four decades later—vanished from stores in 2009, and developers stopped processing the stuff for good on New Year's Day 2011. The company has closed scores of plants, laid off more than 10,000 employees, and reported quarterly losses for years on end.

What happened? Technological advances gave consumers choices that Kodak's fat bureaucracy was unwilling to provide. Writing in the *Wall Street Journal* in November 2006, William M. Bulkeley explained how the implications of this insight ranged far afield from the world of processing photographs:

> Photography and publishing companies shouldn't be surprised when digital technology upends their industries. After all, their business success relied on forcing customers to buy things they didn't want. Photo companies made customers pay for 24 shots in a roll of film to get a handful of good pictures. Music publishers made customers buy full CDs to get a single hit song. Encyclopedia publishers made parents spend thousands of dollars on multiple volumes when all they wanted was to help their kid do one homework paper. The business models required customers to pay for detritus to get the good stuff. . . . Eastman Kodak and Fuji Photo Film had a highly profitable duopoly for 20 years before digital cameras came along. They never dreamed customers would quickly abandon film and prints.

When given real choice, especially the choice to go elsewhere, consumers will drop even the most beloved of brands for options that enhance their experience and increase their autonomy. We have all witnessed and participated in this revolutionary transfer of loyalty away from those who tell us what we should buy or think and toward those who give us tools to think and act for ourselves. No corner of the economy, of cultural life, or even of our personal lives hasn't felt the gale-force winds of this change.

Except government.

Think of any customer experience that has made you wince or kick the cat. What jumps to mind? Waiting in multiple lines at the Department of Motor Vehicles. Observing the bureaucratic sloth and lowest-common-denominator performance of public schools, especially in big cities. Getting ritually humiliated going through airport security. Trying desperately to understand your doctor bills. Navigating the permitting process at your local city hall. Wasting a day at home while the gas man fails to show up. Whatever you come up with, chances are good that the culprit is either a direct government monopoly (as in the providers of K–12 education) or a heavily regulated industry or utility where the government is the largest player (as in health care).

Unlike government and its subentities, Kodak can't count on a guaranteed revenue stream: If consumers abandon its products, sales will be zero, and the company will disappear. The history of private-sector duopolies and even monopolies is filled with such seemingly sudden disappearing acts: The A&P supermarket chain—if you're under forty years old, you probably haven't even heard of it— enjoyed a U.S. market share of 75 percent as recently as the 1950s. Big-box music retailers and bookstores were supposed to bestride the land like colossi at the turn of our new century, but Virgin megastores have all but disappeared, and Borders has just gone bankrupt. Dominant newspapers in one-paper towns were able to book some of the economy's highest profit margins for four decades—more than 20 percent a year, on average, positively dwarfing such hated industrial icons as Walmart—yet with the explosion of Web-based competition, these onetime mints are now among the least attractive companies in the economy.

There is a positive correlation between an organization's former dominance and its present inability to cope with twenty-first-century change. As technology business consultant Nilofer Merchant has aptly put it, "The Web turns old industries on their head. Industries that have had monopolies or highly profitable duopolies are the ones most likely to be completely gutted when a more powerful, more efficient system comes along." This book is about hastening the inevitable arrival of that more efficient system on the doorstep of America's most stubborn, foot-dragging, reactionary sector—government at the local, state, and especially federal levels—and its officially authorized customer-hating agents, the Democrats and Republicans.

We believe the most important long-term trend in American politics is the four-decade leak in market share by the country's political duopoly. In 1970, the Harris Poll asked Americans, "Regardless of how you may vote, what do you usually consider yourself—a Republican, a Democrat, an Independent, or some other party?" Fully 49 percent of respondents chose Democrat, and 31 percent called themselves Republicans. In 2009, those figures were 36 percent for Democrats and 26 percent for Republicans. The only real growth market in politics is voters who decline political affiliation, with independents increasing from 20 percent of respondents to 31 percent. These findings are fully consistent with Gallup surveys as well. In January 2011, Gallup released its latest study on the question of political affiliation and reported that the Democrats were at their lowest point in twenty-two years (31 percent), while the GOP remained stuck below the one-third mark at 29 percent. The affiliation now with the highest marks? Independent, at 38 percent and growing.

Voters free from the affiliation of party membership are more inclined to view political claims with the skepticism they so richly deserve, to hear the dog whistle of tribal political calls as deliberate attacks on the senses rather than rousing calls to productive action. By refusing to confer legitimacy on the two accepted forms of political organization and discourse, they also hint strongly that another form is gathering to take their place.

When duopolies bleed share of a captive market, something potentially revolutionary is afoot. The Bush-Obama era of bailout economics and perennially deferred pain has produced a political backlash that has been evident every time voters have had an opportunity to vent. When blue-state California was allowed in May 2009 to pass judgment on its political class, via a five-part budget-fix referendum (including "onetime" infusions of income tax and lottery proceeds) that a nearly unanimous cross section of major politicians, newspapers, and interest groups supported, the slate lost by an average of thirty percentage points, despite opponents being outspent by an average of seven to one. Eight months later, unknown Republican Scott Brown won Teddy Kennedy's old Senate seat in a three-to-one Democrat Massachusetts. Congressmen mostly canceled their traditional August town hall meetings in 2010 after getting too many earfuls in 2009, GOP establishment candidates for Senate were upended by Tea Party insurgents from Delaware to Kentucky to Nevada, and at the several antigovernment rallies the two of us have attended, protesters have been most enthusiastic when declaring their lack of major-party affiliation.

For the first time in recent memory, participants in the political process, many of them newly engaged, are openly imagining and pushing for a world other than the one they currently live in. A certain spell is on the verge of breaking, with impacts we can only guess at.

In considerably graver circumstances, Václav Havel wrote about a similar, if more severe, phenomenon. The year was 1975, the regime was totalitarian, and the writer was about the only human on the planet who foresaw the process by which communism could suddenly collapse. Greengrocers in Prague, Havel noted in his essay "The Power of the Powerless," displayed "Workers of the World, Unite" signs in their store windows as part of the "dictatorship of the ritual," in which ideological statements no one pretends to believe in are mandated under threat of force to keep citizens too demoralized to effect political change. But what if, suddenly, people stopped going through the motions? "The entire pyramid of totalitarian power, deprived of the element that binds it together, would collapse in upon itself, as it were, in a kind of material implosion." *The Declaration of Independents* is a call to wave away the clouds of obfuscating political malarkey, to call things (in Havel's phrasing) "by their proper names," identify governance for what it is, expose how it sells itself, and inject into the political sphere the same forces of innovation, individualization, and autonomy that are bettering the way we live in every other sense.

The book you are holding is organized into three sections: "The End of the World as You Know It" (Chapters 1 through 3), "The Democratization of Just About Everything, or Case Studies in Making Life Richer, Weirder, and Better" (Chapters 4 through 8), and "Operationalize It, Baby!" (Chapters 9 through 11). "The End of the World as You Know It" maps the ground of the contemporary scene in unconventional terms that have, we think, the advantage of actually corresponding with the world as it is, not as dead-enders in the GOP or Democratic Party wish it were. This first chapter reminds us that duopolies—even, or especially, those we most take for granted—not only can but do change all the time. The way that most of us talk about politics—as an epic struggle between two eternal and essentially immortal adversaries—is as misguided as assuming that entities like Kodak and Fuji, Macy's and Gimbels, or even the Free World and the Iron Curtain will last forever. Yet, everything in our political discourse pushes us toward the worst sort of existence bias. Still, change is not only possible but constantly occurring in ways that are rarely acknowledged or fully appreciated.

Chapter 2, "The Pit and the Pendulum," deconstructs contemporary narratives about seemingly "permanent governing majorities" that have flipped from Team Red to Team Blue and back again with all the speed and drama of a season of *Survivor*. The political parties and the mainstream media (itself a cartel that we will discuss at length) are heavily invested in defining everything in dualistic terms—Republican/Democrat, conservative/liberal, right wing/left wing—even though such antinomies explain less and less of our world and command less and less loyalty from ordinary Americans. It's time to stop pretending that the two parties are actually in conflict with one another (as opposed to colluding in a power-sharing agreement at the expense of the rest of us).

Chapter 3, "The Libertarian Moment," defines the basic adjective by which we identify ourselves and shows that throughout American history, the forces of control and centralization of the Right and the Left have been at battle with the forces of decentralization and democratization on the individual level. We emphasize that American society is well into a libertarian moment that spells death for the old way of doing things. We argue that the current moment is filled with echoes of that oh-so-loathed decade, the 1970s: bad economy, overreaching state, endless wars, unpopular politicians. Just as in the 1970s, however, a lifestyle and deregulatory revolution is bubbling under the surface, making much of our lives better—the part not controlled by statehouses and Washington, DC. We know that things are getting better every time we order online, enter a Starbucks, and attend our gay friends' weddings and baby showers. But to seize fully the libertarian moment and move beyond a stultifying political duopoly, we need (1) to recognize all that is great and good happening around us and (2) to replace attempts to control our economic and social freedom with a decentralized governing structure that devolves power to the people, who ultimately bear responsibility for and the costs of their own decisions about health care, education, retirement, and lifestyle.

The second section of *The Declaration of Independents*, "The Democratization of Just About Everything," is filled with case studies in the decentralization of power and the empowering of the individual. Chapter 4, "Keep on Rockin' in the Free World," begins in Europe in the 1960s, when future Czech leader Václav Havel insisted on the right of filthy, Velvet-Underground-influenced rock musicians to grow their hair out and play the music they liked under a totalitarian dictatorship. As a direct result, Havel launched a dissident movement that would eventually help topple a communist government, usher in a historic wave of global democratization and liberalization, and provide the source code for humble citizens of lousy dictatorships everywhere, from Egypt to Burma to Cuba, to stand up to their oppressors. And his inspiration to accomplish all this was a bunch of degenerate rock musicians who exported a uniquely American vision of a world beyond politics.

Chapter 5, "You Are Now Free to Move About the Country," explains how getting beyond politics brought domestic air travel to the American masses. The story of airline deregulation and Southwest Airlines CEO Herb Kelleher is a classic example of government decontrol busting up a corporatist industry-Washington nexus that actively harmed consumers for decades, stifling anyone who had the audacity to try a new idea. It was the first big postwar case of deregulation at the consumer level, and it unfolded in a totally counterintuitive manner vis-à-vis our contemporary politics, with such heroes as Ted Kennedy, Ralph Nader, and Jimmy Carter leading the way. The Southwest story, broadly understood, points to how economic and political change happens due to the power of ideas and market forces. And airline deregulation shows how and why markets are better than mandates when it comes to spreading the spoils of free enterprise.

At Southwest, Kelleher famously transformed working conditions from dreary to fun. Chapter 6, "The Disorganization Man (and Woman)," charts how the work world has changed in every way possible since the heyday of postwar megafirms that promised cradle-to-grave jobs and relief from competition in the marketplace. In the wake of the "organization man" comes a new breed of individuals, such as baseball stat nerds Nate Silver and Bill James, who created not only highly personalized careers but even the field in which they work. Jobs have been opened up to women, minorities, and people without connections not because of government edicts but because markets reward hard work more than legacy and family connections. The result is a less structured, more fluid and individualized workplace.

Chapter 7, "Rise of the Mutants," suggests that workplaces are more interesting, in part, because the individuals populating them are more interesting. Freed of old cultural and social identities, we're all mutants now, and that's a good thing. A decade before he was unmasked as a sex-addicted Buddhist, Tiger Woods blew apart every conceivable racial, ethnic, and class category as a self-described "Cablinasian" (Caucasian, black, American Indian, and Asian). In this, he is increasingly representative. Whether we're talking about skin color, sexual preference, or self-presentation, we live in a world beyond categories, with endlessly proliferating identities that are as personally liberating as they are generally terrifying to conservative and liberal bean counters alike. There's a reason the X-Men are so popular, and it's not because we're into cookie-cutter culture.

Back in the early 1980s, a parade of rock stars took to the airwaves to proclaim their right to participate in a mini media revolution: "We want our MTV!" demanded Pete Townsend, Cyndi Lauper, and others. Chapter 8, "We the Media," looks at how the Internet and other forms of ubiquitous, low-cost communications continue to radically restructure means of personal expression and personal consumption. We are now well into our second decade of full-blown legacy-media panic, where organization men from dinosaur networks and money-losing newspapers and imperious record companies confuse their own belated job insecurity with the decline of media overall. In fact, nothing could be further from the truth. The world, led by the United States, is in the midst of a culture boom in which the audience has shifted from passive receptacles to active producers, repurposing content and creating infinitely more (and better) content than ever before. Using tools created by such democratizers as Evan Williams (founder of both Blogger and Twitter), building on the do-it-yourself theories of everyone from Marshall McLuhan to Malcolm McLaren, and benefiting from the underappreciated euthanasia of the Fairness Doctrine, we the people have become we the media.

The final section of the book, "Operationalize It, Baby!" brings us back to the political arena. Politics is a lagging indicator of change in America, the last person in the room to get the joke, the last man to buy the Nehru jacket or stock in Snapple. Yet, because the political realm exercises so much influence on the basic operating of our lives via taxation and regulation, it must be reformed so that it facilitates rather than stymies the democratization of opportunity and decentralization of power. Chapter 9, "We Are So Out of Money," makes the case that enormous political change is coming for two reasons. First, the burgeoning ranks of independent voters are sick and tired of the two main parties and ideological perspectives that don't represent how they feel and think. In a world where our choices are limited to John Boehner and Nancy Pelosi, the survivors envy the dead. Second, and perhaps more importantly, we're out of money at every level of government. A decade into the twenty-first century and an unprecedented spending binge, the public sector has maxed out its credit cards and our future. Despite Barack Obama's best intentions to keep increasing the debt ceiling until it punches through the ozone layer and the GOP's insistence that unrestrained Medicare and defense spending are equally sacrosanct entitlements, the era of big government is over, not because of politicians' wisdom and restraint but because of their profligacy and inability to adapt to the new circumstances.

Much of *The Declaration of Independents* illustrates how we've all routed around the government in important areas of our lives. Chapter 10, "Your Mind, Your Health, and Your Retirement Are Terrible Things to Waste," lays out policy fixes to escape the dead hands of local, state, and federal government in the areas over which they still exercise near-total control. Virtually everything in American life has gotten better over the past forty years. There are three great exceptions: K–12 education, health care, and retirement. Each is firmly ensconced in a public sector that refuses to participate in the service revolution. Here's how to blow up the last major citadels of top-down bureaucracy.

Chapter 11, "The Permanent Nongoverning Minority," surveys recent disruptions in politicking as usual, including the Tea Party, the controversial right-of-center populist revolt over big-government spending and corruption; the Ron Paul REVOLUTION, which made an obscure, Fed-hating, goldbug congressman-cum-obstetrician from Texas into a youth favorite in the 2008 presidential race and a *New York Times* best-selling author; California's Proposition 19, the nation's most serious attempt to legalize pot, which polled higher than expected; and the 2004 Howard Dean campaign, which revolutionized political organizing before ending in a strangled scream of defeat. How do we turn Dean's widely mocked cry into a full-throated, Whitmanesque "barbaric yawp," a full-throated expression of the energy and dynamism of the American people? Politicians are at their most afraid—and most responsive—when they can no longer count on blocs of votes. We can change the system by refusing to play by the rules of a game designed to open our wallets and shut our mouths. Americans who secede from political tribes, yet remain fully or sporadically involved in politics, scare the bejesus out of politicians. Through peaceful resistance, ephemerally organized swarms, blatant disregard of immoral laws, and more, we can create a permanent nongoverning minority, where blocs retain their potency by refusing to be co-opted and focusing on ways that the government is conspiring to keep them less free.

For decades in the private sector, power has been flowing out of traditional established centers toward the hinterlands; never before have individuals had so much variety, personalization, and innovation at their fingertips. This sort of centrifugal force is taken for granted when it comes to buying vegetables or coffee, trying out new clothes or new identities, or building vast do-it-yourself universes of toys, food, music, and media. It is resisted only in politics, where the last remaining gatekeepers are desperate to maintain a cobra clutch on power and money. But the same inexorable logic of choice, competition, and cooperation is coming home to roost in city halls, statehouses, and federal buildings all over the land. The question is how to speed up Judgment Day via not just the right policies but the best understanding of the recent past.

If we do declare independence not just within politics but from the politics, we will deliver on the liberatory aspirations hinted at in the epilogue, "The Future's So Bright . . ." If we remain slavishly devoted to the status quo, to the existence bias that tells us we must put up with the false choices offered between Republican and Democrat, conservative and liberal, right wing and left wing, Kodak and Fuji, then eyewear will be the least of our worries.

CHAPTER 2

THE PIT AND THE PENDULUM

Do you remember where you were at the exact moment the "permanent Republican majority" finally clicked into place after, what, more than a century of wandering through an electoral desert? After such historic low points as the assassination of William McKinley, Thomas Dewey's ersatz defeat of Harry S. Truman, Watergate, Reagan's declaring ketchup a vegetable, the first President Bush's puking on the Japanese prime minister, and the ousting of latter-day Marat, Newt Gingrich, from the House of Representatives not by his first, second, or third wife but by his own "revolutionary" comrades, the wind was finally filling the GOP's sails.

Whether you lean left, right, libertarian, or none of the above, if you want to understand why everything you think you know about the political present and future is wrong, take a short trip down memory lane to recall your coordinates when the GOP kicked the Democrats' sorry donkey ass to the curb once and for all, when the party of Jimmy Carter was hosed down the sewer like a case of Billy Beer, never to be seen again except in Ken Burns's barfumentaries about how we saved the twentieth century itself by creating the Department of Interior.

But first, a quick explanation of this chapter's title. In 1840, Edgar Allan Poe published the short story "The Pit and the Pendulum," a macabre tale set during the Spanish Inquisition that opens in medias res with its hero strapped to a gurney in a torture chamber, watching a long, ultrasharp scythe swing slowly back and forth, back and forth. With each pass, the blade lowers inexorably closer to the chest of our hero, who realizes with mounting horror that he is about to be nicked, then sliced, then finally cut to ribbons. How did the anonymous protagonist end up in such a situation? Well, he really has no idea: "Where and in what state was I?"

And this brings us back to contemporary American politics: Where and in what state are we? At every given moment, if you listen to the professional hysterics who serve as the color commentators for our sport of politics, we are in a brand-new place that is both wholly unrecognizable and cemented in stone. Dial the Wayback Machine to 2001, when George W. Bush snuck into the White House via the tightest presidential race in more than a century, after six years of full-throttled, double-chinned GOP dominance of Congress. As Bush entered office, the pants-wetting cognoscenti fell over themselves, trying to figure out whether presidential adviser and acknowledged "boy genius" Karl Rove's dream of a "permanent Republican majority" had finally washed over the iron gates of 1600 Pennsylvania Avenue. It's hard to recall the memory now through the burnt-out ends of smoky days, but even *Vanity Fair* editor Graydon Carter, who would eventually attempt to cash in on the last fetid days of Bush derangement syndrome, initially courted the Bush dynasty like Machiavelli kissing up to the Médicis. Carter, who famously (and wrongly) pronounced an "end to irony" after the 9/11 attacks, tried proving it through heroic Annie Leibovitz photoessays of Bush's war cabinet, lavish fashion spreads of the women in

Forty-Three's life, and paeans to Dubya's dad, the greatest one-term president since the Peanut Farmer from Plains. Condoleezza Rice bestrode the media and the world stage like Ilsa, She-Wolf of the SS, decked out in thigh-high leather boots; Karl Rove haunted the halls of power like Leatherface in *The Texas Chainsaw Massacre*, cutting down enemies and opponents for the sheer joy of it, all before sitting down for a family dinner of fresh liberal meat. And don't get us started on First Dog Barney, who would later star in a series of surreal, Buñuelesque Christmas videos that would make even orphans swear off Santa Claus (in one bizarre, yet oddly prescient, scene from 2006, then Treasury secretary Hank Paulson explains to Barney that the pooch can't put on a holiday pageant because "we're out of money"). Even Ford administration retreads Dick Cheney and Don Rumsfeld were accorded the status of twenty-first-century management wizards rather than the hubristic, power-aggrandizing Nixon revisionists they were later revealed to be.

After George W. Bush won the presidential election via a 5–4 vote of the Supreme Court, the press and most Democratic operatives hailed Rove as a James Bond–level supervillain. If this guy could get an empty suit like Bush (or missing suit, in the case of Bush's supposed dereliction of duties for the Alabama Air National Guard during Vietnam) elected president over sharp-as-nails (read: C student at Harvard during the last years of the college's era of the gentleman's B) Al Gore, there was no telling what else he might pull over the eyes of a powerless America.

Bush inhabited his supposedly transformative role from the get-go, pushing through tax cuts that went from "impossible to inevitable" just months after taking office and teaming up with Teddy Kennedy to double down on the federalization of K–12 education via the No Child Left Behind Act. After a quick initial stumble in the immediate aftermath of 9/11 (his upside-down reading of *My Pet Goat* was only the most visible sign of seventy-two hours' worth of rudderless confusion), he rallied to deliver a memorable speech from Ground Zero and fired a strike over the heart of the plate in Yankee Stadium to start the World Series. He passed a Medicare prescription-drug benefit that was pure pork for seniors, already one of the wealthiest groups in the population, regardless of their demonstrated need for free or reduced-price pills.

All of this was Rove's transformational doing, foes and allies alike agreed. He was "Bush's brain," according to one popular account, and, oh, what a brain it was. In August 2004, *New York Times* columnist and "progressive conservative" David Brooks started laying out the blueprint for a "permanent governing majority" for the GOP. Who could disagree?

The anxieties of the chattering class and Democrats more broadly had only grown deeper and more troubled by November of that year, when Bush not only won reelection handily over another Harvard layabout, John F. Kerry, but managed to earn a clear majority of the popular vote (the first time a president had done so since his dad had in 1988) plus even greater majorities in the House and Senate (a historical exception). For God's sake, Bush, the first and only president not just to speak Spanish but actually to seem comfortable pressing the flesh with mestizos, even jacked up his Hispanic vote in his second election by a whopping twenty percentage points. Didn't Republicans hate Mexicans? What the hell was going on? The GOP's permanent governing majority was here to stay!

When Senate Minority Leader Tom Daschle (D-SD), precisely the sort of well-coiffed nonentity who passes for a wise man in Washington, DC, was sent packing after the election, it became plain as day that the Democrats were, in *New York Times* speak, "baffled in loss." As old-time Democratic hands such as Jesse Jackson yammered on about reaching out to poor white southerners, then Arizona governor and future Department of Homeland Security secretary Janet Napolitano mumbled her way through vague martial metaphors every bit as dispiriting as the ballot results: "You can't write off everything from Atlanta to California," she moaned. "You've got to find some beachheads there." The tentative trickle of Democratic doomsday books published in the run-up to 2004—such as *What's the Matter with Kansas?* and *Don't Think of an Elephant*—turned into a fire hose of liberal panic after King Bush's triumphant second coronation.

Bush and the Republicans now moved in for the kill. The president announced that he was going to use his considerable "political capital" to *really* start throwing his weight around. Social Security reform, comprehensive immigration reform, White House Read a Book campaigns orchestrated by the First Lady—everything was a go. As an analyst at *National Review* gloated, "In view of congressional Democrats' past obstructionism, the president's plans might be dismissed as wishful thinking, except for this: Bush now has the near-unanimous support of the selfsame voters who gave America the Reagan Revolution two dozen years ago." All things seemed possible, even irrevocable.

And then, of course, the 2006 midterm elections changed all that. Democrats picked up six seats in the Senate (two of them belonging to independents) for a new 51–49 majority, plus a huge thirty-one seats in the House. The permanent Republican majority, a notion that had been seared into the national consciousness for six years, was flushed down the memory hole faster than remaindered copies of former GOP House Speaker and wrestling instructor Dennis Hastert's flaccid memoir *Lessons from the Coach.* Arguably even more stunning in 2006 was the Democratic resurgence at the state level, where Mr. Jefferson's party captured a majority of statehouses for the first time since 1994, the very year that made the permanent Republic majority possible.

And then came 2008, when Democrat Barack Hussein Obama, a short-time senator from Illinois and an African American to boot, decisively kicked old-timer war hero Senator John McCain into electoral oblivion. Now it was time for the Democrats' permanent governing majority, founded on such solid footing that Obama could suffer even the presence of logorrheic Senator Joe Biden on his ticket (in recent memory, Biden has made headlines for plagiarizing his life story from a British politician, making bizarre comments about how Asian Indians run his state's convenience stores, and describing Obama in the most hidebound racial terms as "clean, articulate, bright"). The Democrats managed to deliver a veto-proof majority in the Senate, electing people in such legendary Republican strongholds as New Hampshire, North Carolina, Virginia, and New Mexico. In the House of Representatives, the Democrats squeezed out the last remaining Republican congressmen from New England, as ten-term incumbent Chris Shays of Connecticut was sent packing. What a difference four years made!

Fast-forward just two years, and we have yet another "realignment" on our hands, as Tea Party enthusiasm and general voter anger at a sputtering economy sent Democrats back into a minority in the House of Representatives while delivering the biggest state-level gains for Republicans since before World War II. Even before the full results were announced on Election Night 2010, the president's own party members were whispering about possible primary challengers from the left in the next election, and the publishing houses began cranking out new pamphlets on the permanent governing whatever-we'll-have until at least November 2012.

It's rousing stuff, this horse race politics, with shifts as seemingly surprising, unexpected, and irreversible as a drunken, late-night dorm-room game of Risk. And it tells you as much about politics as moving plastic armies from Yukon into Irkutsk.

Large, seemingly watershed partisan upheavals have, of course, been part of the fabric of American politics since the Federalists and Democratic-Republicans, led by John Adams and Thomas Jefferson, duked it out in the early nineteenth century before fading into the same oblivion that would soon swallow the Whigs. In the quarter-century period between Lyndon Johnson's historic shellacking of Barry Goldwater and the retirement of Ronald Reagan, the conventional wisdom held that the Republican Party could elect presidents but not congressional majorities. The same silent majority that was ready, willing, and able to vote for Richard Nixon in 1972 in record percentages just couldn't stomach the notion of House Speaker Gerald Ford or Senate Majority Leader Hugh Scott. After Bill Clinton snuck into office in 1992 with a piddling 43 percent of the popular vote (the lowest percentage since Nixon himself squeaked past Hubert Humphrey and George Wallace in 1968), then lost congressional majorities two years later, the smart money was betting on the Democrats disbanding and re-forming as something else altogether. The Democrats had become your father's Oldsmobile, a tired, worn-out brand that offered nothing worth buying in contemporary America.

Such seesaw battles are entrancing, to be sure. Like Poe's protagonist, when you're strapped to the gurney in the dungeon, when you seemingly can't waggle even a finger, all you can do is stare transfixed at the blade swinging from one extreme to the other and brace for the inevitable slicing of flesh. For every sad-sack, yet gruesomely compelling, book such as *Why Mommy Is a Democrat*, there's an equal and appalling reaction, such as *Mommy, There's a Liberal Under the Bed* (yes, those are actual titles). Democrats or Republicans, stuffing or potatoes, Yankees or Red Sox, Beatles or Stones—American politics, it would seem, is inherently Manichaean and duopolistic. As with arbitrary tribespeople drawn up for another season of *Survivor*, so much depends on the question, Are you Team Red or Team Blue?

These partisan contests are the three-card monte of American life, misdirecting our attention from what really matters most. When you lift your gaze from what's *supposed* to be important and focus instead on longer-term trends, you see in politics a muted version of exactly what you see everywhere else in American society: a loss of brand loyalty and the increasing assertion of independent individual choice.

This is readily understood when it comes to, say, automobiles, where the once-mainstream idea of a family remaining loyal to Chevrolet or Ford or even Toyota is now laughable. When confronted with anything resembling choice, most of us are now readier than ever to hop from one make or model to another. Insurance, food, clothing, colleges, beer, wine, you name it—Americans, away from the political sphere, have learned how to demand what they want, and in a world of rapidly increasing choices, they are happy and excited to try out new things and move on once they get bored or disappointed with what's on offer.

In politics, of course, that choice has been artificially and drastically restricted to effectively two options. In the most Soviet-like grocery store in America (which, we can sadly testify, is the Safeway on Seventeenth Street NW in Washington, DC), you can still buy about fifty kinds of toothpaste. At the ballot box, however, in our first-past-the-post system of candidate-with-the-most-votes-wins, it's still Crest or Colgate. There have been moments when minor parties have played important parts in elections or even emerged as major parties themselves (as the Republicans did back in the mid-nineteenth century). But such episodes are few and far between, especially in the past half century. And when third parties do play a role, such experiences tend to be one-offs, built around the fleeting enthusiasms of a single entrepreneurial figure rather than a broad-based coalition.

Hence, George Wallace's American Independent Party in 1968 turned the election for Nixon, and Ross Perot's Reform Party helped sink George H. W. Bush's bid for a second term in 1992. Yet, no one talks about either party anymore (who would have predicted that

9/11 truther Jesse Ventura couldn't build Perot's Reform Party into a viable national electoral vehicle?). Ralph Nader tipped the election to George W. Bush as a Green Party candidate (winning 100,000 mostly left-of-center votes in Florida, where Bush's 537-vote margin over Al Gore proved decisive). Nader insisted he was doing it to build a viable third party, then seceded from the party in question for widely ignored runs in 2004 and 2008. The Libertarian Party, established in 1971 and long claiming to be the third-largest political party in the country, has almost certainly cost a handful of elections for Republicans. Writing in 2002 in the *New York Times*, conservative journalist John J. Miller sighed over the GOP's "Libertarian problem" and wept that the defeat of incumbent South Dakota senator Jon Thune marked "the third consecutive election in which a Libertarian has cost the Republican Party a Senate seat." Still, on the whole, long-lived third-party successes are rarer than steak tartare.

A different picture emerges when you focus on the flagging enthusiasm for the market leaders, as measured by public opinion polls dating back over the past forty years. Whoever asks the questions, the answers are the same: More and more of us call ourselves "independents," and fewer and fewer of us define ourselves as Republicans or Democrats. During the Nixon years, almost 50 percent of Americans thought of themselves as Democrats. These days, the percentage is in the low thirties. Despite the fact that many more Americans consider themselves ideologically conservative, the GOP has always had trouble getting even one-third of adults to think of themselves as Republicans.

Who can blame us? In a world increasingly characterized by hyperpersonalized service and money-back guarantees, Democrats and Republicans still insist that you sign up for a bundle package that even the most truculent cable operators would be embarrassed to foist on captive customers. Like Kodak and Fujifilm forcing customers to develop twenty-four pictures to get the one or two shots they want, the major parties insist that partisans buy the whole megillah. There is no necessary connection between ostensibly Democratic causes such as artistic freedom and higher marginal tax rates or between Republican causes such as free trade and anti-flag-burning amendments. The whole point of party ideology is to make a ragtag bunch of beliefs appear to be seamlessly integrated. Shortly after the 2010 midterms, Senator Jim DeMint (R-SC) actually said that it was impossible to be "a fiscal conservative and not be a social conservative," which was news to large numbers of gay Republicans who supported tax cuts and opposed Don't Ask, Don't Tell.

And when the parties are not trying to load up our shopping carts with unwanted items, they are simply misrepresenting themselves in ways that are nearly impossible to pull off in the age of Angie's List, Yelp, Rate My Professor, and any number of services that rate reputation. The Democrats and Republicans rarely govern as advertised.

Barack Obama came to power largely on the antiwar vote, vowed for two years on the campaign trail to reassert international norms in America's War on Terror, and said he'd close Guantánamo Bay as one of his first acts in office. As president, Obama has actually tripled down on the war effort in Afghanistan, asserted his right to assassinate even U.S. citizens without trial, and kept both Guantánamo and the dubious legal justifications for open-ended internment in place indefinitely. Even in Iraq, where the winddown proposed by George W. Bush is supposedly under way, a nontrivial force of 50,000 soldiers and tens of thousands of private contractors still keep what passes for the peace.

Democratic voters (and key party donors such as billionaires George Soros, John Sperling, and Peter Lewis, who are the main financiers of pro-pot legislation) like to believe that they're for legalizing soft drugs. Yet, President Obama has laughed off the notion of even discussing marijuana decriminalization, dispatching his drug czar to join the previous five in lobbying against California's pro-legalization Proposition 19 and continuing to send federal agents to raid medical-marijuana dispensaries in the few places they're legal. Democrats are united in opposition to Republican gay baiting; yet, Obama is personally against gay marriage and took two years to instruct his Justice Department to stop enforcing the Defense of Marriage Act, which Bill Clinton supported (we might add that he and his party dragged their feet in eventually repealing Clinton's homophobic Don't Ask, Don't Tell military-service policy). Democrats especially like to believe they are absolutists on free speech, but the Obama administration's former solicitor general, Elena Kagan, who now sits on the Supreme Court, argued in front of that body in 2009, "Whether a given category of speech enjoys First Amendment protection depends upon a categorical balancing of the value of the speech against its societal costs." The law Kagan unsuccessfully attempted to defend, she said then, could reasonably be used to ban political books.

The GOP, too, is not the tribe it claims to be. While controlling the White House and both houses of Congress during George W. Bush's first six years in office, the party of "limited government" produced the biggest expansion of federal spending since Lyndon Johnson. Routinely blamed for the "deregulation" that allegedly precipitated the financial crisis, Bush & Co. actually presided over the biggest regulatory expansion since Richard Nixon, setting all-time records for regulatory spending, increasing regulatory staff by more than 90,000 employees, and even jacking up financial regulatory spending by 29 percent (compared to Bill Clinton's cutting it by 3 percent). Bush created the biggest new entitlement in decades (Medicare Part D), made a show of cracking down on Wall Street (Sarbanes-Oxley), and asserted a primary federal role in the policing of political activity and speech (McCain-Feingold); he even happily signed legislation phasing out incandescent lightbulbs starting in 2012. He did all that in addition to initiating two "nation-building" wars of the kind he routinely disparaged when campaigning for president.

To turn out their base, Republicans try to convince voters that Democrats are weak-kneed socialists, even though all recent GOP presidents have been bigger spenders than Bill Clinton ever was. Democrats, on the other had, try to mobilize their base by convincing voters that Republicans hate minorities and personal freedom, even though Democrats in office often take the exact same positions on the most relevant laws. It's a wearisome act, but the good news is that even while the pendulum has swung back toward the GOP for the short term, voters, in the long view, are accelerating their defection from the two-party tribalism that got us into our current mess.

What's happening to the rapidly vanishing conservatives and liberals (terms easily understood as rough proxies for "Republicans" and "Democrats")? What does the growing plurality of independent voters hold near and dear? What are the self-described moderates moderating toward? They are embracing and pursuing a broadly libertarian vision of limited government and social tolerance, of what the magazine we work for, *Reason*, has long dubbed "Free Minds and Free Markets." We'll define "libertarian" more fully in the next chapter, but suffice it to say for now that there is widespread disenchantment with the idea of ceding more money and more power to authorities in city hall, the state capitol, and Washington, DC. There's also a growing recognition that disagreements about lifestyle, drug use, the role of religion, and more are better hashed out in the marketplace of ideas rather than through the passage of contentious laws. Those pushing for smaller government are not members of some sort of reactionary John Birch Society recoiling from a world that might pollute our precious bodily fluids. By all indicators, Americans are more comfortable with ethnic, social, gender, cultural, and religious differences than ever before.

A *Washington Post*/ABC News poll taken in January 2010 found that 58 percent of adults generally favored "smaller government with fewer services" over "larger government with more services" (38 percent), as compared to 50 percent and 46 percent in June 2004. A 2009 Ayers-McHenry poll asking the same question showed 69 percent of Americans calling for a smaller government and only 21 percent rooting for a bigger one.

What is America's problem with big government? Writing in *The Battle*, Arthur Brooks of the American Enterprise Institute points to specific complaints about government efficiency and efficacy. When Pew Research asked Americans in 2009 whether they thought "government does more to help or more to hurt people trying to move up the economic ladder," 50 percent of respondents said the government hurts people, while 39 percent said it helped. At root, especially in an era of runaway deficits and ballooning entitlement obligations, is a fear that the government simply cannot be trusted with what matters most to people: their ability to earn a decent living and leeway to spend it more or less how they see fit. Recent surveys from Pew and CNN show about two-thirds of the population saying that the government can't be trusted either all or most of the time.

At the same time, other surveys show that Americans are becoming increasingly comfortable with alternative lifestyles. A January 2010 *Washington Post*/ABC News poll found that 46 percent think that "small amounts of marijuana for personal use" should be legalized, the highest total ever recorded. While 51 percent oppose any legalization, that total was over 70 percent just a decade ago. Other lifestyle issues show an unmistakable movement toward tolerance. According to stat master Nate Silver, for instance, bans against gay marriage are losing roughly two percentage points of support each year. His model "predicts that by 2012, almost half of the 50 states [will] vote against a marriage ban, including several states that had previously voted to ban it. In fact, voters in Oregon, Nevada and Alaska (which, Sarah Palin aside, is far more libertarian than culturally conservative) might already have second thoughts about the marriage bans that they'd previously passed."

A 2010 study titled "The Libertarian Vote in the Age of Obama," published by the Cato Institute, underscores the important and growing role of what authors David Boaz and David Kirby call "fiscally conservative, socially liberal" voters. While there are competing definitions of what "libertarian" means, the simplest understanding attaches to people who believe that government is less efficient than the private sector, that people should be left alone as much as possible to live their own lives, and that tolerance is the most important social value. These are people who, by and large, prefer to see the government spend less and have a smaller reach but are also positive toward immigration, gay rights, drug legalization, and similar issues. By the strictest criteria, Boaz and Kirby identify about 14 percent of voters as libertarian, though they note that other tallies identify as many as 59 percent of registered voters as leaning at least somewhat in the libertarian direction. Given the relatively recent rise of libertarianism as an electorally significant disposition, it's not clear how those numbers stack up compared to, say, fifty years ago. But even taking the low-ball estimate of 14 percent, a voting bloc of that size is clearly more than capable of tipping virtually any national, state, or even local election, especially if its members declare themselves free agents at the ballot box. During the 1980s and generally up through the mid-2000s, libertarian voters were more comfortable with Republicans and clearly helped the GOP win Congress in 1994 (indeed, the rhetoric—though not the actions—of the so-called Republican Revolution was often explicitly libertarian).

As the big-government presidency of George W. Bush wore on, however, libertarian voters deserted the Republican big tent and became swing voters, swarming toward and away from candidates and parties. Bush received 72 percent of the libertarian vote in 2000 (compared to Al Gore's 20 percent), according to Boaz and Kirby, but just 59 percent in 2004 (to John Kerry's 38 percent). Even after running on a more openly liberal campaign of nationalizing health care and repealing free trade agreements, Barack Obama still received 27 percent of the libertarian vote, though John McCain drew a strong 71 percent. Meanwhile, libertarians' party identification, while leaning solidly Republican, has been volatile: 32 percent were independent in 2000, 46 percent in 2004, and 26 percent in 2008. A similar, overlapping phenomenon can be found with the large bloc of independent voters, who were crucial to the Obama/Democratic rout in 2008 but just as important in the party's dramatic reversal of fortune in 2010. In just over a year from 2009 to 2010, independent approval ratings for Obama plummeted from 56 to 38 percent.

Such shifts make clear that the libertarian and independent votes are in play, are powerful forces, and, most importantly, are clearly unencumbered by traditional party affiliations. If the Dems and Reps are interested in gaining and keeping power, they would do well to understand and court these blocs. Boaz and Kirby argue that the libertarian vote in particular has been systematically underappreciated for at least two reasons. Political scientists have for a half century or more routinely pigeonholed politics into a Left-Right or liberal-conservative spectrum that may simplify storytelling but fails to map our more diverse reality accurately. Political scientists, that is, are every bit as much prisoners to *The Pit and the Pendulum* mentality as the duopoly they take for granted.

More interestingly, Boaz and Kirby suggest that many libertarian voters do not fully recognize or name their own tendencies. They too are blinded by the conventional categories through which political campaigns and analysis are expressed. That latter point is certainly changing, and fast, as younger voters and tired veterans alike search for a twenty-first-century paradigm that gets at what they actually care about. The rise of a self-consciously libertarian movement (comprising institutions such as the Reason Foundation, the Cato Institute, the Institute for Humane Studies, Students for Liberty, the Mises Institute, and more) has raised the profile of the label, as has the emergence of a raft of high-profile celebrities who self-identify as such, including Drew Carey, Penn Jillette, and the creators of *South Park*. Mix in libertarian noises coming from such traditionally nonlibertarian sources as Glenn Beck and the more traditional conservatives who populate Tea Party gatherings, and the cultural heat of the adjective "libertarian" is making the club more and more inviting.

This is not to say that libertarian alternatives need much help from celebrities or high-profile politicians. As the party affiliation data show, the conventional Right-Left, liberal-conservative, Democratic-Republican duopoly has done a great job of smothering zeal for the status quo. On the presidential level, with the exception of Ron Paul and Barack Obama, who presented starkly different platforms from the other major-party candidates, there was little new or different about the policy choices offered by the dozens of Democrats and Republicans who ran for the White House in 2008.

While American life is increasingly fueled by a do-it-yourself ethos of individualized service, culture, and consumer products in infinite combination ("You want soy with that decaf mocha frappuccino?"), politics continues to be the exact opposite. The eventual 2008 general election survivors, even the initially new-sounding Democrat, ended up channeling the most shopworn agendas and tired identities to a body politic desperate for anything new. That McCain and Obama both voted for George W. Bush's Troubled Asset Relief Program, the single biggest event in recent political history

(McCain, in fact, tried to cancel a presidential debate so he could fly back to Washington and vote yes), tells you all you need to know about substantial differences between the two. They represented not "maverick" thinking on the one hand and "hope and change" on the other but massive chronic fatigue syndrome in the body politic.

But let's be fair: Looking to Democrats and Republicans for the next big thing is like asking General Motors and Ford circa 1975 to map out the future of the auto industry. Legacy market leaders are inevitably the last to notice that their top-down traditions are losing steam in a world hurtling toward bottom-up business and culture. As Chris Anderson documented in his 2006 bestseller *The Long Tail: Why the Future of Business Is Selling More of Less*, technological innovations, especially the rise of the World Wide Web, have produced customer expectations that the consumer experience will be driven by personalization, choice, and autonomy.

Anderson's title refers to the archetypal supply-and-demand curve, whose tail slopes down and toward the right. The thick head of the tail, which represents popular items, is getting shorter; the tail, which represents less popular and more heterogeneous items, is getting longer and more important in terms of total sales. Hence, the online bookseller Amazon stocks several million titles, but more than half of its sales comes from books ranked lower than its top 130,000. In terms of goods and services, Anderson argues, we are turning "from a mass market into a niche nation." The era of the blockbuster and the bestseller has been replaced by a world in which individuals are free to express themselves by tapping into millions of different book titles at Amazon, tens of thousands of different songs at Rhapsody, and hundreds of different beers at a typical supermarket. Smart retailers realize that the key to the future is to give the customer more choices, not to act as a stern schoolmaster who keeps his charges on the straight and narrow. In a similar way, social networking sites such as Facebook and Twitter do not dictate the specifics of interaction as much as provide a relatively free space to facilitate it. Individual users tailor the experience to their own desires rather than submit to a central authority.

Only one candidate in the 2008 election cycle tapped into what might be called "long-tail" politics, campaigning on ideas copacetic to the Internet generation while leveraging the traditional American values of decentralization and choice. That was Rep. Ron Paul, the eleven-term congressman from Texas who is gaining influence even while remaining a punch line for many political jokes.

To be sure, by all conventional measures, Paul's presidential bid was an abject failure—not a single primary win and only a fistful of delegates at the Republican National Convention. Yet, the once-obscure figure managed to raise more than $20 million, virtually all of it online, and inspired an army of hyperdevoted and mostly youthful followers using a pitch—and a style—that will have much more to do with twenty-first-century politics than whatever models of Oldsmobile and Mercury the Democrats and Republicans eventually crank out in 2012. The candidate pulled together over 67,000 people at the social networking site Meetup (more than twenty times the number who signed up for Barack Obama). He won raves from quarters as disparate as conservative commentator George Will (who called Paul "my man" on ABC's *This Week with George Stephanopoulos*), punk icon Johnny Rotten (who gave "Dr. No" a celebratory shout-out on *The Tonight Show*), and a self-explanatory group called Strippers for Paul.

What explained the ability of this odd politician, with an inept campaign-management team and a stage presence straight out of an Asperger's syndrome conference, to attract gobs of money and enthusiasm and a nontrivial number of votes? It was the fact that only Ron Paul said something truly distinct in 2008 about the very nature of power—namely, that government should have less of it on all levels and in every instance. "I don't want to run your life," Paul said. "I

don't want to run the economy. . . . I don't want to run the world."
Such sentiments are simultaneously radical and fully in the Jeffersonian tradition of governing best while governing least. The right to be left alone, as Justice Louis Brandeis once put it, is at the very center of the American experiment because it allows individuals and the communities they form to pursue happiness in competing, peaceful ways. This is especially true in long-tail America, where people are not only increasingly tolerant of alternative lifestyles but constantly on the hunt for ways to augment and hyphenate their own lives. It's no accident that Paul's campaign attracted people who might otherwise have nothing to do with each other politically—antiwar lefties, antimonetarist economists, pro-drug anarchists, Constitution-toting conservatives.

Ron Paul's message, in short, was the only one in recent memory that appealed directly to the independently minded libertarian folk who are increasingly weaving the social fabric of American life in a twenty-first century that has so far been nothing less than a disaster. For a thousand reasons (ranging from his age to his conspiracist belief in the nonexistent North American Union to his role in disseminating racist newsletters in the early 1990s), Ron Paul is in no way a viable candidate for anything other than his safe congressional seat in a bizarrely drawn district that meanders between Houston and Austin. But to focus on the messenger (who managed to park a couple of books on the *New York Times* bestseller list, including one calling for the abolition of the Federal Reserve) and ignore the message is to turn away from the future of American politics.

Democrats and their enablers in the media learned this the hard way in November 2010. After two years of frantically searching for any reason other than those clearly printed on protesters' signs to explain the sudden presence of a potent, grassroots small-government movement—leading theories ran the gamut from a resurgence in racism (in a country with a freshly elected African

American president), to the Supreme Court's January 2010 decision in *Citizens United v. Federal Election Commission*, to the insidious puppetry of billionaire philanthropist brothers Charles and David Koch—mainstream opinioneering was left with the awful conclusion that a growing and increasingly powerful cohort of Americans was having at least some of what Ron Paul (and his son Rand, the first Tea Party–certified member of the U.S. Senate) was smoking. And the people driving this change were emerging, seemingly fully formed, from the bottom up, using the radical, decentralized organizational infrastructure of the Internet. The only ideological message with obviously positive trend lines over the past few years is the big-tent, cross-cultural notion that, as Henry David Thoreau famously pointed out, that government is best which governs least.

Yet, even in the flushed and flustered postelection glow, as yesterday's permanent governing majority becomes today's permanent grassroots revolt and vice versa, it's important to keep one key notion in mind: Politics is a lagging indicator in American life. The 2010 midterms, like all midterms, will not produce innovative policy that turns around the creaky ship of state or even keeps it from capsizing. Even before they took power, House Republicans walked back their election-season commitment to cutting $100 billion (about 2.6 percent of the total) from current government spending. Contrary to the myths perpetuated by liberals and conservatives alike, the winning and losing of elections is not transformative of what matters most.

The grotesque 1896 Supreme Court decision *Plessy v. Ferguson*, which institutionalized the South's Jim Crow laws, is an instructive example here. The case came about as a response to a private Louisiana railroad's willingness to buck decades' worth of racist codes by selling first-class tickets to black passengers. The Court decision did not change the status quo; it ratified it, in a decision pushing back radical capitalists ahead of their time. Similarly, the decision that cast out the separate-but-equal doctrine, 1954's *Brown v. Board of Education of Topeka*, didn't change the world. More concretely, it ratified the anti-*Plessy* consensus, which had been building for decades, that America was overdue in delivering on its founding promise of equal justice for all. Society, not the courts, produced the important changes; justices merely codified them. As left-leaning legal scholar Mark Tushnet has observed, the Court "can have some influence on the margins," but overall "it fluctuates around the trends" rather than creates them. The same can be said even for abortion, which was already effectively legalized first in cultural practice, then in state law, and finally in federal law. Or in drink: When state legislatures finally got around to striking down colonial-era blue laws in the 1970s, they were merely catching up with what people had been doing for decades. There are exceptions to this rule, but the fact of the matter is that the political and legal process trails behind where Americans in society and business have already arrived.

A decade into the twenty-first century, political America is, without question, in a rut. On the world stage, we are a lumbering, unwieldy hegemon, bogged down in two seemingly endless wars and (just as importantly) the mentality that got us into them. The federal government is dead broke but still addicted to endless spending; virtually every state is even more broke than the feds, and, most importantly, there is a massive and still-growing disconnect between politics and culture. Despite their demonstrated incompetence, our elected leaders at all levels are calling for more centralization and more power to solve the problems they created, even as Americans are fleeing their traditional masters in every other sphere and living lives that are more decentralized than ever (indeed, even population densities continue to decline in every major city and suburb in the country outside of Washington, DC).

It is well past time for politics to catch up with the American people. We need an operating manual for the twenty-first century that speaks not to the desires of leaders but to the dreams of individuals. It is time to leave behind the torture chamber of Right-Left, conservative-liberal, Democrat-Republican, and to demand a politics that expresses rather than confounds the potential that is everywhere around us, respecting our diverse and infinitely hyphenated values about governance.

It is time, in short, to free ourselves from both pit and pendulum. In Poe's horror tale, the narrator manages to pull himself off his table only to find the floor literally disappearing beneath his feet. Just as he is about to fall to his death in a deep, fiery pit, he is saved by an invading army: "There was a loud blast as of many trumpets! There was a discordant hum of human voices! There was a harsh grating as of a thousand thunders! The fiery walls rushed back! An outstretched arm caught my own as I fell, fainting, into the abyss. It was that of General Lasalle. The Inquisition was in the hands of its enemies. The French army had entered Toledo."

Needless to say, we don't have time to indulge in fantasies of salvation from without (perhaps especially those involving the French army). The tragicomedy of U.S. politics is that we pretty much get the government we demand. How we arrived at our current situation is not a tale of mystery or imagination but a tightly plotted horror story that we can readily understand and analyze. This is a good thing, however depressing the reading might be. If we know how we got here, then we can figure out how to get out of here.

The first step is to acknowledge what we've all been doing in our own ways, big and small, over the past forty years. Each and every one of us has been authoring a personal declaration of independence, a statement about how we want to be free to live and love, to buy and sell, to enter and exit. Those choices define our time on the planet, and they are too important to leave to other people, especially politicians whose insight is every bit as suspect as their motives.

CHAPTER 3

THE LIBERTARIAN MOMENT

We hold this truth to be self-evident in the twenty-first century: We need independence not just *in* politics but *from* politics. As any reader of the original Declaration of Independence can tell you, like all supposedly self-evident truths, this one needs more than a bit of context and explanation. To fully explain what we're talking about, we need to take a rollicking, seatbelt-free road trip through the past four decades of the American experience.

Our current moment is reminiscent of nothing so much as the early 1970s, and not simply because of economic torpor, miasmic overseas war, and elephant-leg jeans. If you focus on Washington, DC, things are depressingly similar: A divisive first-term president who drives his political opponents into some dark conspiratorial corners while earning a reputation for running an insular White House faces an emboldened opposition party after the midterm elections. The president's approval rating six weeks after his party took a "shellacking" (his word) sits near 50 percent, victim in part to a recession that has sent unemployment to its highest level in years. To combat the economic crisis, the president and an activist

Democratic Congress push through what is routinely described as the most sweeping new economic intervention since the New Deal. With it goes the broadest and deepest new regulatory push in four decades. Frantic attempts to boost home ownership rates through federalizing housing finance fail to change the reality that two-thirds of American families own their homes. On the foreign front, the public is growing ever more fatigued by a war the president inherited, campaigned against, and then escalated, including new bombing incursions into a neighboring country. A whistle-blower from within the defense establishment helps leak to the press many thousands of pages of classified documents on the war effort, and the administration reacts with furious charges of treason and terrorism against both the leaker and the primary publisher of his documents.

It's not that Richard Nixon and Barack Obama are similar: Aside from their both being fiercely proud, unapologetically ambitious, self-made lawyers who could write a bit, the personal commonalities really do run out in a hurry. If anything, the opposite is the point. Two men as fundamentally dissimilar as Richard Milhous Nixon and Barack Hussein Obama have, through the responsibility and temptation of power, the reductionism of our modern politics, and the shocking narrowness of what is considered acceptable government action, managed to steer Washington policy through the same well-worn ruts.

Richard Nixon, in his inaugural address, described a nation "ragged in spirit," "falling into raucous discord," and "torn by division, wanting unity." Barack Obama in his inaugural identified the "sapping of confidence across our land; a nagging fear that America's decline is inevitable," while promising to deliver "hope over fear, unity of purpose over conflict and discord." This boilerplate in rhetoric is matched by a boilerplate in ideas. For forty years now, we have been trying to solve public-education mediocrity with more money, more teachers, and smaller classes, and since 1970 this formula has produced the exact same results—only costing twice as much money. Nixon codified the drug war with the Controlled Substances Act of 1970; Obama, despite running on a promise to be a kindler, gentler drug warrior, has maintained drug war spending at his predecessor's level, continued federal raids on medical-marijuana dispensaries, and had his attorney general threaten Californians with imprisonment for smoking pot even if the Golden State legalized marijuana. Both first-termers signed major legislation requiring lenders to write their customer contracts in clear language; surely this time it will work. Nixon created the money-losing government-owned railroad company known as Amtrak; Obama and his famously Amtrak-promoting vice president threw billions of dollars of stimulus money down that long-gaping budget sinkhole. With exceptions so rare as to be essentially endangered, Democrat and Republican politicians each look upon the world's problems as protruding nails, reaching for the hammer of government ten times out of ten to pound things into place. If the blunt force doesn't work—if it's proven, say, to fail for four decades—they just reach for a bigger hammer.

Now, if someone looked you in the eye in the early 1970s and said, "Man, you know what? We're about to get a whole lot freer," you might reasonably have concluded that he had gone mad from taking too much LSD and staring directly into the sun. Back during those polyester days and Day-Glo nights, Richard Nixon faced an economy groaning under the strain of record deficits, runaway spending on elective and unpopular overseas wars, and newfangled entitlements such as Medicare and Medicaid. He then announced one of the most draconian economic interventions in Washington's inglorious history: a freeze on wages and prices, accompanied by an across-the-board 10 percent tariff on imports and the final termination of what little remained of the gold standard in America.

Though the world wouldn't learn until later that this president was using federal law-enforcement agencies to attack his real and imagined enemies, Tricky Dick's well-established yen for paranoid secrecy and executive-branch power mongering provided an actuarial foreshadowing of corruption. The Democrats of the time were statist in their own way: In 1972, their presidential nominee called for more economic intervention than Nixon. Widely (and rightly) considered the most liberal Oval Office candidate in decades, George McGovern actually claimed that wage and price controls were applied "too late—they froze wages but let prices and profits run wild." And individual states were passing personal income taxes like so many doobies at a beachside sing-along.

Four decades ago, environmental Armageddonism had reached a pitch that would pop the eardrums of even the biggest Al Gore fan, with biologist Paul Ehrlich arguing in the 1968 bestseller *The Population Bomb* that "in the 1970s and 1980s hundreds of millions of people [would] starve to death," and "India couldn't possibly feed two hundred million more people by 1980." That tome, which led to regular appearances by Ehrlich on *The Tonight Show*, was followed up in 1973's *Limits to Growth*, a report by the overtly Malthusian Club of Rome, which concluded there were just too many people living on Spaceship Earth to support. Northern Ireland, the Middle East, and the Indian subcontinent were in flames.

In the United States, crime rates were soaring everywhere and an endless procession of movies—from *Dirty Harry* to *Death Wish*, *The Omega Man*, *Soylent Green*, *Looking for Mr. Goodbar*, *The Warriors*, and *Escape from New York*—imagined urban America as an unlivable nightmare from which there was no escape. Terrorist bombs exploded in record numbers in the early 1970s, right-wing politicians like George Wallace and left-wing pornographers like Larry Flynt were crippled by gunmen, and planes were skyjacked for loot and hijacked to Cuba on a seemingly daily basis.

Yet, even during that dark night of the American soul, with all its eerie echoes of today's historic economic interventions, unpopular wars, limitless surveillance, and executive-power expansions, there were premonitions aplenty of liberty-loving green shoots for those who knew where to look. The contraceptive pill, which gave women unprecedented control over their sexual and reproductive lives, had been made legal for married women in 1965 and was on the verge of becoming legalized for unmarried women too (yes, it took until the 1970s for that to happen). Free agency in sports, music, and film, triggered by a series of legal battles and economic developments, ushered in a wild new era of individualistic expression and artistic independence, from Joe Namath's panty hose to Stevie Wonder's *Innervisions*. It was an unfree world, but as bestselling author (and eventual 1990s-era Libertarian presidential candidate) Harry Browne could attest, it was one in which you could find plenty of freedom.

Widespread middle-class prosperity gave the average American the sort of oh-my-god-I-might-lose-it-all anxiety that had once been the sole province of the wealthy. Generally increased access to the good things in life, from higher education to consumer electronics to designer clothes, gave the broad middle class the tools and the confidence to experiment with a thousand different lifestyles, giving us everything from gay liberation to encounter groups, from back-to-the-garden communes to back-to-the-old-ways fundamentalist churches, from *Bob & Carol & Ted & Alice* to *Looking Out for #1*. In 1968, the technohippies at the *Whole Earth Catalog* announced, "We are as gods and might as well get good at it." A year later, a new technology allowing university computers to communicate with one another went live, laying the foundations for what would become the Internet. Radicals at the publication we write for made what might have been the craziest argument of all during the age of Nixon: If you abolish the Civil Aeronautics Board and get the federal government out of regulating "every essential aspect" of the airline business, down to determining the ingredients of airline "food," then air traffic will grow while prices fall and safety increases.

By the end of the 1970s, the Civil Aeronautics Board was in the dustbin of history, sharing much-deserved space with price controls, the reserve clause in sports, and back-alley abortions. What started out as a decade marred by pointless war and Soviet-style central planning ended up being the decade that ended military conscription and—arguably even more stunning—regulation of interstate trucking and freight rail. The personal computer introduced possibilities few people had ever dreamed of, a property tax revolt in California spread like a brush fire across the country, and the Republican Party went from the big-government conservatism of Nixon and Nelson Rockefeller to the small-government rabble-rousing of Barry Goldwater and Ronald Reagan. Even the decentralist and frankly utopian Libertarian Party scored, winning 1 electoral vote in 1972 and 921,299 popular votes in 1980 (still about double its second-highest total).

Most importantly, individuals burned through the 1970s with the haughty grandeur and splashiness falsely predicted of Comet Kohoutek. Stagflation be damned: Americans finally learned to live, dammit, in a no-collar world where both electricians and executives dressed like peacocks and women started earning real money, not just as entertainers but as doctors and lawyers. Boys grew hair longer than girls', and girls started playing Little League baseball. As Tom Wolfe wrote in his era-naming 1976 essay "The Me Decade and the Third Great Awakening":

Once the dreary little bastards started getting money . . . they did an astonishing thing—they took their money and ran! They did something only aristocrats (and intellectuals and artists) were supposed to do—they discovered and started doting on Me! They've created the greatest age of individualism in American history! All rules are broken!

All that was sacred was made profane, and everything solid dissolved into the Bermuda Triangle, or at least a long series of *Chariots of the Gods* sequels. During the 1970s, we undoubtedly felt superdiscombobulated (Hal Lindsey's millenarian *The Late Great Planet Earth* and Richard Bach's New Agey *Jonathan Livingston Seagull* shared space on the bestseller lists), but there is no question in retrospect that we were considerably more free, even by the time Margaret Thatcher had padlocked the coal mines in Olde England and the Reagan Revolution had ushered in the 1980s as a glorious decade of greed. Most important for the topic at hand, these sorts of things happened despite politics rather than because of them. The midget leaders of men back then—Gerald Ford, Jimmy Carter, Nelson Rockefeller—had virtually no new ideas or forward vision. The deregulation successes (detailed at length in the chapters ahead) happened because of an Ivy League academic and a ballsy lawyer in Texas; the personal computer sprang up in splendid isolation from anything going on in Washington, DC; and the seeds of a revolution in quality food, coffee, and alcohol sprouted from places such as Seattle, Washington; Austin, Texas; Berkeley, California; and Portland, Oregon.

Just as in 1971, there is in 2011 no shortage of reasons to be deeply troubled about the state and future of American liberty. The twenty-first-century version of Nixon's wage-and-price-control debacle was the George W. Bush–led, bipartisan, trillion-dollar bailout of the undeserving financial industry in late 2008, with its open-ended invitations to nationalize whole swaths of the economy, starting with the mortgage-lending businesses. Like the PATRIOT Act that opened the new millennium, the Troubled Asset Relief Program (TARP) was bum-rushed through Congress before even the

authors of the bill had time to read the damn thing, much less debate its likely "unintended" outcomes. Do-something statists, from
David Brooks to Michael Bloomberg, argued openly that the details
of the package didn't matter; the most important thing was showing
that the government was ready to act. TARP has since been ap-
pended by 2010's financial regulatory reform, which dictates what
sorts of products, rates, and fees the government allows the consumer finance industry to offer. After jawboning about the evils of
the "too-big-to-fail" doctrine, the new regulations actually enshrine
it as official policy, charging the government with managing more
and more of Wall Street in the name of minimizing "systemic risk."
Before losing its legislative majority, the first Barack Obama Congress managed to push through a series of bureaucratic, top-down
control systems for health care (essentially locking the existing
flawed system into place and turning health insurance into a government utility) and even pushed its way into oversight of school
lunches across the country.

Whether in international security, finance, health care, the environment, or even the cultural arena, the answer to everything
seems to be a new clampdown. Years after the signing of a free trade
agreement with Mexico and Canada, it is no longer possible to
cross a North American border without showing a passport, reveal-
ing biomedical information, and being entered into a database for
decades. Every day across this great country, some city council
is finding a new private activity to ban, whether it's selling food
cooked with trans fat, using a cell phone behind the wheel, or
smoking a cigarette outdoors. Cities from Los Angeles to Washington, DC, have cracked down on the dread menace of increasingly
sophisticated mobile food carts serving everything from bacon-
wrapped hot dogs to Mongolian barbecue. Plastic shopping bags
and online adult-services classifieds are as criminalized as short-
selling stocks. At all levels, elected and appointed officials cannot

conceive of a life worth living unless all aspects of it are officially sanctioned by some governmental unit.

Yet, if the age of Nixon contained a few flickers of light in the authoritarian darkness, our current moment also remains chock-full of halogen-bright beacons shouting, "This way!" Turn away from the overhyped importance of Washington, DC, and all the dreary, government-expanding policies and politics that go with it, and the picture is not merely one of plausible happy endings to our current sob stories of mortgage-finance meltdowns and ever-lengthening war but something far more radical, more game changing, than all that we've grown to expect. We are in fact living at the cusp of what can only be called the libertarian moment, the dawning not of some fabled, clichéd, and loosey-goosey Age of Aquarius but rather of a time of increasingly hyperindividualized, hyperexpanded choice over every aspect of our lives, from 401(k)s to hot and cold running coffee drinks, from online dating services to lifesaving decoding of individual human genomes.

Let us hack our way to a workable definition of *libertarian*, the only positive political adjective (as opposed to the relatively refusenik category of "independent") that seems to be gaining in cachet and adherents. No less an arbiter of trends than *New York* magazine declared in December 2010 that "there's never been a better time to be a libertarian." In the past few decades, figures ranging from William F. Buckley to Noam Chomsky, Bill Maher to the creators of *South Park*, Rep. Ron Paul to former New Mexico governor Gary Johnson, Camille Paglia to Julian Assange have used the term to describe themselves. Add to that spread the many acolytes of Ayn Rand (whose celebrants reportedly include Brad Pitt and Angelina Jolie) and Milton Friedman, your gold standard purists, sidewalk privatizers, Second Amendment enthusiasts, proponents of the World's Smallest Political Quiz, and groupies of the band Rush, and the term is almost bound to be confusing.

At its root, libertarianism is about a default preference for the freedom to peaceably pursue happiness as we define it without interference from government. It's the belief that the burden of proof should rest not on the individual who wants to sell lemonade, paint his or her house purple, hop on an airplane, ingest intoxicants, or marry someone from the same sex (though preferably not in that order) but on any government seeking to thwart or control such victimless activities. Like the magazine we write for, we agitate for the aspirational goal of "free minds and free markets," celebrating a world of expanding choice—in lifestyles, identities, goods, work arrangements, and more—and exploring the institutions, policies, and attitudes necessary for maximizing their proliferation. We are happy warriors against busybodies, elites, and gatekeepers who insist on dictating how other people should live their lives. Like John Stuart Mill, we're big on "experiments in living." Within the broadest possible parameters, we believe that you should be able to think what you want, live where you want, trade for what you want, eat what you want, smoke what you want, and wed whom you want. You should also be willing to shoulder the responsibilities entailed by your actions. Those general guidelines don't explain everything, and they certainly don't mean that there aren't hard choices to make, but as basic principles, they go a hell of a long way to creating a world that is tolerant, free, prosperous, vibrant, and interesting.

Often described as socially liberal and fiscally conservative, we think that individuals and the groups they form voluntarily should be given more rather than less space to try to create their patch of heaven on Earth. We take care to define *libertarian* less as a noun than as an adjective, and even as a prepolitical impulse. While we may nurture our own fevered utopian dreams, we reject the use of coercion and force to make those who feel differently live by our terms. Though there are a thousand different intralibertarian debates over what qualifies one to claim the *L*-word, for the purposes of our discussion here (and elsewhere), there will be no dogmatic checklist of qualifying policy preferences. Rather, we see libertarianism as more of a tendency: Does a particular person, politician, policy, social development, or technology increase the scope of individual freedom and expression? If so, then it deserves to be considered libertarian.

Look around you at the world you live in and the things you do. Despite the long and seemingly intractable recession, on this planet it's now arguably more possible than ever to live your life on your own terms; it's an early, rough-draft version of libertarian philosopher Robert Nozick's glimmering "utopia of utopias." Due to exponential advances in technology, broad-based increases in wealth, the ongoing networking of the world via trade and culture, and the decline of both state and private institutions of repression, never before has it been easier for more individuals to chart their own course and steer their lives by the stars as they see the sky.

This new century of the individual, which makes the Me Decade look positively communitarian in comparison, will have far-reaching implications wherever individuals swarm together in commerce, culture, and (eventually) politics. Already we have witnessed gale-force effects on nearly every "legacy" industry that had grown accustomed to dictating prices, products, and intelligence to its customers—be it the airlines, automakers, music companies, or newspapers (it was nice knowing all of you). Education and health care, handicapped by their large streams of public-sector, hence revanchist, funding, lag behind, but even in those sorry professions, practitioners are scrambling desperately to respond to consumer demands and compete for business.

A declaration of independence for our political moment means taking the insights, attitudes, and technologies that have revolutionized our private and commercial lives and applying them to the provision—and limitation—of government. It is recognizing, at long last, that treating government like an ATM machine that alternates between two spendthrift owners is no longer tolerable because they have run out of our money while disrespecting our diverse values. It is treating citizens and other residents like customers, not unwitting bankrollers who might luck into some patronage if they make the right friends. And it is acknowledging that the typical customer no longer belongs to a traditional political tribe, making her much more skeptical of, and even hostile to, partisan projects to put a man on the moon, or on Mars, or in a high-speed rail carriage.

What insights can undergird this transformation from party chair to citizen, from groaning bureaucracy to fleet-footed innovation? First is the reaffirmation that, all things being equal, and even in the midst of global economic squeeze, markets and competition remain the best way to organize an economy and unleash the means of production (and its increasingly difficult-to-distinguish adjunct, consumption). The Bush-Obama instinct to nationalize economic problems, from mortgage finance to the auto parts industry, is expensive, illegal, and ultimately doomed to failure. If state involvement correlated with industrial success, we'd all be watching French films and driving Ladas. Allowing for market competition, including in the delivery of government services, should be the default setting. Second is the recognition that at-least-vaguely-representative democracy, with the political freedom it almost always strengthens, is the least worst form of government (a fact that even recalcitrant, antimodern regimes in Islamabad, Tehran, and Berkeley grudgingly acknowledge in symbolic displays of pluralism).

Both points seem almost banal now, but they came under constant attack during the days of the Soviet Union and are still subject to wobbly confidence anytime capitalist dictatorships like

China seem to grow ascendant in a time of domestic economic woe. As *New York Times* columnist and tin-pot wise man Thomas Friedman wrote in 2009, flush with exasperation over the inability of President Obama to push through Friedman's preferred energy policy, "There is only one thing worse than one-party autocracy, and that is one-party democracy, which is what we have in America today. . . . One-party autocracy certainly has its drawbacks. But when it is led by a reasonably enlightened group of people, as China is today, it can also have great advantages. That one party can just impose the politically difficult but critically important policies needed to move a society forward in the 21st century." Though every dip in the Dow makes the professional amnesiacs of cable TV and the financial pages turn in the direction of Mao, there is no going back to the Great Leap Forward.

Or to the Great Society, for that matter. Try as politicians might, citizens continue their great escape from grand designs. Financially ruinous entitlements such as Social Security and Medicare are going nowhere slowly, but all of us are getting better at finding ways to work around stultifying bureaucracies. Virtually across the board, the government's pension plan is becoming less important to retirees, and the medical cartel is slowly losing its death grip on providing basic services. Even across old Europe, government spending as a percentage of GDP has fallen over the past several decades. The Heritage Foundation's Index of Economic Freedom has charted nothing but global increases since it began in 1995. Throughout the 1990s, virtually all of the developed countries in the world (the nations belonging to the Organization for Economic Cooperation and Development) reduced government spending as a percentage of GDP and flourished as a result. Once the current recession abates, in part due to the austerity measures pushed by countries such as Germany and Ireland, look for the downward trend in government spending to proceed apace.

The ne plus ultra change agent is the revolutionary, break-it-down-and-build-it-back-up power of the Internet and all the glorious creative destruction it enables at the expense of lumbering gatekeepers and to the benefit of empowered individuals. No single entity in the history of humankind has been so implicitly and explicitly libertarian: a tax-free distributed network and alternative universe where individuals, usually without effective interference from government, can reshape their identities and transcend the limitations of family, geography, and culture. It's a place where freaks and geeks and regular folks can pool their intelligence and compete (even win!) against entities thousands of times their size.

The generation raised on the Internet has essentially been raised libertarian, even those members who have never heard the word. Native netizens now entering college exhibit a kind of broad-based tolerance toward every manner of ethnic, religious, and sexual-orientation grouping in a way that would have seemed like science fiction just a generation ago. Generations Y and later all swim in markets—that is, in choices among competing alternatives—the way those of us who grew up in the 1970s frolicked on Slip 'n Slides. They didn't sign up for Barack Obama because he wanted to use TARP funds to bail out Chrysler factories and spread xenophobic rumors about the U.S. Chamber of Commerce being financed by foreigners; they signed up for Obama because he symbolized cosmopolitan tolerance, promised to ease back on presidential powers to imprison and abuse enemies, and seemed less likely than Republicans to embrace the drug war. Every one of these strands of hope was explicitly libertarian, and Obama has dashed each of them since attaining office. No wonder young people sat out the midterms.

In the twenty-first century, power—economic, cultural, political—will paradoxically accrue to those people who recognize that it's over for existing power centers. The command economy, the command culture, and the command polity are all in the process of being replaced by a different model—that of a consultant, a docent, a fixer, a friend. The individuals and groups that will flourish in this libertarian moment will be those who open things up rather than shutting them down. President Obama will find this out the hard way if he follows through on his administration's threats to prosecute nonviolent marijuana smokers in any state that has the temerity to vote the plant legal.

The single biggest piece of good news in the past twenty years (and arguably the past ninety) was the collapse of the Soviet Union and, with it, the final discrediting of Marxism as an economic and social model. Communism had ironically sided with the producer rather than the consumer, the factory owner rather than the workingman, by trying without success to shove unwanted commodities on unmanageable customers. If the end of World War II hastened the end of old-style colonialism (by the mid-1960s, virtually all the conventional old-world empires had been thoroughly dismantled), the end of the Cold War marked the end of countless proxy wars between the two major superpowers. The erosion of top-down hegemony resulted not in chaos (as many feared) but in a new era of freedom and mostly peaceful coexistence. While recent years have seen some reversals, as of the end of 2010, Freedom House ranked 87 of 193 countries as "free," 60 as "partly free," and 47 as "not free," which is up from 81/57/53 in 1997 and 58/51/51 in 1987.

Not only are countries increasingly independent and free, but thanks to global trade, they are increasingly prosperous as well, with an estimated 600 million people lifted out of poverty in China alone over the past three decades. War is declining too: As the political scientist John Mueller documents in 2004's *The Remnants of War*, armed global conflicts in which 1,000 people have died yearly have been declining for decades.

Here at home, we've seen an explicit backlash against the expansionist state, as voters weary of a bailout economics they never signed on for try to remind their elected representatives that you can only survive so long flouting any time-honored strain in American politics. The limited-government tendency might comprise a majority only in the rarest of cases, but it has been one of the basic subcategories of U.S. political thought since before the nation's founding, and at a time when the federal government's spending has jacked up from one-fifth of Gross Domestic Product to nearly one-fourth in a matter of months, reasserting this bipartisanly disrespected tradition feels like a basic act of self-defense.

When the gap grows too wide between voter desire and government policy, between the way people actually live their lives and the way government wants them to behave, then a situation that looks relatively stable can turn revolutionary overnight. The pendulum swings get faster and wider, and they are likely to cut more deeply when they strike flesh. Richard Nixon may have been sitting pretty in 1972, having won a second term by a historic margin, but he was sent packing to San Clemente by 1974. Barack Obama built off a surprising Democratic wave in 2006 to win his first term in the White House by the biggest margin since Ronald Reagan drubbed the hapless Walter Mondale in 1984; yet, he was in the public doghouse by 2010. Four years after Nancy Pelosi became the first female Speaker of the House, she's back to being a ranking member. That may not exactly be progress, but it is indicative of the disconnect between politics and the larger American society.

It also points to the central truth of this book, of the past forty years, and (hopefully) of the next forty: We need not only a declaration of *independents in* politics but a declaration of *independence from* politics. Chapter 2 charted the huge declines in affiliation by party, which is all to the good. Why would anyone with half a brain pledge undying loyalty to the party of John McCain or John Kerry, to name the two most recent losers in presidential elections? Only a madman or a mental defective would take a punch for Nancy Pelosi or John Boehner. Would even their family members donate a kidney for Harry Reid or Mitch McConnell? We exaggerate only slightly to drive home the obvious: Partisan politics as it has existed for lo these many decades is your father's Oldsmobile—embarrassing, defunct, way too big, and no longer in production.

We need a retreat, a general evacuation from the area of human activity in which a majority, however slim, acquires the right to control the lives and property of the minority. Unlike the commercial or cultural realms, politics is essentially a zero-sum game. There is one way to do things, and that particular way is enforced against all and at all costs. The innovation and plurality of approaches taken for granted in, say, the prepared-food industry are virtually unknown in politics. This is due to many forces—special interests, power tripping, lack of feedback from affected parties, absence of competition, cover-your-ass syndrome, and more—but no one mistakes the public sector for a world of swift and responsive change. Because the stakes are so high and the world so Manichaean in politics, the best approach is to shrink it to its smallest functional size, so that it covers fewer aspects of our lives.

Why should any of a practicing Catholic's tax dollars pay for a museum exhibition in which ants crawl all over a crucifix? Why should people who hate baseball in the municipal disaster that is Washington, DC, see any of their hard-earned doubloons go to evict local business owners and build a shiny new stadium on behalf of a billionaire busy laughing his way to the bank? Why should those of us who believe that market capitalism requires the freedom to fail be on the hook for auto companies or airlines that cannot manage to succeed? Take the government out of nonessential functions, and the endless disputes that separate us become the subject of friendly

dinner arguments, not life-and-death battles over our own confis-
cated money.

Even as politics should retreat from our world, however, there's
an excellent argument for voters retreating from politics by becoming self-conscious, die-hard independents. Once you have no dog in
the hunt of national politics, we can both testify from experience,
much of what passes for important discourse is revealed quickly to be
absurd, truth-destroying theater. The *St. Petersburg Times*, God bless
'em, has the stomach to watch ABC News's *This Week* every Sunday
and deliver a fact-check on the routinely gaseous statements from
politicians and commentators. Browsing the site just before Christmas in 2010, we found that of twenty statements reviewed on the
site's front page, seven were judged flatly "false," three "barely true,"
six "half true," one "mostly true," and one a "pants-on-fire" lie. Did
Polifact find any true statements? Yes, exactly two, or a miserable
10 percent. Chairman of the Joint Chiefs of Staff Mike Mullen correctly pointed out that historically, Senate ratification of arms-
control treaties has been "bipartisan" (seriously, we're talking about
this level of assertion), and Senator Kent Conrad (D-ND) was right
when he said that federal spending is "the highest it's been as a share
of our economy in 60 years," while revenue "is the lowest it's been as
a share of our economy in 60 years."

Politics is corrosive to a person's constitution (to say nothing of
our nation's Constitution). The underlying business, marketed
with such benign and munificent phrases as "public service," is, at
its base, a system for extracting money from citizens and institutions under threat of imprisonment and then sloshing it around
with intentional inefficiency (for instance, by requiring "prevail-
ing wages" for employees working on government contracts) on
projects, programs, and bureaucracies whose selection and ongoing
sustenance are products of political expedience and patronage. We
would not, to cite one of ten thousand possible examples, hand out

billions of taxpayer dollars to ethanol producers every year if the decision-making process was remotely meritocratic. (Even Al Gore has repudiated his once-vocal support for the program, saying in late 2010, "It is not a good policy to have these massive subsidies for first-generation ethanol." The former vice president attributed his earlier position to special-interest politics: "I had a certain fondness for the farmers in the state of Iowa because I was about to run for President".) And even if you don't subscribe to such a cynical (or realistic!) point of view about the grubby nature of political power, you can surely observe the warp and damage it inflicts on its most energetic participants and even spectators. "Political language," George Orwell wrote in his famous essay on the topic, "is designed to make lies sound truthful and murder respectable, and to give an appearance of solidity to pure wind."

Taking your talking points from political-team membership is a shortcut around the truth and a fast track to intolerance for your fellow man. It's also an abdication of responsibility. As Václav Havel wrote during the latter days of communism, in a critique of Western peace activists, "Why bother with a ceaseless and in fact hopeless search for truth when truth can be had readily, all at once, in the form of an ideology or a doctrine? Suddenly it is all so simple. So many difficult questions are answered in advance! So many laborious existential tasks from which our minds are freed once and for all!" Stepping off the political treadmill can be disorienting at first, as your legs and eyes get used to a world standing still. But suddenly people and things that seemed so important are revealed to be ridiculous. You no longer have to pretend to take Cryin' John Boehner seriously when he pledges to bring fiscal accountability to government this time. The *New York Times* editorial page's inexhaustible supply of the word "must" becomes less an occasion for solemn thought and more like a word search: "Mr. Obama must not be drawn into nickel-and-dime cuts"; the Supreme Court "must let candidates who need public support have enough public dollars to compete effectively"; the United States "must be much more vigilant and aggressive" with China; ad infinitum. Away from the greenhouse-gas emissions of professional politics, you begin to notice that the stuff that matters most in life has little, if anything, to do with Democratic fund-raising totals for the third quarter. The communities you cherish most—your church, your baseball team, your *Star Trek* fan club, your PTA, your death metal Twitter friends, the tolerable half of your family—are not defined by politics and, in fact, would be riven asunder if politics became the prime directive. The stuff you love consuming or using—the Web, your iPhone, vegan pizza, gourmet kimchi tacos from a food truck—was not produced by a benevolent government looking to enrich your life. The world is infinitely more interesting than the insincere debates about politics at or near the centers of political power.

To declare independence in and from politics does not, of course, mean that individuals and the groups they form will shrink from activity that impacts the broadly defined public interest. Indeed, the history of charity in America before the advent of the modern welfare era in the early twentieth century was precisely a tale of private charities providing the model for what the state would do. To assume that the hungry will starve, the naked will go unclothed, and the ignorant will remain uneducated if government spending declines as a percentage of GDP is as misguided as assuming no one would go to church absent a state religion. The opposite is true: Given more money, more time, and more freedom to pursue their lives, individuals will innovate and experiment with new ways of delivering so-called public goods while also continuing to innovate and experiment with conventional business models and cultural apparitions. There's an important reason why religion in the United States—which, thanks to the First Amendment, has no official creed—is more robust, varied, and, dare we say, competitive than it is in, say, England, where the state has its very own church.

There is a learning curve at work here, one that human beings have been struggling with for 40 years, 400 years, 4,000 years. In context, only recently has the concept of individual liberty been prototyped and subjected to testing in anything approaching real-world conditions. Advances are inevitably followed by setbacks, and we stagger into the future punch-drunk, bruised more like Muhammad Ali than like Rocky Marciano.

The power to swarm in the direction of freedom is the new technology fueling an idea as old as the American republic itself: No central government shall interfere with our life, liberty, or pursuit of happiness. The libertarian moment is taking that self-evident truth and organizing it into a comprehensive approach toward living. It started where it always does, in business and culture, where innovation and experimentation are rewarded. Statist politicians— it's not fully clear that there is any other kind—will ignore this epochal shift at their peril. And, like Nixon Agonistes, they will eventually be forced to fly to their own personal San Clementes.

The politicians and the increasingly small-in-number but shrill-in-tone dead-enders in both parties fail to understand that we are moving far beyond them and their cramped vision of a world in which politics is the limit of human potential. More and more of us understand, to a degree almost never discussed in day-to-day political and policy discourse, that the driving force behind many of the advancements we most enjoy stems from an unsung, three-pronged source: the democratizers, who through sheer crazed determination have brought new tools and possibilities to a broad swath of the public; the enablers, those few heroic men and women in government who identified, then helped remove, obstacles to the democratizers' progress; and the theoreticians, who dreamed up these possibilities long before sane men thought them possible. Each one of the stories in the next five chapters shows how these unusual trifectas form in nature to produce unalloyed goods, most of which we're happy to use without the slightest bit of knowledge about the oftentimes brutal fights to make them legal, let alone operational. They provide the source code for what the twenty-first century should be looking like, but so far isn't.

PART II

THE DEMOCRATIZATION OF JUST ABOUT EVERYTHING, OR CASE STUDIES IN MAKING LIFE RICHER, WEIRDER, AND BETTER

CHAPTER 4

KEEP ON ROCKIN' IN THE FREE WORLD

The arrival of amplified rock music performed by free-spirited long-hairs was not, to put it mildly, greeted with enthusiasm by the Cold Warriors of the West. Nearly a decade after Elvis's pelvis dislocated social mores and Frank Sinatra denounced rock as "the martial music of every sideburned delinquent on the face of the Earth," rock 'n' roll refuseniks were still crying bloody murder. In September 1964, *National Review* founder and tireless anticommunist William F. Buckley reacted to pop music's British Invasion with a spasm of Victorian disgust: "Let me say it, as evidence of my final measure of devotion to the truth," Buckley huffed. "The Beatles are not merely awful, I would consider it sacrilegious to say anything less than that they are so unbelievably horrible, so appallingly unmusical, so dogmatically insensitive to the magic of the art, that they qualify as crowned heads of antimusic, even as the imposter popes went down in history as 'anti-popes.'"

Twenty years later, the then wife of Democratic senator and Cold War hawk Al Gore cofounded the Parents Music Resource Center (PMRC) in reaction to the heavy metal and early rap genres that,

Tipper Gore claimed, were "infecting the youth of the world with messages they cannot handle." Musicians from John Denver to Frank Zappa were hauled to Washington to argue under oath (futilely) against a warning-sticker censorship regime. Gangsta rappers like Ice-T stood accused of increasing violence against cops, dance-club bonbons like Cyndi Lauper and Sheena Easton glorified sex, and metal acts from Kiss to Iron Maiden were transmitting secret backwards paeans to Satan himself. In her 1987 book *Raising PG Kids in an X-Rated World*, Gore fretted over the demonic import of the role-playing game Dungeons and Dragons and argued that listening to acts such as Ozzy Osbourne was "playing with fire" and all too often led to death and damnation. "Many kids experiment with the deadly satanic game," she warned, "and get hooked." Gore claimed to be against censorship but instructed her readers to "file petitions with the Federal Communications Commission in Washington to request inquiries into the license renewals of television and radio stations that violate the public interest."

Though such outbursts always look comical in retrospect—Buckley ended up befriending John Lennon in the 1970s, and Tipper Gore attempted to rehabilitate her uptight image by insisting during her husband's 2000 campaign that she'd been a reliable Deadhead all along—the gag reflex that produced them is alive and well. Radical Islam has replaced communism as the existential bogeyman requiring eternal vigilance, and some vigilantes have drawn a link between the vulgar pop culture of the West and the murderous religious radicalism of the Middle East, most notoriously in conservative Dinesh D'Souza's obscene 2007 book *The Enemy at Home: The Cultural Left and Its Responsibility for 9/11*. "Conservatives," D'Souza wrote, "must stop promoting American popular culture because it is producing a blowback of Muslim rage. With a few exceptions, the right should not bother to defend American movies, music, and television. From the point of view of traditional values, they are indefensible. Moreover, why should the right stand up for the left's debased values? Why should our people defend their America? Rather, American conservatives should join the Muslims and others in condemning the global moral degeneracy that is produced by liberal values."

If music has become ever more morally degenerate—and one need only look at the PMRC's now-pedestrian "Filthy Fifteen" list from 1985 to see the long tumble from Twisted Sister (whose "We're Not Going to Take It," a by-the-numbers rave-up, supposedly promoted violence) and Cyndi Lauper (whose forgotten hit "She Bop" promoted masturbation) to GWAR (whose albums include *This Toilet Earth* and *We Kill Everything*) and Slipknot (who wear scary masks and subtitled one album *The Subliminal Verses*)—then it would stand to reason that the era of globalized hip-hop, video game violence, and pornography would have set back the cause of human freedom by generations. In fact, the exact opposite has happened.

Freedom House, a U.S. government–funded international non-profit founded in 1941 by Eleanor Roosevelt and Wendell Willkie, has been conducting "Freedom of the World" surveys since 1973, measuring by a set of stable, if subjective, criteria whether countries are "free," "partly free," or "not free." The group's initial analysis of 151 countries found that nearly half (46 percent) were not free, compared to 29 percent free and 25 percent partly free. The collapse of totalitarian communism beginning in 1989 resulted in free countries outnumbering the unfree for the first time, and by 2010, with 194 countries to choose from (itself an indication of increased freedom), the numbers from 1973 had almost exactly reversed: 46 percent free, 30 percent partly free, and 24 percent unfree.

We're not just talking about correlation between the spread of pop culture and international freedom: There is direct, observable causation. The remarkable two weeks of Egyptian street protests that led to the resignation of longtime dictator Hosni Mubarak were populated mostly by leaderless young people who could no longer tolerate being censored (Mubarak's attempts to shut down the Internet may well have been his fatal mistake). For more than a decade, the Egyptian regime had waged a brutal and eventually losing battle against a burgeoning homegrown heavy metal movement in a crackdown known as the "Satanic Panic." As Cairo's unofficial metal historian Sameh "Slacker" Sabry told journalist Richard Poplak in 2009, "My question to you is: Would you stop listening to the music you loved if someone was going to throw you in jail for it? If the answer is yes, then you don't love the music enough. I have been charged for Satanism; I have been called a devil worshipper. Many times. My name has been in print—with my age, my school—I was waiting for them to come for me. I did not change. I did not hide. You want a piece of me—come get it."

Poplak, writing in a book on pop culture and Islam that came out six months before the historic events in Cairo, concluded on a prescient note:

> What I had seen that night was on some small level a revolution—or at least a concentrated act of defiance—played out to the fuzz and wail of heavy metal music. I had seen kids assert their right to rock. There is this expectation, a shared if unarticulated belief that these bands—like the legendary [Czech band] Plastic People of the Universe, who carried the ethos of revolution inside the psych-swirl of their avant-rock—herald some hope for future freedoms. Regardless of lyrical content, simply by existing, merely by banging head, [the Egyptian bands] Wyvern, Deathless Anguish and company are harbingers of change. What sort of change?

Some of the architecture of that change was spelled out in the Alexandria Declaration, a March 2004 statement from Middle Eastern intellectuals advocating a series of liberal reforms, above all "guaranteed freedom of expression in all its forms, topmost among which is freedom of the press, and audio-visual and electronic media." The Alexandria Declaration, as the German newspaper *Der Spiegel* reported in February 2011, is a "'Charter 77' for reform in the Arab world."

Charter 77, just like the Plastic People of the Universe, is a relatively obscure reference in twenty-first-century America. Yet, its 1970s-era call for freedom of expression in communist Europe is at the very center of the single most foundational story of how supposed Western cultural decadence combined with dissident aspirations in the unfree world to produce not just unprecedented liberation but a usable blueprint for oppressed people everywhere to cast off the shackles of their masters. Standing at the center of that story is the literal author of the blueprint, a rumpled star child of the 1960s whose love and understanding of rock music helped free his country and inspire freedom in so many others: Václav Havel, the leader of what came to be known as the "Velvet Revolution."

That story begins with another story, that of the Velvet Underground, a band whose best-known member, Lou Reed, chafed not under the oppression of Russian tanks but under the strictures of postwar Long Island suburbia. A hippie-hating countercultural figure, the teenaged Reed had been given electroshock treatments to "cure" his homosexual tendencies. Reed would later find a mentor in the legendarily alcoholic poet Delmore Schwartz, before gaining fame for singing about drug abuse and cross-dressing and fronting a band that openly sang about soul-sapping heroin rather than consciousness-raising LSD during 1967's Summer of Love.

No one is exactly sure how a copy of *The Velvet Underground & Nico* found its way to Czechoslovakia before Soviet tanks crushed the cultural opening of the Prague Spring in August 1968. After all, the March 1967 debut album by Andy Warhol's nihilistic house band barely sold in America, peaking at just #171 on the

Billboard charts before quickly disappearing. Rock critics would not come around to declaring it one of the best albums ever made until decades later. There is that famous line, variously attributed to superproducer Brian Eno or R.E.M. guitarist Peter Buck, that "only a thousand people bought the record, but every one of them started a band." And though Czechs were starting bands right and left, as part of an all-too-brief cultural reemergence that saw artists such as filmmaker Miloš Forman and novelist Milan Kundera gain international prominence, there was a lot of catching up to do in 1967 and 1968 for a country that had until recently outlawed William F. Buckley's least favorite band. "It is so strange," the singer of a Czech Velvet Underground cover band would muse a few years after communism's demise, "that Prague was so up-to-date."

Whatever the source, this influential piece of dissonant, drug-saturated, hyperurban yet occasionally gentle music, with the flat everyman vocals of Lou Reed alternating with the morose German female baritone of supermodel Nico, wound up in the hands of a teenage butcher's apprentice and budding rock bassist named Milan "Meijla" Hlavsa. "The Velvet Underground was something very different, very new, very real," Hlavsa recalled a quarter century later, "because their music was a part of their life. . . . It brought us America in a real way. It was good to see that in the States there were normal people who had problems like us." One month after the 1968 Soviet invasion, Hlavsa and some buddies started a band called the Plastic People of the Universe. Named after the song "Plastic People" by future Tipper Gore foil Frank Zappa (though perhaps also influenced by the Andy Warhol/Velvet Underground "Exploding Plastic Inevitable" multimedia extravaganzas that the band would go on to emulate), Plastic People was mostly a cover band at first, singing versions in heavily accented English of Zappa, the Doors, the Fugs, and the Velvets. "The base of our music was the Velvet Underground," Hlavsa said.

Though the passage of time has dulled the shock value, the Velvet Underground in its time was like a needle in the eye even to seasoned Western rock audiences. One of the only music magazines to take contemporary note of *The Velvet Underground & Nico* called it "a full-fledged attack on the ears and on the brain." Legendary *Rolling Stone* critic Lester Bangs in 1969 called the band a "bunch of junkie-faggot-sadomasochist-speed-freaks who roared their anger and their pain in storms of screaming feedback and words spat out like strings of epithets." And he *liked* them. The songs were about heroin, hitting your girlfriend, scoring drugs, and the pathos of planning for the next Manhattan party. The drummer was a girl (no normal occurrence in those days), who played standing up, with mallets. "The real question is what this music is about—smack, meth, deviate sex and drugdreams, or something deeper?" wondered Bangs. "The most important lesson [about] the Velvet Underground," he concluded, was "the power of the human soul to transcend its darker levels." This was not the sort of material that either Dinesh D'Souza or Tipper Gore could bop along to.

Now, imagine how it might have gone over in a totalitarian country where longhairs like Hlavsa were arrested, literally, for having long hair, as well as for the crime of possessing unapproved music. Rock bands in Czechoslovakia required a license from the government, and in those days of communist "normalization," the Plastic People's was soon revoked. The band continued to play, but only at weddings (one of the few activities beyond the government's control) and at secret, onetime shows advertised through paranoid word of mouth. The Plastics acquired a Warholesque "artistic director," the crazed alcoholic imp Ivan Martin Jirous, and eventually replaced its English-language repertoire with a bunch of Czech originals derived from the poetry of various banned authors. The songs weren't political in any conventional sense, but when the state dictates culture, all unapproved acts become political, like it or not.

The actual Velvet Underground back in the United States was being used as a cautionary tale for parents about their drug-addicted teens. "The light show, the intensity of the sound, the wild dress and appearance of the musicians has turned many adults away from listening to the lyrics," the Utah *Deseret News* quoted one cult-awareness seminar leader as saying in 1974. "But if heeded, the words vividly convey a message of confusion, searching, longing, destruction, and morbidity." At the same time, the band's Czech apprentices were being portrayed on propagandistic communist television shows as dangerously nihilistic longhairs who might just convince wayward teens to hijack an airplane. Forced underground by the censors, the Plastics and their followers christened their own artistic movement as "the underground" (in English), or *druhá kultura* ("second culture"). It was alternative before there was Alternative. As Hlavsa would tell an interviewer in 1997, "Our community, which was, probably imprecisely, referred to as 'underground,' was a pocket of normal life. . . . People with feelings similar to ours were coming to our concerts. Their music preferences were not necessarily similar, but music wasn't as important there as meeting people and being together in a normal environment for a while. I don't know if anything like that would be possible had the Plastic People of the Universe not existed then."

By 1976, the regime could stand it no more. At a festival celebrating *druhá kultura*, four members of the Plastic People, along with many other festival attendees, were arrested on charges of disturbing the peace, no small offense in communist Czechoslovakia. It was a move that would not only backfire on communist authorities but help create source code for citizens of any lousy country to stand up to their oppressors. Dissent itself was about to be democratized, planting seeds that would eventually free hundreds of millions of people.

Václav Havel, by this time, was not your typical rock 'n' roller. At age thirty-nine, this disheveled, chain-smoking playwright with the awkward stammer, son of one of the richest families in modern Czech history, spent much of his time with his regal wife futzing about the garden of their vacation cottage outside of Prague, under the perpetual surveillance of the police. As an enthusiastic participant of the 1960s—"That was an extraordinarily interesting, fertile, and inspiring period, not only here, but in the culture of the entire world," he told an interviewer in 1975—Havel was a rock guy. He preferred the Stones to the Beatles and took from amplified music "a temperament, a nonconformist state of the spirit, an anti-establishment orientation, an aversion to philistines, and an interest in the wretched and humiliated," he would later write. This may help explain why, the year before, after more than a half decade of depressed indolence brought on by normalization and the experience of being banned in his own country, Havel had uncorked a piece of literary and political punk rock whose ramifications are still being felt.

In April 1975, Havel sat down and, knowing that he'd likely be imprisoned for his efforts, wrote an open letter to his dictator, Gustáv Husák, explaining in fearless and painstaking detail just why and how totalitarianism was ruining Czechoslovakia. "So far," Havel scolded Husák, "you and your government have chosen the easy way out for yourselves, and the most dangerous road for society: the path of inner decay for the sake of outward appearances; of deadening life for the sake of increasing uniformity; of deepening the spiritual and moral crisis of our society, and ceaselessly degrading human dignity, for the puny sake of protecting your own power."

It was the big bang that set off the dissident movement in Central Europe. For those lucky enough to read an illegally retyped copy or hear it broadcast over Radio Free Europe, the effect was not unlike what happened to, well, those few people who bought the Velvet Underground's first record: After the shock and initial pleasure wore off, many said, "Wait a minute, I can do this too!"

By standing up to a system that had forced every citizen to make a thousand daily compromises—indeed, by identifying those compromises and vowing to forgo them in the future—Havel was suggesting a novel new tactic: Have the self-respect to call things by their proper names, never mind the consequences, and maybe you'll put the bastards on the defensive. "In general, I believe it always makes sense to tell the truth, in all circumstances," he told interviewer Jiří Lederer three weeks after issuing the letter. Besides, "I got tired of always wondering how to move in this situation, and I felt the need to stir things up, to confront others for a change and force them to deal with a situation that I myself had created."

A Czech, then Slovak, then Polish, then communist-bloc dissident movement sprang up around Havel's letter, producing entire genres of literature within the confines of samizdat. Writers grew their hair out a bit, joked out loud about the secret police, and began looking for a cause célèbre. When the arty longhairs of the Plastic People got charged with disturbing the peace, it became a turning point in both Havel's life and the future of the world. "What Havel realized was that this represented something very dangerous," said Czech-born British playwright Tom Stoppard, whose award-winning 2006 play *Rock 'n' Roll* centered on a Plastic People fan becoming radicalized in communist Prague, in 2009. "Now the state could put you into jail simply for being the wrong sort of bloke." As Havel would later recall, "Everyone understood that an attack on the Czech musical underground was an attack on a most elementary and important thing, something that in fact bound everyone together: it was an attack on the very notion of living within the truth, on the real aims of life."

Havel's 1976 essay on the Plastic People trial—which he and his friends brazenly attended every day, shocking officials in the courtroom—has the rushed and liberated tone of someone who has just crossed a personal point of no return, or has just heard the Sex

Pistols' *Never Mind the Bollocks* for the first time. "It doesn't often happen and when it does it usually happens when least expected," the piece begins. "Somewhere, something slips out of joint and suddenly a particular event, because of an unforeseen interplay between its inner premises and more or less fortuitous external circumstances, crosses the threshold of its usual place in the everyday world, breaks through the shell of what it is supposed to be and what it seems, and reveals its innermost symbolic significance. And something originally quite ordinary suddenly casts a surprising light on the time and the world we live in, and dramatically highlights its fundamental questions."

Ivan Martin Jirous and his compadres, Havel writes, may not have "had any other aim in mind than persuading the court of their innocence and defending their right to compose and sing the songs they wanted," but through the absurd theatrics of totalitarianism they became "the unintentional personification of those forces in man that compel him to search for himself, to determine his own place in the world freely, and in his own way, not to make deals with his heart and not to cheat his conscience, to call things by their true names . . . and to do so at one's own risk, aware that at any time one may come up against the disfavor of the 'masters,' the incomprehension of the dull-witted, or their own limitations." Havel and his friends began to experience "the exciting realization that there are still people among us who assume the existential responsibility for their own truth and are willing to pay a high price for it." Suddenly, "much of the wariness and caution that marks my behavior seemed petty to me. I felt an increased revulsion toward all forms of guile, all attempts at painlessly worming one's way out of vital dilemmas. Suddenly, I discovered in myself more determination in one direction, and more independence in another. Suddenly, I felt disgusted with a whole world, in which—as I realized then—I still have one foot: the world of emergency exits."

The essay ends with a classic description of Havel bumping into a film director who doesn't understand his sudden enthusiasm for defending a bunch of derelict, possibly drug-addled rock musicians. "Perhaps I'm doing him an injustice," Havel writes, "but at that moment, I was overwhelmed by an intense feeling that this dear man belonged to a world that I no longer wish to have anything to do with—and Mr. Public Prosecutor Kovarik, pay attention, because here comes a vulgar word—I mean the world of cunning shits."

With this middle finger pointed at commie censors and other cunning shits, Václav Havel and his friends then launched Charter 77, arguably the most influential human rights organization in modern history. The charter of the organization's name was an ingeniously clever petition: Like Martin Luther King Jr. asking for the "promissory note" of the Declaration of Independence to be enshrined in official policy, the Czech and Slovak signatories of Charter 77 merely asked their government to abide by its own laws—specifically, the 1960 Czechoslovak Constitution, plus the human rights provisions in several international treaties that the country had signed on to to shore up its image, most critically the 1975 Helsinki Final Act of the major Cold War diplomatic effort, the Helsinki Accords.

The Final Act, signed by President Gerald Ford, was roundly criticized at the time by American conservatives—and especially neoconservatives—as a "betrayal" since, among other things, it codified the existing postwar borders of Europe, which meant accepting in treaty form the imperial Soviet subjugation of the Baltic countries of Latvia, Lithuania, and Estonia. But the act also included important covenants on civil, political, and economic rights. Living up to Helsinki would have meant allowing free expression, "freedom from fear," freedom of religious practice, and other rights then quashed by totalitarians and authoritarians everywhere. The narrow, legalistic tactic of petitioning the government to follow its own laws was a built-in defense against charges of political subversion and a clever way to attract the attention and support of international activists and governments. It started with Charter 77, spread to the Committee for the Defense of Workers in Poland, then to the Moscow Helsinki Group, and on and on. In the West, Helsinki helped spawn Helsinki Watch, which would later become Human Rights Watch, which linked up with the fate of Eastern Bloc dissidents, and by the time Ronald Reagan was negotiating with Mikhail Gorbachev about nuclear warheads and the Strategic Defense Initiative in the mid-1980s, the Final Act was a handy spotlight with which to expose communist hypocrisy: a crowbar wedged into the seams of the Iron Curtain.

Czechoslovak authorities initially responded to Charter 77 by trying to suppress the document and harass its authors, but the petition had gone global and was being beamed back into the country through Radio Free Europe and Voice of America. Emboldened even in the face of a new round of arrests and show trials, the chartists launched the Committee for the Defense of the Unjustly Persecuted, and Havel even brought the just-back-from-prison Plastic People over to his country house to record their 1978 album, *Passion Play*. The wind now in the anticommunists' sails, Havel in October 1978 uncorked his most famous and influential essay of all, "The Power of the Powerless." The lead essay in what was supposed to be a joint Polish-Czechoslovak dissident forum, Havel's meditation on the meaning of dissent and the architecture of lies required by totalitarianism had a profound impact across the Eastern Bloc and beyond. It was a how-to guide for regular people to create daily acts of subversion just by choosing to live and act honestly and openly.

Solidarity activist Zbygniew Bujak once told Havel's English-language translator (and former coconspirator of the Plastic People), the great Canadian journalist Paul Wilson,

> This essay reached us in the Ursus factory in 1979 at a point when we felt we were at the end of the road. . . . Reading it gave us the

theoretical underpinnings for our activity. It maintained our spirits; we did not give up, and a year later—in August 1980—it became clear that the party apparatus and the factory management were afraid of us. We mattered. And the rank and file saw us as leaders of the movement. When I look at the victories of Solidarity, and of Charter 77, I see in them an astonishing fulfillment of the prophecies and knowledge contained in Havel's essay.

Havel spent most of the next five years in jail. But such arrests only served to make the plight of the dissidents more internationally famous and to drain what remaining sympathy there might have been among Western intellectuals for the projects of communism and Marxism. Like George Orwell, another self-described "man of the left" obsessed with the meaning of words and the endless search for truth, Havel became one of the twentieth century's most effective anticommunists.

And, like Orwell, Havel saw political and ideological tribalism as the great impediment to that search. Personal independence, he has said for decades, is the prerequisite for living in truth. Havel's Civic Forum movement, which rose up against and eventually took power from the Communist Party, was intentionally designed as a unified front against communism. In the first months of his presidency, which began in 1989, he championed "nonpolitical politics," and even when that ideal disintegrated upon contact with modern democratic realities, Havel refused to ever join a political party. As he wrote in his 1991 book *Summer Meditations*,

All my adult life I was branded by officials as "an exponent of the right" who wanted to bring capitalism back to our country. Today—at a ripe old age—I am suspected by some of being left-wing, if not of harboring out-and-out socialist tendencies. What, then, is my real position? First and foremost, I have never espoused any ideology, dogma, or doctrine—left-wing, right-wing, or any other closed, ready-made system of presuppositions about the world. On the contrary, I have tried to think independently, using my own powers of reason, and I have always vigorously resisted attempts to pigeonhole me.

By the time communism imploded in 1989, Havel and his comrades had been preparing for the moment for over a decade, through exhaustive debate, peer review, coalition building, and acts of enormous personal courage. It was no accident that Czechoslovakia's liberation, as compared to the rest of the region, would be among the least violent and most poetic, that it would be called the "Velvet Revolution." As then president Havel told a startled Lou Reed when he met the Velvet Underground's former front man in 1990, "Did you know that I am president because of you?" Nine years later, during his last presidential visit to the Bill Clinton White House, Havel made two musical requests: Get Lou Reed to play a set, then bring over the Plastic People. To celebrate the last Soviet troop leaving Czechoslovak soil, the Czech president organized a star-studded concert featuring Paul Simon and Frank Zappa (it was the last live show by Zappa, who would die of prostate cancer). There is a reason why there's a revolution named after the Velvet Underground, a pariah even in the Free World, and none after Van Cliburn, the classical pianist pushed endlessly on American audiences as the high-cultural equivalent of Russian piano masters. The Velvets represented a do-it-yourself culture, while Cliburn represented a straitjacketed approach to official recognition.

November 1989, with its Velvet Revolution and breaching of the Berlin Wall, was the most liberating month of arguably the most liberating year in human history. As preeminent modern Central European historian Timothy Garton Ash wrote in a 2008 essay, 1989 "ended communism in Europe, the Soviet empire, the division of Germany, and an ideological and geopolitical struggle . . . that had shaped world politics for half a century. It was, in its geopolitical results, as big as 1945 or 1914. By comparison, '68 was a molehill." Without the superpower conflict to animate and arm scores of proxy civil wars and brutal governments around the globe, authoritarians two decades ago quickly gave way to democrats in capitals from Johannesburg to Santiago. Endless war was replaced by enduring peace in Central America. Nations that had never enjoyed self-determination found themselves independent, prosperous, safe, and integrated into the West. More people now live in freedom, peace, and nonpoverty than at any time in human history.

Even these numbers only begin to capture the magnitude of the change. The abject failure of top-down central planning as an economic organizing model had a profound impact even on the few communist governments that survived the 1990s. Vietnam, while maintaining a one-party grip on power, launched radical market reforms in 1990, resulting in some of the world's highest economic growth in the last two decades. Cuba, economically desperate after the Soviet spigot was cut off, legalized some foreign investment and private commerce. In perhaps the single most dramatic geopolitical story between 1989 and 2011, the country that most symbolized state repression that year when it rolled tanks at peaceful protesters in Tiananmen Square has used a version of capitalism to pull off history's most successful antipoverty campaign. Although Chinese market reforms began in the late 1970s and were temporarily halted after the Tiananmen Square massacre, China's recognition after the collapse of the Soviet Union that private enterprise should trump the state sector has helped lift hundreds of millions of people out of poverty, giving the Western world vapors about competing with a country where people had only recently starved to death in the tens of millions. While China has far to go in even approximating acceptable standards of political freedom and living, its citizens are unquestionably better off materially than they were a generation ago.

Perhaps the least appreciated benefits of the Cold War's end were those enjoyed by the side that won. Up until 1989, mainstream Western European political thought included a large and unhealthy appetite for government ownership of the means of production. The original Marshall Plan was an almost desperate attempt to prevent the kind of domestically popular (if externally manipulated) communist takeover that would submerge Czechoslovakia in 1948. Upon taking office in 1981, socialist French president François Mitterand nationalized wide swaths of France's economy. By the time the Berlin Wall was pulled down at decade's end, it was the rule, not the exception, that Western European governments would own all their countries' major airlines, phone companies, television stations, gas companies, and much more.

But this would not hold true for much longer. In the long battle of ideas between Karl Marx and Milton Friedman, even the democratic socialists of Europe had to admit that Friedman had won by a landslide. Although media attention was rightly focused on the dramatic economic changes transforming Asia and the former Eastern Bloc, fully half of the world's privatization in the first dozen years after the Cold War, as measured by revenue, took place in Western Europe. Since then, European political and monetary integration has opened up the free movement of goods and people across once-militarized borders. London is crawling with Latvians, Paris with the Polish, and international marriages are increasing even faster than living standards in the former Warsaw Pact countries. And two decades of state sell-offs in the West have given even Scandinavians more basic respect for capitalism than their American counterparts. It was no accident that, in the midst of Washington's recent bailout of U.S. automakers, Swedish enterprise minister Maud Olofsson, when asked about the fate of struggling Saab, tersely announced, "The Swedish state is not prepared to own car factories."

Charter 77, meanwhile, has proven an inspiration to more than a dozen freedom movements in authoritarian countries the world over. Using the same blueprint of asking oppressive governments to abide by their own laws, the sons of Charter 77, often with the explicit assistance of Havel, have continued to shock consciences, trigger backlashes, and occasionally bring down bad governments. Liu Xiaobo of China's Charter 08 was awarded the Nobel Peace Prize in 2010 after heavy lobbying from Havel. Over 10,000 Chinese have signed Charter 08's call: that "freedom, equality, and human rights are universal common values shared by all humankind, and that democracy, a republic, and constitutionalism constitute the basic structural framework of modern governance." A similar Varela Project in Cuba has produced vicious crackdowns by the communist government there. Belarus's Charter 97 was getting hammered by government goons at press time for this book. Nonviolent resistance movements openly modeled on Charter 77 and Civic Forum have changed governments in Serbia, Georgia, Ukraine, and Kyrgyzstan. Similar stirrings have attempted to dislodge authoritarians in Lebanon, Burma, Iran, Tunisia, Egypt, and seemingly everywhere else in the Middle East.

The Alexandria Declaration, like the original Charter 77, holds Arab-world governments accountable to international treaty obligations (the Universal Declaration of Human Rights, the International Covenant on Civil and Political Rights, the International Covenant on Economic, Social and Cultural Rights, and so on) and goes further in listing other treaties countries should join if they haven't already. It calls for free and regular elections, nondiscrimination against women, a transparent and independent judiciary, political term limits, and a host of other Free World artifacts largely unknown in the broader Middle East. Many of the declaration's basic principles have already been adopted by the successful pro-democracy protesters in Tunisia and mouthed by the mostly young crowds massing against autocrats in Algeria, Yemen, Jordan, Syria, Lebanon, and elsewhere.

It's far too soon, as of press time for this book, to declare 2011 the most consequential year for global freedom since 1989. If that proves the case, however, we'll have plenty of trashy Western culture to thank—not just for helping spark Václav Havel's defiance and the replicable Charter 77 movement but also for exerting its specifically liberating influence on Arab and other still-closed societies themselves. Whether it's post-Taliban Afghanis getting Leonardo DiCaprio haircuts and digging up banned VCRs once the mullahs were deposed, Iranian kids texting each other in English to set up trysts and/or protests, or Egyptian "Metaliens" braving possible arrest to see live sets by Hate Suffocation, citizens of unfree countries are using, adapting, and spitting back out the artifacts of surplus Western culture in ways that lead inexorably toward greater personal autonomy, outgroup bonding, reconsideration of stifling cultural traditions, and ultimately liberalization in the countries themselves. And it's not just Western culture, either—India's sexy/corny Bollywood industry (with its traditionalist tales and many Muslim stars) now counts the Middle East as its third-largest overseas market, with world premieres and even a proposed theme park taking shape in Dubai.

As Metalien historian "Slacker" Sabry tells author Richard Poplak in 2010's *The Sheikh's Batmobile: In Pursuit of American Pop Culture in the Muslim World*, "It is the same here in Egypt as it is everywhere, is it not? . . . A gathering of friends who love a small piece of culture beyond anything else. Here are young Egyptians and Saudis trying to find their identity. Through this, we assert some kind of difference from the crowd. This is the way of the Western childhood since the fifties, no? It *can't* be a bad thing."

No, it can't, no matter how many times Republicans and Democrats or conservatives and liberals try to convince you otherwise. In the late 1950s, as his career was about to go into a decadelong eclipse before he came back as a nostalgia act, Frank Sinatra spoke for record-burning Bible Belters and Stalin-friendly folkies like Pete Seeger alike when he hissed, "Rock and roll smells phony and false. It is sung, played, and written for the most part by cretinous goons." Such dismissive critiques of rock music and other American ephemera like comic books, movies, and video games ("Step away from the video games," counsels Barack Obama, who admits to not having played one since the days of Pong) proceed apace. Whether driven by heartfelt concern, fears of political dissent, or bald moral panic ("More often than not," wrote Tipper Gore in 1987, "when teens gather to indulge in the occult, heavy metal is there"), agony over popular culture actually pays tribute to its potential liberatory effects, which range far beyond any particular form of entertainment.

If the critics of pop culture typically lack perspective, its practitioners often lack a sense of irony. In October 1989, a month before Germans pulled down the Berlin Wall and six weeks before the Velvet Revolution unfolded in Czechoslovakia, Neil Young released an album called *Freedom*, which featured the sardonic song "Rockin' in the Free World," intended as a snarky attack on Ronald Reagan's legacy and George H. W. Bush's removal from brutal realities ranging from school violence to a thinning of the ozone layer. "We got a thousand points of light," snarls Young, "for the homeless man / We got a kinder, gentler / Machine gun hand." A minor hit in the United States, the song took on anthemic dimensions among the peaceful revolutionaries of Central Europe, who sang along with the chorus unironically while expressing themselves for the first time with something like unfettered abandon.

In Havel's Czechoslovakia, the consumption and production of pop culture generally and rock music specifically helped engender a political revolution, just as it seems to be doing in the Arab world. In the United States, these same things helped loosen things up too, of course. When rebellious 1950s teens across American grew up, the same insight that caused them to question the censorious tastes of their parents led to a soberer reconsideration of the economic nature of government power; the same thing happened with their own kids and then their grandchildren. Antiauthoritarianism—at least for an increasingly forgotten moment—led to altogether different types of democratization egged on from surprising quarters indeed.

As we'll see in the next several chapters, just as things seemed darker than midnight in the jungles of Vietnam and the domestic economy, when it came to commerce, the workplace, personal identity, and the very means we use to express ourselves, a thousand flowers—along with a thousand microbrews, websites, ethnicities, and so much more—were about to start blooming.

CHAPTER 5

YOU ARE NOW FREE TO MOVE ABOUT THE COUNTRY

If rock music and heavy metal have provided a bass line for political and social revolution, the history of the seemingly unsexy topic of airline deregulation sheds light on one of the indisputable ways we are better off than we were forty years ago. The delicious new freedoms and advances in prosperity and possibility we take for granted even in the midst of economic downturns emanate from a variety of sources. But much of the credit belongs to the democratizers of commerce, the men and women who insisted that luxury technologies be made available to average consumers, so that they in turn could be freed up to pursue maximum happiness in their lives.

For at least the first twenty years of the Cold War, Americans tended to look up at the skies with a sense of dread, half expecting to see Soviet missiles raining down like arrows at Agincourt. Few Americans had viewed their country from on high. Up through the late 1960s, just 15 percent had taken a single plane trip. How and why that changed is a case study in how independence from politics can transform our everyday lives.

In 1970, the year before Southwest Airlines CEO Herb Kelleher finally won, once and for all, the Texas Supreme Court case that ended forty-three months of uphill legal battles to obtain government permission to launch even a single goddamned plane, there were fewer airplane trips than there were Americans: 169 million for a population of 203 million. Four decades later, the flight-per-American ratio has tripled, the number of international flights has increased ninefold, and Southwest alone carries nearly 100 million passengers per year. Air travel over those four decades has gone from rarified luxury item to easily attainable commodity. And no single company is more responsible for the transformation than Southwest Airlines. As the company says in its ads, "You are now free to move about the country."

"The people of Southwest Airlines are crusaders with an egalitarian spirit who truly believe they are in the business of freedom," wrote management consultants Ken and Jackie Freiberg in *Nuts! Southwest Airlines' Crazy Recipe for Business and Personal Success*, their 1996 book-length portrait of the company. "Their mission is to open up the skies, to give ordinary people the chance to see and do things they never dreamed of." As Roy Spence, who has run advertising campaigns for the company, told the Freibergs, "What Southwest has done is create democracy in the airline business." All this is old hat to frequent flyers on the low-cost, joke-cracking airline. Less known and almost totally unappreciated is how much the federal government tried to prevent that democratization from ever taking place.

"This was another planet, another world," says Kelleher, with a characteristic twinkle and another drag on his cigarette. "One of the [government's] fundamental purposes was to throttle competition."

Another world? That's putting it mildly. In 1970 America, an airline could not fly between two states without first receiving federal

Civil Aeronautics Board (CAB) permission to exist as a company and fly that particular route instead of another existing airline (this was subjected to a seven-point test); the airline then had to agree to a fare set by Washington regulators after laborious rate hearings. The result was a government-managed cartel of major carriers that were utterly shielded from competition. "The CAB had effectively closed the industry to outside firms and guaranteed firms already in the industry relatively stable market shares," a young man we'll get to later wrote in 1982's *Instead of Regulation*. "Between 1950 and 1974, the board had received 79 applications from firms wishing to enter the industry—it granted none." Recalls Kelleher, "Their thesis was that if a new airline was gonna take one passenger—one, that's what they said—*one* passenger away from an existing airline, it can't be certificated."

It's important to note here that the regulatory regime, cemented during Franklin Delano Roosevelt's second term after a dozen years of policy zigzagging, was inspired by laudable-sounding goals that sound familiar to our modern ears. Lawmakers wanted to encourage the development of a nascent industry with clear implications for national security. They wanted to make sure that mail got delivered, that rural communities received new technologies, and that planes didn't crash. These impulses produced a regulatory pattern that has been replicated by enterprises from airlines to tobacco companies to investment banks: The big existing companies, those ostensible targets of the regulation, got the federal government to consolidate their market shares, protect them from new competition, and even hand out direct subsidies.

This is what Nobel laureate James Buchanan and other postwar economists described in formulating what has come to be known as public choice theory—the observation that government actors and those they regulate will work in their mutual self-interest to produce "regulatory capture" by an industry of its regulators. Politicians get to protect jobs (and pocket campaign contributions), CEOs get to protect their market share and income stream, and the public gets to take it in the ear unless and until opposition to the inherently unfair, intellectually indefensible practice is marshaled and concentrated enough to overcome market participants with a bigger personal stake and more access to power. It is why Mattel ends up supporting (and winning exemption from) new federal regulations on Chinese toys enacted after some Mattel imports were found to be toxic. It's why subsidies for ethanol continue to be shelled out (including as part of the great Republican-Obama tax compromise of December 2010), even though not a single person outside the state of Iowa can support them with a straight face. It's why Phillip Morris and its corporate successors support tobacco regulation by the Food and Drug Administration, why Walmart supports minimum-wage increases, and why Big Pharma shelled out so much money in favor of ObamaCare, which was sold as explicitly anti-Pharma. It's why no one loved Obama's financial regulation overhaul more than Goldman Sachs and other major Wall Street financial institutions, who emerged from the Troubled Asset Relief Program with a bigger market share than before.

How much did federal regulations cement into place the airline status quo? This much: Three of the four main airlines operating at the time of the 1938 Civil Aeronautics Act had basically the same market share thirty-four years later. In 1972, United Airlines had gone from 22.9 percent of the market to 22.0, Eastern from 14.9 to 11.6, and TWA from 15.1 to 11.9. Only American Airlines saw a substantial change, but it too was still going strong with 15.0 percent market share after dropping from 29.6 percent in 1938. "The fact that the existing airlines had 90 percent of all the revenue passenger-miles in 1938, and also had 90 percent of all the revenue passenger-miles in 1978, at the time of deregulation, would give you somewhat of a hint," Kelleher says.

Try to think of any industry in the modern-day United States in which the exact same four companies have dominated the market for the last four decades. The rules sound like science fiction to us now, but they were the law of the land during our lifetimes. Airlines wishing to change a fare had to announce their intent thirty days beforehand. If a competing carrier (most popular routes had just one to three airlines servicing them) objected to the price, the CAB would hold hearings and eventually hand down a ruling. If an airline union won better wage concessions, its employer would get the government to pass along the cost increases in the form of increased (competition-protected) ticket prices. Everything down to the contents of airline food was subject to federal regulators—that is, on interstate flights.

Southwest Airlines exists because Texas is big. Like the now-forgotten Pacific Southwest Airlines (PSA) in California, Southwest was not subject to all those onerous interstate regulations and could fly multiple routes in a large and populous state. The two airlines served as a field experiment to test—and demolish—the federal government's half-century-old theory that the airline industry, in the absence of tight regulation, would jack up prices, abandon small-town routes, and hinder the development of the industry itself. Still, even to fly within its single state, Southwest had to clear legal hurdles that, with the passage of time, look insane.

Southwest Airlines applied to the Texas Aeronautic Commission in November 1967 to fly between Houston, Dallas, and San Antonio. Three months later, the application was approved, then promptly greeted with a restraining order from competitors Continental, Braniff, and Trans Texas, which argued that the markets were fully served already and could not support a new entrant. (It was not enough, apparently, to let Southwest discover that unhappy fact using its own money.) A trial court in the summer of 1968 sided with the incumbents over the upstart. Another seven months later, the state court of civil appeals upheld that ruling. Southwest's investors had blown their $500,000 of seed money on legal fees. Their lawyer, Herb Kelleher, legendarily vowed to pay out of his own pocket if they lost their Texas Supreme Court appeal. Kelleher won. The plaintiffs then appealed to the U.S. Supreme Court, which in late 1970 refused to hear the case, upholding Southwest's victory. But Braniff et al. still weren't done and filed a complaint with the Civil Aeronautics Board against Southwest's even existing. The CAB, perhaps surprisingly, rejected that claim in June 1971, at which point the legacy airlines filed one last restraining order back in a Texas court. On June 17, 1971, the Texas Supreme Court shot down the injunction, and on the very next day, nearly five years after hatching the idea of providing lower-cost air service to the Texas Triangle, Southwest Airlines launched its first commercial flight.

"I thought, this is one heck of a hoax they're perpetrating here!" says Kelleher, whose tireless work during the long legal fight ended up putting him in the CEO's chair. "And then I realized, essentially this was the way they lived. That's why there wasn't a lot of competition."

This was hardly the end of Southwest's legal problems (or its last brush with the U.S. Supreme Court). To this day, the company is the sole target of an infamous U.S. amendment, named after former Speaker of the House Jim Wright, expressly forbidding it from using Dallas's lonely Love Field Airport, which sits a stone's throw from company headquarters, in flights to forty-six states. Managing to get flights into the air, however, allowed Southwest to usher five key innovations into a sclerotic air-travel industry that had changed little in a half century: (1) unheard-of speed in turning around airplanes for their next flight, (2) a preference for unloved regional airports, (3) variable pricing between flights on the same route, (4) getting out of the meal-serving business, and (5) a conscious puncturing of jet-age cool with corny, down-home friendliness. All these changes were made in the service of one overarching goal: "Our basic thinking [was that] Southwest would democratize the skies," Kelleher says. "Which we did. I mean, a couple of years ago 85 percent of [Americans] had flown at least one commercial flight as opposed to 15 percent in 1966. And, of course, during the 1990s, the Department of Transportation issued a report that said Southwest represented 90 percent of all low-fare competition in all of the United States of America."

Southwest's first television commercials featured forty stewardesses in go-go boots serving Bloody Marys to businessmen on an 8:00 a.m. Dallas-to-Houston flight called the "Love Bird." When deep-pocketed Braniff matched the credit card–maxing Southwest's ridiculously low $13 fare from Dallas to Houston in early 1973, Southwest responded by offering passengers a fifth of Chivas. Instead of going to court over an advertising copyright infringement claim by another aviation company, Kelleher, born in New Jersey and educated in New York City of all places, challenged the opposing CEO to a public arm-wrestling match—and won. Texas ate it up.

While Southwest quickly became the world's greatest advertisement for the futility and obstructionism of ostensibly well-meaning federal regulations, we wouldn't be talking about the company today, or in this book, had its operations remained confined within the borders of the Lone Star State. While 1971 may have been the year of the "Nixon Shock"—when on a single day an American president, and a Republican to boot, established an across-the-board ninety-day wage and price freeze, a 10 percent tariff on all imports, and the end of the U.S. dollar's peg to gold—it was also the year of not only Southwest Airlines' first flight but the tentative beginnings of a remarkable coalition, spanning from Ralph Nader to Teddy Kennedy to Gerald Ford to Republican-leaning economists to future Supreme Court justices, that would, before the end of the decade, dismantle federal airline regulation as we knew it.

In the revolutionary month of May 1968, when European students were rioting en masse, a Boston University undergraduate named Lanny Friedlander mimeographed and stapled together some journalism and argument influenced by Ayn Rand's philosophy of objectivism and called it *Reason*, promising to bring into the arena of public discourse "logic, not legends" and "proof, not belligerent assertion." (Both of us, eventually, would become editors of what has become the largest libertarian publication on the planet.) One of the first subscribers was an aerospace engineer and fellow Randian named Robert W. Poole. "I'd never written anything for publication, but because I was interested in aviation, [Friedlander] got me to write a piece about airlines and aviation policy," Poole recalled in a 2008 *Reason* retrospective. "I did a hell of a lot of research, which was fun, but even more fun was seeing it in print, having it be the cover story of what became the first offset printed issue." The article, "Fly the Frenzied Skies," was reprinted in the libertarian journal *The Freeman* and elsewhere and spread like an intellectual virus. One of the first explicit calls to deregulate all aspects of the airline business, it began like this: "A private business whose sales volume had increased 15–20% annually for seven years (and showed many signs of continuing to do so) would probably view its future with eager anticipation. In the government-controlled, privately 'owned' cartel known as commercial aviation, however, the expected growth in air travel is viewed . . . in horror."

Not everyone interested in improving air travel by reducing government's role in it was an Ayn Rand fan. In 1971, a Cornell University economics professor and liberal Democrat named Alfred E. Kahn came out with an influential book called *The Economics of Regulation*. Kahn, after surveying the landscape of how the best intentions so frequently produced unintended consequences, concluded that the solution certainly for the airline industry was deregulation. "If the regulators could be omniscient, then regulation could work perfectly well, but the essence of the case for the free market is unknowability," he explained in 1989 to Poole, who'd been editor of *Reason* for over a decade. "Anybody who is a strong antitruster ought to be opposed to regulation."

That this sounds like a strange argument to be coming from a liberal Democrat in 2011 is a testament to how much liberal Democrats have forgotten their own recent history. Though the academic case for airline deregulation had been building up since economists began studying the question in earnest after World War II, the early 1970s were a high-water mark for a broad-based, left-of-center distrust of authority. Writing in the *Los Angeles Times* in December 2010, liberal cultural historian and Teddy Kennedy biographer Neal Gabler got this history almost exactly backward: "In the days of FDR, the Democratic Party, despite its factions and disagreements, coalesced around one overriding tenet: muscular government action, especially in behalf of the powerless. After FDR, Democratic presidential nominees Harry Truman, Adlai Stevenson, John Kennedy, LBJ, Hubert Humphrey and even the much-maligned George McGovern and Walter Mondale subscribed to this liberal ideal without apology. Belief in the efficacy of government was a prerequisite to gaining the nomination," Gabler wrote. "[But] sometime in the 1970s, the Democratic Party . . . stopped pressing government action as an overriding binding principle and began instead to appeal to individual interest groups."

Gabler's theory, widely echoed in contemporary America, skips over some pretty important milestones in left-of-center discontent. Popular sentiment against the Democrat-launched and -escalated Vietnam War was already derailing the presidential ambitions of Lyndon Johnson and Hubert Humphrey by 1968, a year also notorious for serial political assassinations, race riots, and police violence against antiwar demonstrators at the Democratic Party's very own convention in Chicago. The Pentagon Papers, released in 1971, shattered many illusions by detailing how four successive U.S. administrations had persistently lied to the American people about Vietnam. Revelations about appalling abuses at J. Edgar Hoover's FBI began dribbling out in 1971, ultimately culminating in a 1975–1976 Church Committee series of congressional investigations exhuming official government activity that retain the power to shock nearly four decades later. David Halberstam's reputation-making *The Best and the Brightest*, released in 1972, is an explicit and devastating attack on the entire notion of enlightened technocratic (and often specifically Democratic) competence. Even movie theaters at the time were filled with paranoid anti-government ruminations, from *Parallax View* to *The Conversation* to *Three Days of the Condor*. By the time Richard Nixon gave his final peace sign in 1974 from the helicopter pad on the White House's South Lawn, Gabler's mythical "belief in the efficacy of government" was pretty much toast—and deservedly so.

This fertile antiauthoritarianism led many on the left to question the alleged enlightenment of government regulation across a variety of stodgier areas, from "urban renewal" schemes that bulldozed entire neighborhoods of low-cost minority housing to arcane regulations that roadblocked interstate trucking. As Kahn explained to Poole, "So it was the convergence of the free-market people and the antitrust tradition, in which [John F.] Kennedy is very strong. We had a most interesting political alliance of the National Association of Manufacturers and Ralph Nader. We had Common Cause and we had the National Federation of Independent Businesses. We had the Ford Motor Co. and we had the Consumer Federation of America."

That deregulatory coalition had at its center a man whom Neal Gabler of all people should know all too well: Teddy Kennedy. "Senator Kennedy's decision to hold oversight hearings on the CAB was the crucial factor in the emergence of airline deregulation as a politically visible and important issue," Stephen G. Breyer and Leonard R. Stein claim in *Instead of Regulation*. If the name of the first author sounds familiar, it should: Not only was Breyer special counsel to the Kennedy-run Senate Committee on the Judiciary from 1974 to 1975, but he was also appointed two decades later to the U.S. Supreme Court, where he holds down the liberal end to this day. Breyer comes from the Alfred Kahn school of deregulation-as-antitrust. "Governmental intervention intended to serve the public interest proved to be working to the serious detriment of the American consumer," he and Stein write.

The Kennedy hearings, held in February and March of 1975, established in the public eye the fact that low-cost intrastate airlines like Southwest were making a mockery of every argument the CAB and corporatism-loving airlines raised for the regulatory status quo. Far from blocking service to rural and regional airports, Southwest was introducing commercial air travel to cities such as Lubbock, Odessa, and Harlingen, which had long been frozen out by big airlines. Instead of retarding the industry, Southwest and PSA were expanding it. "The Dallas-Houston market went from thirty-second largest to fifth largest in the United States within a couple of years. And all the other carriers were carrying more passengers than they were carrying before we started, because we expanded the market so tremendously," Kelleher says. And the low fares they offered weren't suicide pacts—to this day, Southwest has made a profit for a record of thirty-seven consecutive years.

Kennedy's subcommittee concluded that current airline regulation was inherently unfair and anticonsumer, driving up prices while shutting out innovation. Featuring an unusual left-right coalition, as well as the visibility of Kennedy, Nader, and other participants, the hearings were a critical and popular success. "Despite the fact that the industry and several unions opposed reform, many legislators supported change, seeing deregulation as, simultaneously, a proconsumer, antiinflation, and less-bureaucracy, less-governmental-control issue," write Breyer and Stein. "Few groups could seriously argue with such legislation." Recalls Kelleher, "The time and the atmosphere were just right for it to happen. Serendipitous, I guess you might say."

Even before the Airline Deregulation Act of 1978, the Civil Aeronautics Board began to dismantle itself from within. After the hearings, President Gerald Ford appointed John Robson as the new CAB head. Robson quickly lifted the moratorium on new airline routes and most activities of charter-plane companies. President Jimmy Carter was such a strong proponent of deregulation that he appointed to replace Robson none other than the regulation-averse academic Alfred Kahn, who sped up the demolition process. The relaxing of government control had—surprise!—set off a price war among new low-cost airlines and panicky legacy carriers, and now the public was thirsting for more. Away went CAB's authority to (rarely) approve new routes; the default was reset to freedom. Fare ceilings and first-class minimums were the next to get tossed. By the time Carter signed legislative deregulation into law, the administrative decontrol had already unleashed a revolution. Breyer and Stein write,

> The reform undertaken by the Kahn board between June 1977 and October 1978 had a dramatic effect on airline prices, passengers, and profits. Despite inflation, the least-expensive fare in many markets actually decreased between 1974 and 1978. Passenger traffic increased over 16 percent from already record levels in 1977. And not only were people flying more, but more people were flying. A 1971 survey by the New York Port Authority revealed that less than 50 percent of the U.S. adult population had ever flown; by 1978, this figure exceeded 61 percent. . . . In less than three years, the Robson and Kahn boards had totally altered the shape and character of the airline industry. Increased competition prompted lower fares, which, in turn, brought air travel within the economic means of many Americans for the first time.

The Airline Deregulation Act (or the Kennedy-Cannon Bill, as it was known in the Senate)—signed into law by President Carter, who actively campaigned for president in 1976 on a deregulatory economic platform—accomplished something unheard of in modern politics, Democratic or Republican: It eliminated a government agency. By 1984, the Civil Aeronautics Board had been phased out, and companies like Southwest were now free to take their intrastate low-cost formula across state lines. The speed at which the revolution took place shocked even the theoreticians and enablers who made it happen. "My dad was saying, 'Ha, ha, comes the revolution! You and I will never live to see any of this come to pass,'" Robert Poole recalled about reactions to his initial article. "I thought Dad was quite right: He wouldn't live to see it. I thought that I maybe would. I have enough confidence in the power of ideas and empirical evidence that [I thought] if we banged on it hard enough we'd overcome, but I thought it would take a lot longer than the seven years from the time that article was published to the [deregulation's] actually coming to pass."

And the results? Study after study has concluded that Americans save around $20 billion per year due to lower airline prices. As noted at the outset, the average American today flies three times as often as in 1970, and yet, despite the congestion, accidents and fatalities are down across the board by 30 to 40 percent. Southwest has become the most profitable and busiest airline in U.S. history. Much of the rest of the world has looked upon the success of deregulation and Southwest's low-cost revolution and gone even further, privatizing airports across Europe (in America they are more than 99 percent government run), getting the federal government out of the air-traffic-control business in Canada, eliminating subsidies (U.S. carriers have received tens of billions of dollars this century), and easing restrictions on foreign ownership of domestic airlines (believe it or not, foreigners cannot own a majority stake of a U.S.-based air carrier). The biggest airlines in the world are now the UK-based, Southwest-aping, low-cost flyers Ryanair and easyJet, and it's now absurdly easy to travel all across Europe for less than $50. Deregulation in the rest of the world has now lapped that in America.

Why did that happen? One reason is that in the debased political imagination of modern America, the word "deregulation" has become, on the left, synonymous with three things liberals hate: Ronald Reagan, Margaret Thatcher, and big corporations. "I kind of idolized Senator Kennedy because of what he did for deregulation," says Kelleher, who describes himself politically as a John Connally–style Texas Democrat. "But you must admit, as a political generalization, he leaned more to getting government into things instead of out of things. People had difficulty comprehending that he was the father of deregulation in the airline industry." Not only have American Democrats forgotten their antiauthoritarian past, but they've credited Reagan for deregulation that happened under Jimmy Carter's watch and conveniently forgotten that in airline deregulation (as in all varieties of industrial decontrol), the most vocal opposition came from precisely those big corporations that the Ralph Naders of the world love to hate. Deregulation isn't the friend of big business; it's the enemy of corporatism-addicted incumbents. Anyone who doubts that should listen to the words of Jimmy Carter himself—for instance, those uttered in his one and only presidential debate with Ronald Reagan. It was Carter, not Reagan, who one week before the 1980 election said in his closing remarks, "I share the basic beliefs of my region [against] an excessive government intrusion into the private affairs of American citizens and also into the private affairs of the free enterprise system. One of the commitments that I made was to deregulate the major industries of this country. We've been remarkably successful, with the help of a Democratic Congress. We have deregulated the air industry, the rail industry, the trucking industry, financial institutions. We're now working on the communications industry."

And yet, in modern politics, airline deregulation is widely denounced as a mistake in urgent need of correction by former *New Republic* honcho Marty Peretz as well as *Washington Post* chin stroker David Ignatius. In 2007, Robert Kuttner, one of the founders of the progressive magazine *The American Prospect*, moaned that Delta hadn't offered a meal for purchase on a Boston to Seattle flight. But his main complaint? "Deregulation allows airlines to adopt any pricing scheme the traffic will bear." The horror! What would such critics' desired reregulation look like? Ask the only major airline CEO who lobbied against the federal government's post-9/11 airline bailout. Kelleher says,

> I think once the American people understood what the consequences of it were, you'd have an insurgency on your hands. Because they may get upset about the fact that they're delayed, they may get upset about the fact that someone with a given airline doesn't treat them the way they'd like to be treated, but if you say, okay, what's the alternative—you're not going to get to see your kids as often, you're not going to go to your grandmother's birthday, you can't expand your business the way that you were hoping to expand it. . . . Well, that would all fall apart. It's all gone. Forget it.

Antiauthoritarianism, government decontrol, and entrepreneurial initiative made people more prosperous and free and, in the process, upset the apple cart of corporate-government stability that had long made the country artificially expensive and boring. The same forces that led Herb Kelleher to make the once-exclusive skies friendly to just about everybody were about to change the very notion of the workplace as we knew it.

CHAPTER 6

THE DISORGANIZATION MAN (AND WOMAN)

In most senses, *Time* magazine's 2009 list of the hundred most influential people celebrated the same categories of exalted superhumans we've come to expect from the kingmakers and ring kissers of the general-interest (read: generally uninteresting) mass media. Despite occasional flashes of something actually new and different, there was little to suggest that this list had to be published in 2009 rather than, say, 1999, or even 1949 for that matter. There were your statesmen (Barack Obama, Hillary Clinton, Nicolas Sarkozy, Gordon Brown), your superstars (Tiger Woods, Brad Pitt, Oprah Winfrey), your CEOs (Ted Turner, T. Boone Pickens), and your scientists (Stephen Chu, Paul Krugman). They had approximately three hundred Ivy League degrees and invitations to Davos among them. Same old, same old.

Yet, smuggled into this straight-outta-Aspen collection of hyperelites and lottery winners was a thirty-one-year-old stat nerd, online poker enthusiast, and consulting firm dropout named Nate Silver.

While interesting in itself, his rise to prominence has broader significance in the contemporary world of work. Silver's highly individualized career is suggestive of larger changes in how more and more of
us go about making a living these days.

Just two years before, Silver had been famous only among a subset of a subset of a subset of baseball fans—consumers of new-school
"sabermetric" analysis who enjoy projection science and consume
the stuff at *Baseball Prospectus*. Within that small if influential
group of regression analysts and standard deviation deviants, Silver
was a star, famous for developing the Player Empirical Comparison
and Optimization Test Algorithm (PECOTA), a system (cheekily
named after obscure Kansas City Royals mediocrity Bill Pecota) for
predicting how hitters and pitchers will perform over the course of
their careers. PECOTA was a hit with fantasy baseball enthusiasts,
sophisticated consumers of baseball analysis, and even major-league
front offices. The formula served as a cornerstone of *Baseball Prospectus*'s series of annual books and subscription-based online content. Silver chugged away at the publication for most of the decade,
concocting several other whimsically named formulas and helping
the company become one of the most successful niche self-publishing
franchises in the two decades since another unknown, Bill James,
upended the very way people understand baseball with his 1980s
Abstracts.

But it wasn't Silver's work in applied baseball mathematics
that landed him in *Time*'s hundred. In 2007, Silver started moon-
lighting from *Baseball Prospectus* on the influential left-liberal "netroots" website Daily Kos. He burst forth with informed critiques of
major-media political analysis, which he found to be innumerate,
unscientific, and inaccurate. Posting pseudonymously under the
name Poblano, Silver began crunching political poll numbers himself better than even the professionals did, rapidly building a loyal
following.

In spring 2008, Silver came out of the closet and went solo, launching his FiveThirtyEight website, so named for the number of voters in the Electoral College. Time and again during the long, slow march to the 2008 election, Silver's amateur parsing of poll numbers and handicapping of primary races proved more valuable than those of the pollsters and political journalists who'd been paid to do this work for decades. He quickly rose through the ranks as a hotshot political analyst, writing for *The New Republic* and showing up on CNN and other cable yak channels. Silver's coup de grâce came in November 2008, when he correctly predicted the winner in every U.S. Senate race and got forty-nine of fifty states right in the contest between John McCain and Barack Obama. *Time* magazine recognized his influence and ballistic career path a year later, followed in 2010 by FiveThirtyEight's getting snapped up by none other than the *New York Times*. In just a few short years, Silver had gone from being another faceless pencil pusher in corporate America to become a marquee name clutched to the very bosom of the Gray Lady.

It's worth lingering a moment to marvel at the velocity of career change now available to those working in the media (and elsewhere). Fifteen years before FiveThirtyEight, there was almost no such thing as a political weblog, let alone one published by a major newspaper. Publishing a daily newspaper back then, and for the half century before that, was among the most profitable of business activities in the United States, with an average annual profit margin of around 25 percent (compare that to Walmart, which is lucky to scrape out 3.5 percent from its stores). Like most monopolistic institutions, newspapers became highly bureaucratized and stultified, requiring rigid credentials from anyone attempting to break into the lucrative fraternity. College grads with their eyes on the upper tier of the business had better come with a journalism education from Columbia or Northwestern, not (like Silver) an economics degree from the University of Chicago. The road to big-market dailies was routed through a gauntlet of tiny-market advertising shoppers and weeklies, at which you were expected to "learn the basics" and move on to incrementally higher-circulation papers, until maybe one day you got a tryout on the city desk of the *Houston Chronicle*. On the content side, it was impossible to access most political polls outside whatever your local daily chose to publish about them, and even with an expensive Lexis-Nexis account, it was beastly work just accumulating, let alone repurposing, the best political data in the country. Beating the pros at their own game, in real time, for an audience of hundreds of thousands, as something to do to blow off steam after a long day of dissecting the line-drive rates of relief pitchers? Get real.

Silver is the twenty-first-century embodiment of what the great economist Joseph Schumpeter called "creative destruction" as it applies to the workplace. With World War II raging, Schumpeter, an Austrian refugee who had ended up at Harvard, channeled Karl Marx and Friedrich Engels of all people to underscore that capitalist society was characterized not by placid burghers lording their wealth and status over lowly villagers but by "gale force winds" of change constantly upending established ways of doing business. The creative spirit of determined entrepreneurs would be the main driver of innovation and economic growth, Schumpeter wrote in his 1942 classic *Capitalism, Socialism, and Democracy*, but the disruptions would come at a cost to the entrenched order and produce a backlash against capitalism by an intellectual class increasingly alienated from the harsh edges of market competition.

The concept of creative destruction is familiar to anyone who remembers the pre-Web Internet or just how great MS-DOS 3.0, Quattro Pro, and WordPerfect seemed back in the day. Ironically, Schumpeter's description bore far less resemblance to the era that immediately followed its publication. Postwar America was marked not by an intellectual embrace of the turbulence of capitalism but by something closer to the opposite: an attempt to enforce rigid models of corporate and societal conformity. Postwar America was the era not of the leapfrogging Lone Wolf but of the nose-to-the-grindstone organization man. Herb Kelleher or Nate Silver need not apply.

The concept of *the organization man*, a term made famous by journalist and urban theorist William H. Whyte's 1956 bestseller of the same name, helped to define what postwar work meant to millions of Americans. His titular creature did not simply work for a large firm but "belonged to it," in the same way a priest belongs to the church—fundamentally and for life. The organization man was at once an aspirational ideal for a burgeoning middle class and a description of how the modern worker developed his sense of individual identity based on groupthink. The group, said Whyte, could be a university, a government unit, or, more popularly, a corporation that structured most aspects of a worker's life. As a good worker, you valued the schools, the tastes, the religion, the you-name-its that your organization valued. The organization derived its power not simply from being mainstream but from being the only stream—the sole source of meaning, identity, and value. Thus defined by the group, the individual adapted to it, rather than vice versa.

Whyte, like postwar society itself, was ambivalent about the organization man mentality for all sorts of reasons. Treating employees like cogs in a machine may have made sense in an industrial age defined by Henry Ford's assembly line, but it went against the long, proud American tradition of cranky individualism. In the new arrangement, the best way an individual could serve his family, his company, and ultimately his country was to not make waves, to sand down all the rough edges that might undermine the team effort necessary to beat the competition, whether it be Coca-Cola or communism, Sperry Rand or the Soviet Union. Conformity became an avenue to distinction rather than the usual route toward repression.

The organization man mentality was both an effect and a cause of what John Kenneth Galbraith and others called the "new industrial state," a political economy dominated by giant, largely unionized corporations thought to be beyond the vicissitudes of the market and competition. Think GM, IBM, Xerox—cradle-to-grave enterprises with robust executive-training programs that identified young comers and bred them into a distinct corporate culture. The society it helped produce was hierarchical, broadly prosperous, and intolerant of deviation from the (law-abiding, white, male, Protestant) norm.

This stultifying ethos, while real, was never as pervasive as cultural critics feared, in part due to the critics themselves. Writers as different in style and temperament as Whyte, David Reisman (*The Lonely Crowd*), Sloan Wilson (*The Man in the Gray Flannel Suit*), Betty Friedan (*The Feminine Mystique*), and Philip Wylie (*Generation of Vipers*) pushed back against notions of conformity. Figures such as Jack Kerouac, Ralph Ellison, and Ayn Rand became celebrities on the power and commercial appeal of their explicit rejection of mass society and the status quo. Rock 'n' roll, epitomized by the thrusting hips of Elvis Presley, the gender-bending of Little Richard, and the sexualized piano pounding of Jerry Lee Lewis, spoke to a world beyond the executive suite, as did the more urbane entertainments produced by Miles Davis, Nina Simone, and Lenny Bruce. For a gray, conformist decade, the 1950s produced a hell of a lot of individualists and antiheroes (Marlon Brando, Paul Newman, and Monty Clift, to name just a few in the movies). The long siege laid against the organization man began even as the concept was being articulated, picked up momentum throughout the 1960s, and was completely triumphant by the time Richard Nixon's one-way ticket to San Clemente had been punched in 1974. Even the "silent majority" was made up of individuals, it turned out.

This basic shift from organization man to the Me generation was the backdrop for the emergence of the revolutionary figure who made Nate Silver possible and who fittingly wrote *Time* magazine's mini profile of Silver for the top one hundred list. Bill James was drafted for the Vietnam War in December 1971 at the age of twenty-two and fit in somewhat worse than Yossarian in *Catch-22*, Hawkeye in M*A*S*H, or Bill Murray's character in *Stripes*. "As a soldier, I failed every test you can fail," he told author Scott Gray. "I simply had no ability to do any of the things the Army wants you to do. I couldn't do push-ups. I couldn't shoot a rifle worth a crap. I couldn't march fast or climb obstacle courses, I couldn't assemble and re-assemble a rifle quickly, I couldn't keep my shoes shined or my shirt-tail tucked in. I was constantly singled out, in training, as the guy who didn't get it." A natural antiauthoritarian and lifelong baseball fanatic, James, after his military tour, parlayed his University of Kansas degrees in economics and English into a job as a night watchman in a pork and beans factory, where he used his ample spare time deploying the scientific method to test out conventional wisdom from baseball organization men he suspected were full of malarkey. Was baseball really "90 percent pitching"? Were batting average and fielding percentage really the best ways to measure the value of hitters and fielders? Did players really peak at age thirty? Do base runners really steal off catchers? Are minor-league statistics essentially meaningless? Through analytical rigor and sheer research doggedness (remember, this was two decades before you could access the raw data with the click of a mouse), James arrived at the emphatic, even countercultural answer of no.

His first self-published mimeographed opus, *The Bill James Baseball Abstract of 1977*, sold all of seventy-five copies. But James's caustic eloquence and outsider's insights slowly found an audience, until Ballantine picked up the franchise in the early 1980s and helped turn it into an annual bestseller. Early readers were not unlike the mythical 1,000 listeners who bought the first Velvet Underground record: Every single one of them started an alternative career of his or her own, be it (like Nate Silver) a direct knockoff or (like contrarian *New Yorker* essayist Malcolm Gladwell) a derivation once or twice removed. Presaging the distributed intelligence of the World Wide Web, James solicited and even published data and analysis from his readers, taking particular relish when it trumped his own. He developed scores of formulas, coined dozens of terms (including *sabermetrics*, derived from "Society for American Baseball Research"), and relentlessly showed his math in an effort to better "organize the thinking" of the informed baseball fan. Meanwhile, as another James-influenced writer, Michael Lewis, observed in his absorbing bestseller *Moneyball*, "Two changes were about to occur that would make his questions not only more answerable but also more valuable. First came radical advances in computer technology: This dramatically reduced the cost of compiling and analyzing vast amounts of baseball data. Then came the boom in baseball players' salaries: This dramatically raised the benefits of having such knowledge."

It took decades for James's radical ideas to penetrate the thick collective skull of Major League Baseball, an institution arguably more resistant to change than the Roman Catholic Church, the Soviet Politburo, and *The Tonight Show* put together. James was long greeted with comical derision from managers, sportswriters, and comfortable guardians of an ossified status quo. But capitalism— even the heavily socialized, grotesquely subsidized version practiced by Major League Baseball—cannot long stand idly by while truthful market information lies around unexploited. James's approach to analyzing baseball was first picked up by the moribund Oakland A's organization in the late 1990s, which proved so successful on a limited budget that a new breed of general managers sprung up nearly overnight—young MBA types with sabermetrics on the tongue and a taste for hiring new statistical analysts. James himself was hired by the Boston Red Sox in 2003 (the team owner, Wall Street trader

John Henry, was still another fan), after which the team won two World Series in short order. In 2006, when *Time* named Bill James one of that year's top one hundred, Henry wrote up the appreciation: "He was an outsider, self-publishing invisible truths about baseball while the Establishment ignored him. Now 25 years later, his ideas have become part of the foundation of baseball strategy."

All of this started as one man's individualistic revolt against the organization man mentality. James wrote in an essay for *Slate* in 2010,

> It is a very American thing, that we don't believe *too much* in obeying the rules. We are not a nation of Hall Monitors; we are a nation that tortures Hall Monitors. We are people who push the rules. I myself am a stubborn, sometimes arrogant person who refuses to obey some of the rules that everybody else follows. I pay no attention to the rules of grammar. I write fragments if I goddamned well feel like it. I refuse to follow many of the principles of proper research that are agreed upon by the rest of the academic world. An editor said to me last year, "Well, you've earned the right to do things your own way." Bullshit; I was that way when I was 25. It has to do with following the rules that make sense to me and ignoring the ones that don't. It doesn't make me a bad person; it makes me who I am.

Bill James and Nate Silver are archetypal examples of what can be called the disorganization man (as we'll see, the descriptor works equally well for women). People who reject cradle-to-grave employment as the Biafra of the spirit create their own jobs (or in James's case, their own industries), and with brains and determination, they inflict meritocracy on institutions hidebound by professional and intellectual protectionism. They light fuses under gatekeepers, then walk through the front door after the explosion.

It would be overly dramatic—and plainly inaccurate—to say that Silver is single-handedly reshaping the *New York Times* or that James runs strategy for the Boston Red Sox, much less the national pastime. Both, perhaps ironically, work, for now, for legacy firms with billion-dollar valuations, but each shows how porous the walls around the castle have really become.

In hurriedly moving from a traditional consulting job at KPMG that he didn't care for—Silver's on record as saying that "spending four years of my life in a job I didn't like" is his biggest regret—to a personally defined job that was literally unimaginable before he created it, Silver embodies a new social type. James is an even more powerful example: He went from guarding franks and beans to helping bring a World Series title to a historically cursed franchise and doing it on his own cranky terms. The stat guru still lives in Lawrence, Kansas, not Boston, still publishes annual books, still argues daily with his readers, and in 2011 is scheduled to come out with a massive book using the scientific method to analyze . . . crime.

The creative destruction of the Internet, along with the trailblazing pre-Internet example of disorganization men such as Bill James across thousands of disciplines, has destroyed corporate monoculture and subservient workplace identity as we know it. The broad forces of democratization and decentralization, which are only now beginning to wreak havoc on politics, have already remade the entire American concept of work. The great skyscrapers of Midtown Manhattan that once signified the supposed efficiency and precision of transhistorical business giants such as Pan Am and AT&T have been humbled like the Great Pyramids of Giza, stripped of their gold-plated veneers and robbed of whatever treasure and wisdom once resided within. They are the tombstones of the organization man's world, and they line the thoroughfares of New York, Boston, Chicago, Detroit, San Francisco, and elsewhere like tidy, well-maintained grave markers in a World War II cemetery, silent reminders of a past and often heroic age. The companies that built and occupied these ruins are not coming back, at least not in the same form.

Consider the General Motors Building near Central Park South, completed in 1968 in signature International House style and once home to the planet's most successful car company. If the organization man had a mailing address, it just might have been 767 Fifth Avenue. Time was, GM was literally the engine of American capitalism and hegemony—it was called "government motors" long before Washington owned even one share of the company's stock. "What's good for General Motors is good for the USA" was a widespread enough nostrum to be parodied in song in the 1950s Broadway version of Li'l Abner, in a number called "What's Good for General Bullmoose." GM has long since relinquished ownership of the skyscraper, and the ground-floor Cadillac showroom has given way to an Apple store. GM has become the poster child for what once was considered great and stabilizing and predictable in America—the bold industrial design, lifetime employment, generous union benefits—but now lies in ruins. In 2007, even before the current recession, the company lost a record amount of money ($37 billion) even while selling a record number of cars (9.4 million). Backward-looking management combined with plush union contracts to create what is widely recognized as a pension fund that happens to produce some automobiles. An ill-advised and illegal federal bailout and managed bankruptcy in 2009 only delayed the inevitable for a company whose customer base is no longer consumers but Washington bureaucrats (the bailout was illegal since the Troubled Asset Relief Program funds used to pay for it initially were only supposed to be available to financial institutions). Like the industrial Midwest from which it sprang, GM has been rusting out for decades, losing market share, reputation, and capital. The company-town ethos it relied on is as dead as, well, Flint, Michigan.

The demise of the corporate automaton would doubtless have come as welcome news for the counterculture (mostly of the politically leftish variety) that sprang up in opposition to it. But a funny thing happened during the long and unhappy death of the organization man: The twenty-first-century Left has become its chief eulogist. Paul Krugman, the Nobel Prize–winning Princeton economist and *New York Times* columnist (and therefore colleague of sorts to Nate Silver), is arguably the most vocal peddler of what free market scholar Brink Lindsey has termed *nostalgianomics*. "The middle-class America of my youth is best thought of not as the normal state of our society, but as an interregnum between Gilded Ages," writes Krugman, who was born in 1953. The period between 1950 and 1970, when income inequality lessened and a broad-based middle class flooded into housing markets, suburbs, and department stores like never before, he writes, was close to ideal. "Middle-class America didn't emerge by accident," Krugman argues. "It was created by what has been called the Great Compression of incomes that took place during World War II, and sustained for a generation by social norms that favored equality, strong labor unions and progressive taxation." By the 1980s, alas, the political forces that championed redistributive taxes and kept Pinkertons from clubbing union members had been routed by Ronald Reagan, ushering in our new, lamentable Gilded Age.

Brink Lindsey rejects "this revisionist account of the fall and rise of income inequality." The postwar flattening of incomes, he argued in a 2009 paper for the libertarian Cato Institute, "was built on extensive cartelization of markets, limiting competition to favor producers over consumers." Worse, especially from a liberal's point of view, "the restrictions on competition were buttressed by racial prejudice, sexual discrimination, and postwar conformism, which combined to limit the choices available to workers and potential workers alike. Those illiberal social norms were finally swept aside in the cultural tumults of the 1960s and '70s. And then, in the 1970s and '80s, restraints on competition were substantially reduced as well, to the applause of economists across the ideological spectrum. At least until now."

Business consultant and freelance visionary Tom Peters, too, has a much different take than Krugman, one that has the advantage of helping describe work as it is currently experienced (including by the likes of *New York Times* columnists and academics at elite institutions). Peters calls Krugman's type of thinking the "false-nostalgia-for-shitty-jobs phenomenon." Private-sector unionism hasn't declined from a high of around 35 percent of workers in the 1940s to just 7 percent in 2010 because some latter-day Andrew Carnegies decided to break the AFL-CIO or Services Employee International Union, Peters says. In a very real and salutary way, unions created to make assembly-line jobs less awful have declined as those jobs have thankfully become less awful or disappeared altogether. What is true for blue-collar workers is also true for white-, pink-, and no-collar workers. Very few of us are mining coal or turning steel or tilling fields these days, nor do we work for employers who assume that all employees are equal cogs in a unified machine. Many more are in service professions and office work, which will always be more individualized, both in responsibilities and measures of productivity, hence compensation. "Oh for the halcyon days when I could sit on the 37th floor of the General Motors Tower passing memorandums from the left side of the desk to the right side of the desk for 43 years," Peters told *Reason* magazine in 1997. "It's just total shit. It really is. Life was not as glorious as imagined."

Peters, whose 1982 coauthored volume, *In Search of Excellence*, attempted to isolate and identify the qualities that made some companies succeed and others flounder, provides a key to the ongoing dialectic of the American workplace. That controversial, trendsetting book, Peters later explained, was a reaction "to the MBA dogma of the 1960s and '70s," the very sort of top-down, professional management mind-set that had helped to make work so stultifying for generations of American office drones. Peters, who served a couple of tours of duty in Vietnam, is equal parts Marshall McLuhan, Stewart Brand, and Tom Wolfe, with a strong dash of P. T. Barnum sprinkled over it all (there are continuing questions, for instance, about how much he cooked his data for *In Search of Excellence*). He speaks in all caps and ends virtually every sentence with an exclamation point. Best to take it all with a grain or two of salt, which, truth be told, only makes it tastier.

For Peters, the ultimate personification of the organization man mentality was Robert McNamara (1916–2009), whose impressive resumé included stints in the Army Air Force's Office of Statistical Control during World War II (where he introduced systematized bomber inventories credited with vastly improving the war effort), at the Ford Motor Company (where he created modern inventory controls), and in Lyndon Johnson's cabinet, where he served as secretary of defense (and introduced his grimmest mathematical formula, the body count). Peters credits McNamara with bringing order to massive, unwieldy organizations but rails against his pretense to omniscience and insistence on conformity, whether in the service of selling Edsels or the Vietnam War. Peters told Virginia Postrel,

> My entire adult professional life is one big effort to exorcise the demon of Robert McNamara. You know, I went to Vietnam. I was not a war protester. I went to Vietnam twice, not once. But McNamara was the closest we've had to a serious, statist planner in this country. And he got away with it three times—once at Ford, once at the Department of Defense, and once with the World

Bank. And my passion is the destruction of everything that McNamara stood for. My life is a passionate statement against statism—statism in the corporation, as opposed to in the nation, if you will.

Peters all too happily crows, "The corporation . . . as we knew/know it . . . is dead!"

The organization—certainly in its IBM-style blue-suit, white-shirt, red-tie manifestation—is dead. Many of the most successful businesses in America describe themselves in distinctly counter-corporate terms, be it the black-turtleneck wearers at Apple or the Foosball-playing ingenues at Google (whose company motto is "Don't be evil"). The starting point for talent and innovation is the individual, decidedly unloyal worker, members of what Dan Pink once called the "Free Agent Nation." In his 2001 book of the same name, Pink, a former speechwriter for Al Gore, argues that the 1950s-era organization man archetype was in fact a tool of control wielded by powerful employers in part to keep workers cowed. In light of an increasingly dispersed and decentralized workforce, as well as temporary or contract-based opportunities, Pink argues that workers would do better to think of themselves as free agents, like professional athletes. In order to gain the freedom to make your own rules, you need to give up certain assurances that came with old-style jobs. It's a bit like how Hollywood works now—above-and-below-the-line talent swarming together on a project, then disbanding until the next one comes around.

It's worth pointing out that the balls-out version of Pink's idyll has not yet come to pass. Self-employed workers as a percentage of the economy have not shifted much over the past few decades, coming in at around 25 percent of all workers. And the median tenure for workers at a given job didn't change much either between 1983 and 2004, sticking at around five years. More important, though, is the psychic connection between worker and company. Few on either side of the relationship, particularly those just entering the workforce, pretend that any job is forever—or that the skill set you start with at age twenty-one is the one you'll end up with when you hit your fifties.

This isn't to say that contemporary employees are amoral paladins, but they do rightfully insist on more autonomy and more individualized work situations and compensation packages. Partly as a result, only seventeen of the Fortune 100 companies and just 29 percent of companies overall still offer traditional defined-benefit pensions, which reward long tenures with the same company and punish frequent movers with high transaction costs. As recently as 1985, a full eighty-nine of those firms offered defined-benefit pensions. Nowadays, the default is a 401(k) plan, which workers own and control themselves. Critics of such arrangements see them as abdication by corporations of the cradle-to-grave security they supposedly once provided. In fact, the same percentage of private-sector workers is covered under pensions as in 1970. So much for what Jacob Hacker and others call the "Great Risk Shift," in which the little guy shoulders more and more of the burden for everything.

But does getting compensated on an individualized basis mean, as Paul Krugman and, before him, John Kenneth Galbraith would have it, that we're all poorer now, except for the mighty few at the top of a hyperstratified income pyramid? No. On the most basic macroeconomic level, median per capita income has nearly doubled, from over $15,500 in 1969 to just over $27,000 in 2009 (both in 2009 dollars), according to the Census Bureau. Americans have spent much of that increase on day-to-day improvements, which is why households in every income quintile are crammed full of stuff: 66 percent of households have an automatic dishwasher (compared to 20 percent in 1971), 86 percent have air-conditioning (up from 36 percent), and 99 percent have a refrigerator (up from 65 percent). Critics focus less, however, on broad-based gains and more on the widening gap between rich and poor. Economists of all stripes note that in the early 1970s, incomes in developed economies started pulling apart. The best explanation for this is simply that the returns not simply on education but on brains became greater as the United States and other developed economies shifted from being based on manufacturing and brute strength to services and strategic thinking. (Incidentally, the shift away from manufacturing employment should not be confused with a decline in manufacturing; by every yardstick, the United States produces more stuff than ever, but, as in farming, we do so with fewer workers.) These are not industries that can be systematized in the same way as assembly-line work, which means that the individual, rather than the group, will continue to be more important at every level.

The real question is not whether this sort of trend is happening but whether, as Krugman and others charge, opportunity is being funneled to the haves at the expense of the have-nots. Simply put, there is no reason to suspect this is true. The democratization of opportunity, a mythic linchpin of American identity, proceeded apace through the presidencies of Reagan, Clinton, and two Bushes. It will also survive the Obama administration. In 1997, Daniel P. McMurrer, Mark Condon, and Isabel V. Sawhill of the liberal Urban Institute analyzed intergenerational mobility in the United States, or the ability of children to rise (or fall) to markedly different class and employment positions from those held by their parents. The "widespread perception that the youngest generation of workers— men, in particular—is not doing as well economically as their parents did," the authors found, was based on the unacknowledged reality that Americans had gotten pretty fat and happy over the past few generations, even after the Great Compression had abated.

Compounding the misperception are structural changes in work—especially the shift from an agricultural economy in the early part of the twentieth century (when one out of three Americans worked on a farm) to an urban, industrialized one. It was relatively easy to abandon the wheat fields for one of the country's many growing cities. But since World War II, the basic sectors of the economy have not changed with the same velocity as before. There has been, as McMurrer, Condon, and Sawhill put it, a "more static occupational structure" over the past several decades than there was in the first half of the twentieth century.

They concluded, "Children today are increasingly free to move beyond their roots—equality of opportunity has increased." How increasingly free are they? Due to historical patterns of gender discrimination, economists often use the changing status of sons and fathers as a proxy for intergenerational mobility. If mobility is fixed, a father's position will predict his son's. Between 1962 and 1973, studies suggest, the variation "directly attributable to [a] father's background fell from 11 percent to 7 percent," while the variation attributable to education grew from 19 to 22 percent. Studies of more recent data (from the 1970s and 1980s) found that the association between starting points ("origins") and where you end up ("destinations") declined by one-third. That is to say, the job world has been becoming steadily more open to more people of differing backgrounds. "Since at least the mid-1970s," according to McMurrer, Condon, and Sawhill, "there has been an increase in circulation mobility, meaning that the links between individuals' destinations and origins are eroding." This helps explain the counterintuitive finding that where you attend college is less valuable than commonly assumed. A 2002 study by Stacy Berg Dale and Alan Krueger found that "students who attended more selective colleges do not earn more than other students who were accepted and rejected by comparable schools but attended less selective colleges." The reason for that? Over time, it's your work that matters, not your connections.

This democratization is broad-based, extending to ethnic minorities and women. Women currently head about 40 percent of all businesses in the United States, and the rate of growth is outpacing that of male-headed businesses. Between 1997 and 2002, for instance, the number of firms headed by women grew 20 percent, while those headed by men grew by 16 percent. Firms headed by minority females grew by 57 percent and those headed by minority males by 30 percent.

Such statistics strongly suggest that work opportunities are increasingly being democratized. It matters less where you come from and more how you perform. At the same time, workplaces are generally becoming more personalized, with a growing number of employees able to set their own schedules. The big bump here started decades ago, especially as women entered the workforce en masse in the 1970s. According to the Families and Work Institute's *2008 National Study of Employers*, "79 percent of employers now allow at least some employees to periodically change their arrival and departure time, up from 68 percent." The study does note that across eighty measures of workplace flexibility, including working from home, maternity leave, and more, there has been a general stability in practices over the past decade. The main changes that can be viewed as negative are that employers are asking workers to fund higher percentages of health benefits, fewer employers are allowing workers to go from full-time to part-time and back again, and telecommuting is down slightly.

Such overall stability may be seen as the settling into place of the disorganization man (and woman) workplace. There are, arguably, as many pitfalls to the careers of the future as there were to those of the past, even if brute labor has largely been replaced with sitting in front of a computer. The difference going forward is that those who bring their individual talents to the office (or what passes for an office these days) will go further than they might have in the past.

That's certainly what worked for Nate Silver and, before him, Bill James, who isolated Silver's contribution to the current moment—and to the very question of meritocratic advancement—this way for *Time*'s 2009 list of the hundred most influential people:

> Let us take, for example, gay marriage. It's not that Silver doesn't have an opinion on the issue; he probably does. It's that he doesn't start his analysis with his opinion; he starts with the data. He finds every vote on the issue of gay marriage that he can—every poll, every survey, all the related factors. Then he looks for aspects that might reveal changing attitudes. Where was the public on this issue in 2004? Where was it in 2006? Where is it now? What are the numbers from Nebraska? What are the numbers from California? How are the numbers from Nebraska different from those from California? After studying all of it, he reaches a conclusion: Gay marriage is gathering voter support by about 2 points a year, and within three or four years, gay-marriage advocates are going to start winning elections, and here's when that's going to happen in California and in Nebraska and in Arkansas.
>
> Is he right? I don't know. The point is not how precisely he calls the results but that after reading his analysis, you actually know something you didn't know when you started. In a world choking on retreaded arguments long worn bald of the facts, this type of analysis has proved to be stunningly—and reassuringly—popular.

If the world is choking on retreaded arguments—and there's little reason to doubt the truth of such a statement—it's also choking on retreaded social identities that bear less and less connection to the increasingly polyglot, mongrelized world in which we live. If our workplaces have become more interesting and varied, it might just be because the individuals showing up there every day are becoming more interesting and varied too. When it comes to contemporary

America, forget about e pluribus unum—from many, one. Nowadays, where there was one, there are many. Who could have guessed that what Marlo Thomas, Alan Alda, and Rosie Grier sang about on the much-mocked, supersaccharine, Ms. magazine–sponsored 1972 concept album *Free to Be . . . You and Me* has finally come to pass?

CHAPTER 7

RISE OF THE MUTANTS

When Tiger Woods burst onto the Professional Golfers' Association (PGA) tour in August 1996, he was nothing short of mesmerizing, and not just to golf obsessives who lay awake at night sweating water traps and misfired nine irons. After a heavily publicized and smartly truncated college and amateur career, Woods turned pro and immediately collected more than $60 million in endorsement contracts with Nike and such top golf names as Titleist. He managed to win two tournaments by year's end and was named both PGA Rookie of the Year and *Sports Illustrated*'s Sportsman of the Year. In spring 1997, he won the Masters, the first of fourteen major tournament victories (so far), second only to the legendary Jack Nicklaus. It was a blazing start to a career that has landed him at the very top of the *Forbes* list of highest-paid athletes with amazing regularity ever since. The magazine for "capitalist tools" estimates that Woods pulled down $105 million in winnings and endorsements in 2010, over $45 million more than the number two sportsman on the list, boxer Floyd Mayweather. That's even after his most recent turn in the headlines and the exposure of a sex life every bit as driven as his golf game.

Of course Woods was mesmerizing. Too-cute clips surfaced of him from the old *Mike Douglas Show* golfing as a two-year-old with his father and Bob Hope. Unlike the often-tortured relationships between sports stars and their parents, this was no *Fear Strikes Out* scenario, in which anguished baseball player Jimmy Piersall freaks out and climbs a backstop due to the unsettling effects of his father's psychic torture. This wasn't an Andrea Jaeger (tennis) or Todd Marinovich (football) or Mike Tyson (boxing) story, in which the athlete is driven to failure and self-destruction due to overbearing or absent parental figures. No, Woods seemed to get along just fine with his parents, no matter how focused they might have been on his golf game in utero. He was the all-American kid, Jack Armstrong reborn, a Wheaties box just waiting to happen. He'd quit Stanford, not some junior college, to hit the pro links. He was young and fit, unlike the blobby, seemingly interchangeable guys named Duffy and Fuzzy and Payne who were playing the game around him. Woods was the Babe Ruth or Red Grange of golf, transforming a sport that has always worried about creating the next generation of recreational players and galley watchers. He was the perfect face for Nike's golf division, which reportedly pays him upwards of $30 million a year to plaster his mug and signature all over their equipment.

Most mesmerizing of all, Woods was a black man in a game whose events took place at country clubs with long and ugly histories of racial discrimination. Before Woods, even golf diehards struggled to remember another black player who was really in the top tier. There was Lee Elder, who was born in 1934 and turned pro in 1959, more than a decade after the color barrier crumbled in football, baseball, and basketball. When Elder won his first of four tour events, the 1968 Monsanto Open in Pensacola, Florida, he had to change clothes in the parking lot because blacks weren't allowed to use the clubhouse. Things had gotten a little better by the time he teed off at the 1975 Masters, the first black to do so. He could use the clubhouse, but he rented two homes in the Augusta, Georgia, area and shuttled back and forth between them to befuddle the racists who had sent him death threats. Beyond Elder, there was Lee Trevino. He wasn't black, but Trevino burned brightly in people's memories as a minority in golf. During his late 1960s and 1970s heyday, Trevino was known by the sobriquet "Super Mex," reflecting his Mexican American heritage, for his ability to pull off impossible shots and for his outgoing personality. The winner of six majors and a fierce opponent of the other greats of his day, Trevino reveled in his ethnicity, even titling his autobiography *They Call Me Super Mex* and signing off on a character with the same name for the 1988 video game Lee Trevino's Fighting Golf. In that popular arcade game, players could choose from a range of avatars with different strengths and weaknesses, most of which adhered to crude ethnic and gender stereotypes. "Miracle Chosuke" was a Japanese fellow and an expert at putting. "Pretty Amy" and "Super Mex" were the best all-around players. "Big Jumbo" was the first coming of the mullet-sporting John Daly, a heavyweight golfer who could crush the ball but was all thumbs on the greens (and all business in the bar).

So much for golf's history with minorities. And then comes Tiger Woods, not just black but on a fast track to becoming the greatest golfer of all time, during a decade that had seen the election of Bill Clinton, himself being touted as the "first black president." Even better, Woods's victory in the Masters dovetailed with the fiftieth anniversary of Jackie Robinson's breaking the color barrier in baseball. His "coronation as the Black Prince of the Country Club," wrote Gary Kamiya in *Salon* at the time, "gave America a chance to engage in its favorite ritual, the recitation of warm . . .

racial platitudes. While blacks celebrated the triumph of one of their own in a lily-white sport, whites wiped away tears and congratulated themselves on their remarkable progress."

There was just one small, complicating factor: Tiger Woods didn't consider himself black. No, he told an audience on *The Oprah Winfrey Show*, he preferred the word "Cablinasian," a neologism that combined his various racial and ethnic components: Caucasian, black, American Indian, and Asian (Chinese and Thai). "Growing up," he explained, "I came up with this name: I'm a 'Cablinasian.'"

As coincidence would have it, Woods's comments came at the same time that the Office of Management and Budget and the U.S. Census were talking about adding a new "multiracial" category to official government surveys (the 2000 and 2010 censuses reflect this category). The last time they'd changed things had been back in 1977, and since then, all respondents had been relegated to one of following discrete racial groups: American Indian or Alaska Native, Asian or Pacific Islander, black, or white. An additional "ethnic classification" included "Hispanic Origin" or "Not of Hispanic Origin." Those choices, noted a Census Bureau report, "have come under growing criticism from those who believe that the minimum set of categories no longer reflects the increasing racial and ethnic diversity of the Nation's population."

Against such a backdrop, Woods's self-description seemed spot-on. He had a multiracial background, and he might as well say so. Weren't we—finally—at a point in history where everyone was ready to move on from simple, either-or categories? Reaction to Woods's self-identification was mixed. Some, including one of us in *Reason* in 1997, hailed it as precisely the sort of individualistic gesture that was long overdue. Woods, this argument ran, was essentially updating and revising Jean de Crèvecoeur, the French-born writer who had famously asked in the 1782 collection *Letters from an American Farmer*, "What then is this American, this new man?": "He is either a European, or the descendant of a European, hence that strange mixture of blood, which you will find in no other country. I could point out to you a family whose grandfather was an Englishman, whose wife was Dutch, whose son married a Frenchwoman, and whose . . . four sons have four wives of different nations. *He* is an American, who, leaving behind him all his ancient prejudices and manners, receives new ones from the new mode of life he has embraced."

Crèvecoeur's blind spots, in retrospect, are disturbingly clear: Not only is the gender of his new American exclusionary, but he pointedly leaves out the blacks he once bought and sold as slaves. And he perhaps says more than he means when he argues that New Worlders, who practiced a form of race-based slavery that had never existed in old Europe, were indeed "receiving" new prejudices. But his larger point—that to be American is to be a mongrel, a mutt, a mix of many preexisting categories—remains inarguable. Woods seemed to be bringing Crèvecoeur into the late twentieth century, in not just a positive way but one that simply described reality more fully than the rigid and fraught categories of black and white.

Golf's new superstar did have his detractors. Reflecting the history of the "one-drop rule," which held that the smallest amount of "black blood" meant the bearer was a second-class citizen or worse, Colin Powell suggested that regardless of what Woods thought, he was African American. "In America," said the man who would go on to become the first black secretary of state, "which I love from the depths of my heart and soul, when you look like me, you're black." California congresswoman Maxine Waters, then chair of the Congressional Black Caucus, was critical of the proposed multiracial category. "Letting individuals opt out of the current categories," she told *Time*, "just blurs everything." Defenders of race- and ethnicity-based affirmative action, which depends on being able to maintain fixed categories by which to assign levels of redress, were not impressed by Woods's self-description either.

Woods dropped the Cablinasian identifier soon after announcing it. Academic George Davis suggested it was due to financial interests. "I had heard that it was Nike who pulled him away from his declaration that he was not 'black,'" Davis wrote in *Psychology Today* in 2009. "There was more money to be made as the only prominent black person in golf. Black and white—that made his story the American story. There was transcendence in it. There was magic. The 'Cablinasian' story! Magic? Not yet!"

Davis's take has a certain cynical logic to it, though we can never know for sure if it's accurate. Whatever the reason for Woods's turn away from talking up his Cablinasianness, his description of himself and our broader society is fundamentally true—and more obvious than ever in 2011. Whether we're talking about skin color, sexual preference, or self-presentation more generally, we live in a world that is constantly pushing beyond assigned categories and creating exotic new ones, with endlessly proliferating identities scattered about the landscape like so many discarded Lady Gaga costumes.

In 1997's *Plenitude*, published on the Web and revised over the years based on reader feedback, anthropologist Grant McCracken dubs this the quickening "speciation" of social groups in North America, Europe, and, increasingly, the rest of the world. Where there was once one, there are now many, says McCracken. And, as importantly, we're increasingly okay with that, just as we are with the relatively new, yet already taken-for-granted profusion of produce at even the crummiest supermarket in America. Growing up, you'd be lucky to stumble across broccoli and cauliflower in the produce section of your local Safeway or Kroger. Now, the same section is likely to teem with broccoflower, a neon-green hybrid, not to mention broccolini and bright yellow cauliflower, a half dozen types of mushrooms, and three or more distinct colors of potatoes. Eggplants once came only in the deepest shade of purple—Italian Americans even used their word for the vegetable, *mulyan*, as a name for blacks. That already makes no sense in a world where eggplants might be white, or "Japanese." Introduced in 1965, Kellogg's Pop-Tarts came in three flavors: blueberry, strawberry, and brown sugar cinnamon. The company now boasts twenty-seven varieties. McCracken writes,

> Teens were once understood in terms of those who were cool and those who weren't. But in a guided tour of mall life . . . I had 15 types of teen lifestyle pointed out to me, including heavy-metal rockers, surfer-skaters, b-girls, goths, and punks. Each of these groups sported their own fashion and listened to their own music. The day of the universally known Top 40 list is gone. Gender types are proliferating. Whole new categories of powerful, forthright femaleness have emerged, while "maleness" is undergoing its own florescence. Gayness, which used to mean adhering to a limited number of public behavioral models, has rapidly subdivided into numerous subgroups. Many of these groups have developed their own literature, music, and even retail communities. They have become social worlds.

There are no clear, bright lines anymore, but everywhere around us there is more complexity and nuance when it comes to social reality and our depictions of it. Arbitrarily starting with the early 1970s, a period in which all the old verities seemed up for grabs, the mainstream has given way to an overarching alt culture with nary a backward glance. *Happy Days'* vision of high school gave way to *Fast Times at Ridgemont High*, which gave way to *Napoleon Dynamite* and *King Dork.* Cher gave way to Madonna, who gave way to multiple versions of herself before giving birth to Lady Gaga. Kareem Abdul Jabbar gave way to Magic Johnson, who gave way to Dennis Rodman, a top-performing professional athlete unthinkable in pre-1980s

America. Simply put, we live in a world where the literal and figurative cast of characters is far richer and more diverse than it was even in the Summer of Love, much less during the postwar high tide for the organization man and the happy homemaker.

In 1997, McCracken was writing *Plenitude* just as the Internet and its best-known manifestation, the World Wide Web, were becoming a truly global phenomenon. Without overselling it, the Net represented the first time that a truly global audience could communicate almost instantaneously and relatively free of traditional forms of government censorship and corporate control. You needn't be uncritically utopian about this to recognize two main results that are still everywhere with us.

First, there has been an unparalleled cultural mixing as the world floods through Web browsers and every locale on the globe effectively becomes connected to every other. The Iranian Canadian journalist Maziar Bahari could tell you that the results can be quite discombobulating in darkly comic ways. In 2009, Bahari was held captive for months by Islamic militants in Iran. When he was finally released, he told CBS News that at least one of his captors had formed an obsessive relationship with a U.S. state that is typically the butt of jokes. "The words 'New Jersey' sounded to him like the most American place that you can be in your life," said Bahari. "He hated me and he was jealous of me at the same time because I had been to New Jersey." As economist Johan Norberg has noted, the cultural aspects of technologically driven globalization have generally been ignored or underacknowledged. While activists in the 1990s focused on economic impacts (both positive and negative), Norberg stresses the social and cultural ones. "Critics of globalization worry about the Disneyfication or McDonaldization of culture, of standardization replacing 'authentic' traditions," he says. "But it's more correct to say that no single culture is becoming dominant. Instead, it's pluralism, the freedom to choose among many different paths and destinations, that is gaining ground due to globalization and greater exchange." That's precisely the dynamic that sets fire to plenitude and breeds speciation like rabbits. There's a reason that governments the world over focus on controlling not simply basic communications but representations of other ways of life. How long will it be before a generation of Iranians, chafing under the yoke of a repressive interpretation of Islamic governance, their fantasies fueled by Springsteen and Bon Jovi ballads and reruns of *Jersey Shore*, insist on their inalienable right to vacation at Seaside Heights and buy pizza by the slice?

As people in one place have greater access to images and representations of others' lifestyles, they often begin to desire and imitate them in ways that upset the status quo. An apocryphal story told about Stalin makes this point. The dictator was supposedly an admirer of the 1940 film *The Grapes of Wrath*, which he believed showcased the depredations of capitalism. He ordered showings of the film throughout the Soviet Union. As immiserated audiences watched the final scenes of the Okies driving west from the Dust Bowl to California, they had an unintended response: "You mean in America, even the poor people have cars?" As it becomes easier to travel from one place to another, both in terms of actually flying from one nation to another and in terms of simply viewing how the other half of the world lives, all sorts of barriers to mixing break down. Something similar happened in communist Romania, where the only American show allowed to air for many years was *Dallas*, again on the grounds that it showcased Western decadence. Instead, as improbable as it may sound, it led to a cult of J. R. Ewing worship and postdictatorship endorsement deals for the actor who played the evil oil baron, Larry Hagman.

Second, the Web and other technological developments have helped significantly lower the costs of producing, distributing, and consuming the sorts of ultrapersonalized cultural artifacts that flesh

135

out plenitude. When you walk into a Starbucks, you are able to purchase one of hundreds of thousands of different types of beverages
in a way that simply was not available a few decades ago. You can
create almost any drink you want. Something similar is happening
with social identity. As McCracken emphasizes, social groups and
identities—ranging from evangelical Christians to Deadheads to
knitting Brooklyn hipsters—create social worlds, replete with stuff
to wear, buy, listen to, and read. "Let your freak flag fly" was an expression of the 1960s counterculture, an exhortation to be who you
wanted to be. It has become exponentially cheaper to create and fly
your freak flag over the decades since the Monterey Pop Festival and
Woodstock, and the vanishing number of squares who don't themselves join in the fun barely raise an eyebrow of disapproval.

Punk icon Johnny Lydon, known as Johnny Rotten when he
was the lead singer of the outrage-inducing Sex Pistols in the mid-
1970s, tells a story of how he personalized his clothing to express
himself. He took a Pink Floyd T-shirt and scrawled across the top,
in bold, unmistakable letters, "I hate." That's a classic case of *détournement*, or "textual poaching," in which a marginal group or individual literally rewrites a mass-marketed product. How far things
have come since then. Sites such as Zazzle and CafePress allow
users not only to create but to sell whatever T-shirts they want,
along with other sorts of items, ranging from sneakers to coffee
mugs. Most interesting of all, one needn't interact with the mainstream to create an identity. Online pornography caters to more
types of fetishes than there are varieties of Pop-Tarts, arguably rival-
ing Starbucks in its ability to slake any and all thirsts.

As importantly, the Web and other forms of online communica-
tion and signaling have hugely reduced the costs of finding like-
minded souls, whether your interest is political dissent, *Star Trek*
fan fiction, or discovering distant family members back in the old
country. Widely feared as an agent of social isolation and alienation

during its early years, the Internet has instead proven to have a beneficial effect on flesh-and-bone activities. It allows people to learn more and get involved more. In 2008, Gallup reported that Americans were "more tuned in to political news than ever," citing the rise of online media as the major reason that the number of people following politics "very closely" had risen about 50 percent since 1996. Twitter, the social messaging system that restricts users to 140 characters per message, has been used as an organizing tool for everything from antigovernment protests in the Middle East to food-truck operators in Washington, DC. According to the 2010 *Survey of the American Consumer*, which polled over 26,000 random adults, Twitter users are "142% more likely to participate in political or environmental causes, 141% more likely to be part of a lobbyist group or similar organization, and 103% more likely to have attended a political rally or event in the past twelve months."

If the Web and other technologically potent means of cultural globalization are having an effect, it is ultimately in "meatspace," or what quaintly used to be known as the real world. With variety—of ethnicities, of genders, of races, of clothing, of food, and more—comes mixing. The percentage of foreign-born residents in the United States is about 12.5 percent, according to the Census Bureau, up from just 4.7 percent in 1970. Not coincidentally, Pew Research reports that one in seven marriages is now interracial or interethnic, an all-time high. While such couplings remain a small fraction, the trend captures an undeniable reality that has been gaining ground for the past few decades.

"In 1961," write Pew's Jeffrey S. Passel, Wendy Wang, and Paul Taylor, "the year Barack Obama's parents were married, less than one in 1,000 new marriages in the United States was, like theirs, the pairing of a black person and a white person, according to Pew Research estimates. By 1980, that share had risen to about one in 150 new marriages. By 2008, it had risen to one-in-sixty." New social realities have given rise to new levels of tolerance and plural-ism as well. In 1987, two decades after the Supreme Court had in-validated the last laws against interracial marriage, only 48 percent of Americans thought it was "OK for whites and blacks to date each other." By 2009, fully 83 percent did. Similar trends can be observed in other areas of personal identity. The Gallup Poll began asking whether "gay or lesbian relations between consenting adults should or should not be legal" in 1977. Just 43 percent then thought they should be legal. Today, that figure stands at 58 percent. "While pub-lic attitudes haven't moved consistently in gays' and lesbians' favor every year, the general trend is clearly in that direction," summa-rizes Gallup.

What is driving not just the creation of plenitude, of quickening speciation, but its acceptance? We are, after all, creating not just more types of people but more acceptance of more types of people. For McCracken, "the marketplace . . . is the great lingua franca of the contemporary world." That is, the overlap between what we see in our produce aisles and our personal lives is incredibly strong. Market-places for food, ideas, and, ultimately, identity revolve around volun-tary exchange and people who bring new things to the table. Nobody is forced at gunpoint to bargain in a marketplace; indeed, market-places should be free from precisely that sort of coercion. In its place is persuasion, what transgendered economist Deirdre McCloskey calls the "sweet talk" of commerce: Try this, it'll make you feel better. You've never had fruit so sweet. You've never tasted anything like this before.

It's no coincidence that as trade barriers have fallen and people have become relatively freer to migrate than in the past, the United States has become more accepting of vastly different ways of life. Similarly, it's no coincidence that as Cuban Chinese restaurants be-gin to flourish in places such as Jersey City, more people might find Cuban-Chinese couples more acceptable. And on and on.

In the previous chapter, we discussed the economist Joseph Schumpeter's concept of "creative destruction" as it relates to the workplace in a relatively open, capitalist society. In 1942's *Capitalism, Socialism, and Democracy*, Schumpeter called the continuing evolution and transformation of goods, services, and desire itself to be "the essential fact of capitalism." Earlier economists, especially those critical of free markets and competition, tended to take supply and demand alike for granted. Economics was more about the proper and efficient distribution of stuff that already existed. Schumpeter was working off another script altogether. In free marketplaces, what people wanted changed all the time and so did what they were willing to pay for it. Producers were constantly on the hunt for something new and different that people might want even before they knew they wanted it. Schumpeter talked of an ongoing process that "revolutionizes the economic structure *from within*, incessantly destroying the old one, incessantly creating a new one." He stressed the role of "mutations," the sort of constant shape-shifting that we see clearly all around us, whether in the stores at a mall or in the people walking around the mall.

Schumpeter helps explain not just how commerce changes but how people change. There's a reason that the X-Men and, more broadly, Marvel Comics characters are dominating the contemporary movie box office, with a new action hero or three coming out every season. Starting back in the early 1960s, when monthly comic books could still sell hundreds of thousands of copies, Marvel Comics stressed the inner turmoil of its heroes, the angst felt by Peter Parker, a nerdy high school student transformed by an accident into the Amazing Spider-Man, or Ben Grimm, the test pilot who became the powerfully strong but hideously repulsive, orange-skinned Thing in the Fantastic Four. They were mutants in the cosmology of Marvel head Stan Lee. This theme was strongest in the X-Men series, which followed the adventures of children who were born different into a hostile, uncomprehending world. By the time the X-Men hit the big screen in 2000, they had evolved themselves, adding and subtracting characters, plots, and subplots. What remained was not simply a ragtag bunch of misfits hunted down by the government for being superpowered oddballs. The most memorable characters, such as Wolverine, were partly freaks of nature and partly freaks of human intervention (Wolverine, for instance, sported an unbreakable skeleton and claws implanted by slightly mad scientists).

The Marvel-based movies struck a nerve with audiences. There have been three X-Men movies, as well as a spin-off, and more sequels are in production (*X-Men: First Class* is the most recent). The Hulk's modern-day update of Dr. Jekyll and Mr. Hyde has been made into movies twice and, despite lukewarm reviews both times, did boffo business. Spider-Man has emerged as one of the most reliable movie franchises in recent memory. Regardless of the specifics, the Marvel universe products share a common core theme: Precisely that which makes individuals unique both alienates them from others and makes others envy them. On a mass scale, these films contemplate existentialist riddles about individual identity, community, and self-transformation. They enact plenitude as they literalize Schumpeter's mutations. They take the freak, the outlier, the misfit, the one of a kind, and make the audience not simply cheer on, but want to be, him or her or it. We walk out of these movies wanting not to be Superman, who despite being the last son of Krypton, brimming with superstrength, heat-emitting vision, and more, could pass for one of us simply by donning an off-the-rack suit and a pair of horn-rimmed spectacles. We want to be Wolverine or Storm, mutants who not only are different from everyone around them but look different too.

In a world where the X-Men have captured the public imagination, where we all drink something at least slightly different at the local coffee bar, where we individualize our online newsfeeds and are increasingly okay with people who look and sound and think and fuck different (to paraphrase Apple Computer's slogan of a few years back), it somehow seems right that Tiger Woods, a black man in the ultimate white man's sport, would turn out to be far more complicated and multilayered than he at first appeared to be. We've gone from Lee Elder changing his clothes in a parking lot due to racism to Super Mex Lee Trevino endorsing a video game to a multiracial Stanford dropout on track to being the greatest duffer in history—all in thirty years.

As his tabloid-rich personal life and confessions of sexual compulsion attest, Tiger Woods clearly has a long way to go as a family man. As a Cablinasian, he represents something that's in all of us.

CHAPTER 8

WE THE MEDIA

It would surely be obscene to describe Fred Eckhardt's 1970 home-brewing manifesto, A *Treatise on Lager Beers*, as a piece of samiz-dat literature. He didn't type the fifty-two pages of recipes and chemical step-by-steps through multiple sheets of carbon paper in order to make extra copies. He didn't have to smuggle the manu-script out of the country to reach an audience. There was no fear of arrest—at least not by the ideological police.

But this spunky little pamphlet with the typewritten text is argu-ably more responsible than any other source for the happy reality that, quite unlike four decades ago, you can now find delicious and variegated American beer just about everywhere alcohol is sold in this country. Like Thomas Paine's *Common Sense*, the *Treatise* became the cranky but ultimately optimistic source code for a revolution whose participants fundamentally understood that in order to put en-lightenment into practice, sometimes you have to break the law.

"IT'S ILLEGAL" warns the subtitle on page six of the *Treatise*. Eckhardt gets right to the point in his terse and colorful introduc-tion: "Homebrew has acquired an evil reputation in this country from the Prohibition period (1920–33) when this was all most people had to drink. It was usually made surreptitiously, hurriedly, and drunk too soon. Bottles exploded, ceilings were covered with the yeasty messes in many homes. The brewers of this country weren't telling their secrets to anyone. . . . The dark ages had arrived." And unbeknownst to most modern-day Sam Adams drinkers, the repeal of Prohibition had nevertheless left in place an infuriating patchwork of inane laws criminalizing harmless behavior, which conspired to nearly snuff out a grand American tradition that long predates such noted home brewers as George Washington and Thomas Jefferson. Eckhardt wrote,

> After Prohibition, it remained illegal to make homebrew (it still is) and so even then there was no light to be shed on the subject. Now more than 35 years after the end of Prohibition we are just beginning to explore the possibilities of home brewing. . . . There are almost no quality beers made in this country, so if you want good old-country style beer you must make it yourself. Even the German beers imported into this country are being made to the so-called American taste. Pablum and pap for babies. You actually can make beer just as good as the great European master brews in your home. This book is only a start.

Was it ever. Sold at first in the storefronts of wine stores in Eckhardt's hometown of Portland, Oregon (the book's publisher was a Portland-based do-it-yourself outfit called Hobby Winemaker), *A Treatise on Lager Beers* traveled down the I-5 to the barley fields of Chico, California, and over the Rocky Mountains to the rugged steppes of Boulder, Colorado. Wherever there was a local source of delicious mountain water mixed with cussed Western independence, the *Treatise* found an eager audience of basement tinkerers tired of telling the old joke about how drinking Budweiser or Coors was the equivalent of having sex in a canoe ("it's fucking near water"). The book rapidly went through seven printings, eventually selling a jaw-dropping 110,000 copies. "We sure didn't expect that!" Eckhardt remembers, nursing an Alt at Portland's Widmer Brothers Brewing. "Covered the printing bill, that's for sure."

Like Robert Poole's 1969 *Reason* article on airline deregulation, Eckhardt's primer on how to make your own lager helped create a world that he pined for but never fully expected to see. And like Poole—whose career for the past two decades has focused on trying to assist governments interested in sensible, market-oriented transportation policy—Eckhardt has been actively involved in implementation. He started the Oregon Brew Crew homebrew club, wrote the country's first regular beer column for the *Oregonian*, and held a stake in several Portland-based microbreweries and beer-related companies. You can still get a pint of "Fred" at downtown Portland's popular Hair of the Dog brewpub, and every year the city celebrates "FredFest" on his birthday, bringing together craft-alcohol makers of all varieties to raise money for charity. He is both bigger than nearby Mount Hood and smaller than your grand-mother, with an upturned, white handlebar mustache and an imp-ish gleam in his eye, and when he's not leading beer-and-cheese or even beer-and-chocolate tastings, he's busy talking up Buddhism or winning gold medals at senior citizen swimming meets. "Fred is one of those larger-than-life kind of people that you are lucky to meet," Hair of the Dog owner Alan Sprints has said. "His influence on my beers and brewing style has been a blessing, but above and beyond beer, he has been a role model for life itself."

Eckhardt's story is straightforward, if in an only-in-America kind of way. As a teenaged marine in Okinawa during World War II, he and his fellow grunts, when they had access to the stuff, consumed beer for purely utilitarian reasons. "We drank it to get shitfaced!" he recalls. But during the Korean War, when he was stationed in Japan as a radio engineer, Eckhardt went hitchhiking on an R&R pass and found himself face-to-face with a bottle of Tuborg beer from Denmark. "You didn't drink it to get shitfaced, you drank it because it tasted good," he says. "I'd never tried that before." Another Eureka moment came in 1967, when, after serving out his tour in the military and going to college, Eckhardt drank a pint of Anchor Steam beer on a visit to San Francisco (the resurgence of Anchor Brewing Company due to the intervention of washing-machine-fortune heir Fritz Maytag is itself an epic story). "I began to wonder if one really could brew a beer like that at home," he recalled in a 2009 piece for *All About Beer* magazine. An inveterate tinkerer, Eckhardt first dabbled in basement wine making, then noticed some recipes lying around the Wine-Art store, and before long was boiling wort, experimenting with secondary fermentation, and connecting with other practitioners of the still-illegal art. Wine-Art owner Jack McCallum suggested Eckhardt write a book, and a craft-brewing revolution was born.

Eckhardt's *Treatise*, along with his 1989 guide, *The Essentials of Beer Style*, landed squarely within the deep American literary tradition of practical-minded, down-to-earth, yet ambitious self-improvement tracts first popularized by Benjamin Franklin in his landmark autobiography. Franklin, who remains the archetypal American scientific tinkerer, populist striver, and mirthful pamphleteer, produced both a rich and complicated literary text and a step-by-step guide to make it in the New World through continuous self-improvement and hard work. Eckhardt's oeuvre contains no strain of social climbing, but there is something quintessentially Franklinian and American about his basic approach: When quality doesn't exist, create it on your own. Once you learn how to do it, show your math to your fellow man through the written word, so he can replicate the results and improve one of the great and simple things in life. Though the work of improving Americans' beer palate sounds like the project of an elitist dissatisfied with the commoners' tastes, it's actually another twist on Southwest Airlines' form of democratization: The conservative, corporate, organization man status quo, in cahoots with a protectionist and illiberal government, colluded for far too long to produce crap. Americans deserve to know better.

When baseball commentary became too stiflingly dull-witted and unscientific in the 1970s, Bill James launched what at first was a revolution in self-publishing, then later flowered into a root-and-branch change in the way at least some people in the sport organized their businesses. The same has happened with home brewing. According to Eckhardt's calculations, when A *Treatise on Lager Beers* came out in 1970, "there were only 73 U.S. brewing companies operating 133 brewing plants in 31 states. Industry predictions told us there'd only be 10 by 1990. One could speculate that they'd all be brewing Budweiser clones by then." Then the first modern American microbrewery opened up in Sonoma, California, in 1976. In that same bicentennial year, a Boulder-based tinkerer named Charlie Papazian self-published a forty-page pamphlet called *The Joy of Brewing* (the title was a nod to 1972's "gourmet guide to love making," *The Joy of Sex*) and soon thereafter launched the American Homebrewers Association. Sierra Nevada opened its doors in 1980, the Great American Beer Festival inaugurated in 1982, and Portland, Oregon, soon became the microbrew capital of the world. There are now around 1,500 breweries and 1,000 brewpubs, terms like *India pale ale* have become commonplace in run-of-the-mill bars, and the corporate giants in the brewing industry are frantically snapping up craft-beer makers in order to cash in on the only sector of the industry showing consistent growth. From being the laughingstock of the beer-making world in 1970, the United States has become, in Eckhardt's and many others' estimation, its "salvation."

Before much of that could unfold, however, there was still the little matter of what Eckhardt described on page seven of his foundational text: "We should all work to have the law changed so that there is no doubt about the home brewer's rights alongside his wine-making brother." Though law enforcement usually went after do-it-yourself brewers only when they tried to sell their concoctions, the maximum penalty was still five years in prison, and you didn't always have to be a big bootlegger to get rung up. As Greg Beato reported for *Reason* in 2009, a couple in Middlesboro, Kentucky, was arrested for making just three gallons of beer in 1962 and charged with "illegal possession of an alcoholic beverage" and "living in adultery." To allow for the unbridled experimentation that would eventually trigger the entire craft-beer revolution, the democratizers needed a government enabler.

And what an unlikely one they found. The marvelously named Barber Conable, a long-forgotten Republican congressman from Rochester, New York, who didn't drink beer, had a constituent who sold beer-making supplies. It sure would be good for business, the constituent pointed out, if his customers didn't face five years in the federal slammer. Conable introduced a bill in 1978 allowing households to brew up to two hundred gallons of beer per year, making the patriotic argument that Americans shouldn't have to "rely on the beer barons" if they didn't want to. The amendment sailed through the House; Democratic senator Alan Cranston from California introduced it as an amendment to another bill, and then, ten days before he deregulated the airline industry, President Jimmy Carter took the federal shackles off basement beer makers. "I'd say over 90 percent of small brewers I talk to today have roots in home brewing," Papazian told Beato. "The creativity and innovation they've brought to the business has been amazing. The American wheat beers. The fruit beers, the honey beers, the chocolate beers. They were all homebrews first."

The beer industry in America now has become a microcosm of two embattled arenas: politics and the media. As in politics, a duopoly—Anheuser-Busch InBev and MillerCoors—soaks up the vast majority (around 80 percent) of market share. As in the media, such gigantism provokes routine calls for antitrust intervention, particularly when the latest merger is announced. As in both, the legacy giants allegedly dominating all comers are steadily leaking market share, innovation, and buzz, while the long-tail upstarts yapping at their heels seem to be having all the fun. In the first half of 2010, U.S. beer sales dropped 2.7 percent, but the craft industry continued its long-term bull run, increasing by a robust 9 percent. Yet, because of existence bias, because of journalism's tendency to focus on the slumbering giants instead of the energized newbies, a story that should be among the most inspirational in modern America (especially for those of us who hate Budweiser) is instead frequently miscast as a case of industry doldrums.

"Crack open a beer this summer. Please," *Advertising Age* wrote just before summer 2010. "The $100 billion U.S. brewing industry is staggering into its crucial selling season from its weakest position in years. Sales for 11 of the biggest brands fell in the four weeks ended May 16." Nowhere did the story mention, say, Boston Beer, owner of the Sam Adams brand. The largest craft-beer company in the country, Boston Beer saw sales grow 12 percent in 2010, and at press time it was trading on the stock market at twenty-nine times earnings, as opposed to twelve times earnings for Molson Coors.

Fred Eckhardt is living proof that the American tradition of impactful pamphleteer activism is more than alive and well. Four decades after publication of the *Treatise*, it has never been easier for self-publishers and other outsiders to build their own seats at the table and elbow the deadweight aside, forcing the top-down cultures of industrial media (and politics and music and beer and a thousand other sectors) to confront their own banal inadequacies and acknowledge (only after kicking and screaming) the newcomers' contributions. Forget Bill James and pollster Nate Silver—consider the case of Rich Lederer, an investment manager by day and sabermetrics dabbler by night at his Baseball Analysts website.

Lederer, beginning in December 2003, spearheaded a one-man campaign to convince the famously stubborn and insular Baseball Writers' Association of America to elect underappreciated 1970s pitching great Bert Blyleven to the Hall of Fame. At the time, Blyleven had never received more than 30 percent of the vote (you need 75 percent to get in). By penning a series of convincing articles and debating individual voting writers (face-to-face, in many cases), this outside dabbler pulled off the unthinkable: He changed a doomed candidate into a 2011 inductee into the Hall of Fame. In a conference call with reporters after his January induction, Blyleven went out of his way to repeatedly thank Lederer, a California investment banker whom he had never met.

This twenty-first-century David-versus-Goliath story contrasts sharply with another Hall of Fame campaign, one that culminated in the 1979 election of outfielder Hack Wilson, who played in the 1920 and 1930s. Wilson's posthumous triumph (he died in 1948) resulted from a crusade led by the country's most influential sports broadcaster, Howard Cosell, using the top-down media of ABC Sports and *Sports Illustrated* magazine. The pamphleteers are now strutting around where only giants once trod.

In far more consequential areas of human endeavor, people outside the traditional power structures of legacy media are using technology and the American tradition of outsider agitation to change the dull, duopolist, or monopolist status quo to express themselves more fully and influentially. Name a subject that dominant city newspapers have walked away from covering intensely—statehouse politics, high school sports, local crime—and you'll find some entrepreneurial characters filling the void with gusto. Four law students in Washington, DC, unhappy with the lukewarm journalistic and legal interest in the bizarre 2006 slaying of a young

District resident in his home, launched a blog called Who Murdered Robert Wone? in December 2008 as a clearinghouse for news, legal theories, and comments about the case (the blog takes no official position on whodunit). The site proved so popular—it's had more than 2 million page views and 37,000 comments to date—that the criminal trial of Wone's roommates was standing room only for a month, the 2010 verdict made the front page of the *Washington Post*, and a civil wrongful-death case will no doubt remain a hotly contested local story throughout 2011.

This new bottoms-up media is more than just motivated amateurs dedicating more energy to a given topic than any journalism professional will or even can muster. There are also the myriad databases, work-arounds, and aggregators enriching our media consumption by better organizing and curating the online world. In 1990, the Internet Movie Database began life as a Usenet group whose information was supplied by hobbyists and movie obsessives and whose existence was supported by donations. It migrated to the Web in 1992, and by 1996 it had incorporated in England. In 1998, a Berkeley film student named Senh Duong decided to build a website where he could compile all available movie reviews about his favorite actor, Jackie Chan. A dozen years later, Rotten Tomatoes gets more traffic—30 million unique visitors a month—than any living film reviewer.

Where there once stood gatekeepers, mediators, and critics telling you from on high what and how you should think, there is now full-fledged retreat and chaos. *Newsweek*, once a powerhouse of received and regurgitated wisdom, legendarily self-appointed to "write the first draft of history," was sold for all of $1 in 2010 and later merged with Tina Brown's gossipy politics/celebrity website The Daily Beast. The once-infallible *Reader's Digest* went bankrupt in 2009. Ostensibly straight-shooting CNN may be "the most trusted name in news," but it's finishing a distant third to more opinionated challengers in the cable-news wars it once dominated. Or consider the career arc of Andrew Sullivan, the blogger who once upon a time was the editor of the once-influential *New Republic*, the opinion magazine cofounded in 1914 by venerable journalist Walter Lippmann. Named editor of *The New Republic* in 1990, the twenty-eight-year-old Brit made a splash publishing an excerpt from the controversial book *The Bell Curve* and a massive attack on Bill Clinton's health-care-reform plan. Gay, conservative, and trim, Sullivan posed seminude for Gap underwear ads. As the 1990s wore on, *TNR*'s reputation suffered mightily in the wake of plagiarism and false-reporting scandals. By then, Sullivan had started blogging as a one-man show. His Daily Dish blog now is far more widely read than anything emanating from his old magazine—and it's more influential to boot: In December 2002, Sullivan, along with other bloggers such as Josh Marshall of Talking Points Memo and David Frum of *National Review*, received credit for bringing Senate Republican leader Trent Lott's career to a standstill. At a hundredth-birthday celebration for Strom Thurmond, Lott enthused that "we wouldn't of had all these problems" if only Thurmond had won the presidency in 1948, when he ran on a segregationist Dixiecrat ticket. For the most part, mainstream media outlets looked the other way. Sullivan, Marshall, and Frum, among others, kept the issue alive, and Lott resigned his leadership post before year's end.

Then there's the shadowy, hacker-inspired, document-dumping powerhouse known as WikiLeaks. By the time this book goes to press, Australian-born WikiLeaks founder and made-to-order James Bond villain Julian Assange may be on trial for sexual assault in Sweden, or wearing an orange jumpsuit in Guantánamo Bay, or quite possibly on the planetary lam from Interpol, uploading document dumps via undisclosed pay phones. Whatever the outcome, the revolution that he began (in the true revolutionary fashion of being an asshole every step of the way) will far outlive Assange's fifteen minutes of fame in the way that unauthorized file sharing has far outlived the quarter-hour allotted Sean Fanning, the creator of Napster. In a relatively short period, this seemingly stateless outsider to the musty mores of journalism has slammed the science of global warming with the first real body blow of popular doubt (by publishing internal communications from the University of East Anglia's Climate Research Unit showing scientists fudging data to produce favored outcomes), made public some of Sarah Palin's private e-mails, broadcast a bone-chilling video of a U.S. Apache helicopter massacring civilians (including journalists), and then made available thousands of original U.S. diplomatic cables while preparing the publication of hundreds of thousands more. "It's not correct to put me in any one philosophical or economic camp, because I've learned from many," Assange told *Forbes* magazine in November 2010, not long before handing himself over to the British authorities for an extradition hearing. "But one is American libertarianism, market libertarianism. So as far as markets are concerned I'm a libertarian, but I have enough expertise in politics and history to understand that a free market ends up as monopoly unless you force them to be free. WikiLeaks is designed to make capitalism more free and ethical."

The legacy-media reaction to Assange and like-minded upstarts is an instructive reminder that the still-dominant journalistic narratives we consume are created by a defensive, self-interested (though not self-aware) elite of people who've come a long way, baby, since the far more countercultural times of the early 1970s, the Pentagon Papers, and opposition to Richard Nixon. The *Wall Street Journal* editorial page, though no doubt tickled by WikiLeaks' East Anglia cache, pronounced after the diplomatic data dump that "Assange is an enemy of the U.S." who should be subject to American "reprisal under the laws of war." The *New York Post* advocated designating WikiLeaks a "terrorist organization," arguing that "acquiescing in such anarchy is . . . unacceptable." As Salon.com's civil-libertarian blogger Glenn Greenwald pointed out after doing a series of media interviews defending WikiLeaks, "What always strikes me is how indistinguishable—identical—are the political figures and the journalists. There's just no difference in how they think, what their values and priorities are, how completely they've ingested and how eagerly they recite the same anti-WikiLeaks, 'Assange = Saddam' script. So absolute is the *WikiLeaks-is-Evil* bipartisan orthodoxy among the Beltway political and media class (forever cemented by the joint Biden/McConnell decree that Assange is a 'high-tech Terrorist') that you're viewed as being from another planet if you don't spout it. It's the equivalent of questioning Saddam's WMD stockpile in early 2003."

Never before in history has it been easier to produce, disseminate, and consume media—preferably at the same time. The customer is no longer captive to Walter Cronkite's wisdom or Dan Rather's armadillo stories and now owns the means of production, attached to history's greatest distribution channel. There are now an estimated 150 million weblogs, 190 million Twitter accounts, and 500 million active Facebook users. "The people formerly known as the audience," in press critic Jay Rosen's apt phrasing, are now practiced in the arts of writing headlines, sizing photographs, shooting and editing video, producing animation, determining the veracity of sources, processing reader reactions, connecting with audiences, networking with like-minded producers, and performing dozens of other activities that, until recently, were mostly the province of credentialed professionals. Instead of greeting the news of an engaged, democratized, easier-to-find audience and source pool with parades down Main Street, the organization men of the legacy media have reacted to these events with barely disguised horror.

Every year, like a pack of crows announcing the arrival of winter, several anxious new tomes from big-media lifers pronounce journalism to be on death's door. In 1999, writing in the introduction to

Bill Kovach and Tom Rosenstiel's *Warp Speed*, legendary author David Halberstam declared, "The past year has been, I think, the worst year for American journalism since I entered the profession forty-four years ago." Since then, obviously, things have only gotten worse. Journalism "may face its greatest threat yet" and could well "disappear," Kovach and Rosenstiel warned in 2001's *The Elements of Journalism*. "The news about the news," according to the subtitle of a 2002 book of the same name by lifelong *Washington Post* editors Leonard Downie Jr. and Robert G. Kaiser, is that "American journalism" is "in peril." In 2009, Downie one-upped himself, cowriting in a white paper titled "The Reconstruction of American Journalism" that not only is accountability journalism "at risk" but "American society must now take some collective responsibility for supporting news reporting."

Within the Möbius strip of media criticism produced, digested, and praised by current and former mainstream journalists, the biggest woe-is-media book in 2009 was Pulitzer Prize winner Alex S. Jones's *Losing the News*, whose gravity is evident right there in the subtitle: "The Future of the News That Feeds Democracy." Jones's potent operating metaphor is that the "iron core" of news—not crime-blotter sensationalism or infotainment fluff but foreign coverage, political watchdoggery, and statehouse reporting—is shrinking, and with it our ability to function as a republic. But the only way to conclude that the iron core is shrinking is to deliberately ignore every new source of news and to focus instead on the reduced output of industrial behemoths.

One of us debated Jones about his book on the online video-debate site Bloggingheads.tv in 2009, on a day when Reason.com's blog had just compiled a list of comically awful last-minute California laws that had recently been passed, culling the information from a Google News search that led to such sources as MTV.com, *Hip Hop Press*, a boating newsletter, and a half dozen small regional papers. Since there's no way the *Los Angeles Times* or *Sacramento Bee* was going to cover all these laws, wasn't this a demonstration of the iron core expanding in such a way as to improve citizens' ability to keep track of their elective representatives? Jones's response was telling: "See, I think that's scandalous. I think that's appalling," he said. "Maybe *Hip Hop [Press]* is a site that inspires you with confidence, but it would seem to me that you're giving away your confidence pretty cheaply."

This edifice-complex viewpoint, from inside the belly of a staggering but still-powerful beast, has important implications for those of us having more fun on the outside looking in. For one, as a matter of basic media literacy, it helps explain why ostensibly "liberal" establishment media so often end up supporting positions that favor government power over individual concerns. When your power is shrinking but still potent, when you take as a basic professional orientation the notion that journalism should be impartial, fair, and above it all (or, in Jay Rosen's again-memorable phrase, "from nowhere"), and when your self-appointed sense of responsibility for the polity's affairs creates a natural peer group of similarly responsible government officials and policy intellectuals, you will inevitably develop an existence bias that accepts as normal the status quo (regardless of how indefensible that may be) and enforces certain mores of acceptable behavior within the circle of trust. Those who do not understand how to speak that language—especially if they emanate from the threatening culture of technology—tend to be greeted with a disproportionate ferocity.

That's part of what happened to Julian Assange, and it's definitely what happened with California's Proposition 19, a marijuana-legalization initiative editorialized against by twenty-six of the Golden State's thirty largest daily newspapers. It's not that there weren't good arguments against Proposition 19: As inveterate drug legalizers ourselves, we winced at the initiative's sheer complicating length and its unclear language governing employers. But the way that the unsigned view-from-nowhere editorialists disapproved of the entire discussion was instructive. The proposed law offended not just their sense of policy but their sense of decorum. "No to Ganja madness!" snickered San Diego's *Union-Tribune*. "What were they smoking?" asked the *Sacramento Bee*. "The legalization crowd would stand a much better chance if some of the stoners speaking up for Proposition 19 would just stay quiet," sniffed Chico *Enterprise-Record* editor David Little (yes, that's the same Chico where Sierra Nevada is brewed and where college students have for decades been breaking federal drug laws with a notable intensity). Gov. Arnold Schwarzenegger—whose unrepentant pot smoking is one of the many highlights of the classic 1970s documentary *Pumping Iron*—warned that California would become a "laughingstock" if Proposition 19 passed. As was the case when the formerly pot-smoking president of the United States snickered at and then dismissed a question at an online press conference about whether he'd be in favor of legalizing pot, the awesome burden of responsibility and seriousness have placed pot-experienced establishmentarians in the position of reflexively mocking anyone who dares challenge the murderous status quo. That 850,000-plus Americans are arrested per year for possession of a relatively harmless drug is unconscionable. So, too, is the federal government's anti-scientific classification of marijuana in the same category as heroin. Those who would realign marijuana laws even partway in the direction of reality and human liberty are by default treated like Tommy Chong at a church picnic.

Existence bias and the policing of in-group mores (against outgroup interlopers) form one side of the view-from-nowhere pathology. On the other you have the bias that dares not speak its name, partly because it is largely unconscious. It is *do-something* bias, or the instinct, shared almost universally by responsible journalists and politicians alike, to respond to crises real and imagined by pragmatically using the world's largest problem-solving tool. In crisis-solving mode, you need not concern yourself with the unintended consequences of well-meaning laws, with the regulatory capture identified by Alfred Kahn and other economists as endemic to the system. Terrorists strike, so we need the open-ended September 14 authorization against terrorism, plus the PATRIOT Act. The financial crisis hits in the fall of 2008, and in the words of do-something New York mayor Michael Bloomberg, "Nobody knows exactly what they should do, but anything is better than nothing." By the time the inevitable flaws of these panicky, bipartisan, media-supported legislative packages make front-page news, there's always a new problem requiring urgent intervention. Then the Michael Bloombergs of the world can get back to lecturing the rest of us on the problems of political "incivility" and how we need a "no-labels" movement to get beyond petty politics and pragmatically solve problems, dammit.

But as the previous chapter showed, these one-size-fits-all colors are fading. Americans are becoming more speciated and individualized not just with their personal identities and consumer choices but with their ideologies and politics too. We are hybrids upon hybrids, thrashing around at the far end of the long tail, instinctively distrustful of the latest snake oil salesman offering a magically nonpolitical solution to the world's problems. The evolution described throughout this book—from a mass culture of political/media recipients to an infinitely more robust and fluid collection of association-forming individuals bearing labels as promiscuous and variegated as tags on a blog post—that train's not stopping. Everybody is coming from somewhere, carrying some baggage, and we are right to reach for our skepticism (and our wallets!) when a group of people in or adjacent to power claim to be descending upon us with an ideological slate as clean as a baby's mind.

The libertarian insight in this case is less about producing policy agreement and more about recognizing that restraining the government from enforcing a one-size-fits-all policy is the best way to allow for true tolerance of a superhyphenated culture. Unfortunately, the same crowd that has been trying to convince us that our glorious culture boom is the worst thing to happen to journalism since Adolf Hitler wrote a column for William Randolph Hearst is now busy lobbying the federal government to intervene on the dinosaurs' behalf.

In March 2009, Robert McChesney, a communications professor at the University of Illinois, and John Nichols, the Washington, DC, correspondent for *The Nation*, penned a widely circulated story for the progressive weekly calling for a journalism "stimulus" costing $60 billion over the next three years. Provisions included a $200 tax credit for newspaper subscriptions, the elimination of postage rates for magazines receiving less than 20 percent of their revenue from advertising, and taxpayer support for "a well-funded student newspaper and a low-power FM radio station" at "every middle school, high school and college." In 2005 that same duo had published a book whose subtitle complained that the American media "destroy democracy." Now they're pitching their plan to save the media as a way to "sustain" the country's "democratic infrastructure." Apparently a lot can change in just four years. "Only government," McChesney and Nichols concluded in the *Nation* piece, "can implement policies and subsidies to provide an institutional framework for quality journalism." Reporting the news "is a public good that is no longer commercially viable. If we want journalism, it will require public subsidies and enlightened policies."

Former *Washington Post* executive editor Leonard Downie Jr. made a similar proposal in his "Reconstruction of American Journalism" white paper, calling for, among other things, a national "Fund for Local News" to be administered by the Federal Communications

Commission. "American society," Downie and coauthor Michael Schudson declared, "must now take some collective responsibility for supporting news reporting—as society has, at much greater expense, for public education, health care, scientific advancement and cultural preservation, through varying combinations of philanthropy, subsidy and government policy." These sentiments would have been considered shocking when Downie's newspaper was butting heads with Richard Nixon in the early 1970s. They are now commonplace not just within the self-conscious media sphere, at places like the *Columbia Journalism Review* and the Poynter Institute, but among the people who run the federal government.

"Not nearly enough is being done to find ways to preserve these institutions that are so critical to our democracy," said Rep. Carolyn Maloney (D-NY) in September 2009, in one of several hearings during the 111th Congress on how to reverse the flagging fortunes of Big Media. Senator John Kerry (D-MA), who chaired a Senate gabfest on the subject, semicoherently expressed his sense of urgency: "The increase in media conglomerates has resulted in an increase in agenda-driven reporting and over time, if those of us who value a diversity of opinion and ideas, and are unafraid to be confronted with pointed commentary and analysis, do not act, it is a situation which will only get worse." In March 2009, Senator Ben Cardin (D-MD) introduced the Newspaper Revitalization Act, which would give papers targeted tax breaks and allow them to restructure as 501(c)(3) nonprofits as long as they stopped endorsing political candidates and agreed to limit the amount of advertising they ran. That same month, Attorney General Eric Holder singled out newspapers for possible preferential treatment under the law. "I think it's important for this nation to maintain a healthy newspaper industry," he said. "So to the extent that we have to look at our enforcement policies and conform them to the realities that that industry faces, that's something that I'm going to be willing to do."

Even President Barack Obama got into the act, telling the *Toledo Blade* that September, "What I hope is that people start understanding if you're getting your newspaper over the Internet, that's not free and there's got to be a way to find a business model that supports that. . . . It's something that I think is absolutely critical to the health of our democracy."

It's an old joke in Washington that you can tell an industry is in its death throes when it finally starts to have some pull on Capitol Hill. The case against government intervention in the media business is not tough to make, and it begins with the First Amendment's famous phrase, "Congress shall make no law." As with other regulations, attempts to shore up certain sectors inevitably end up handing out favors to the biggest corporations in the industry at the expense of upstart outsiders. Nixon's Newspaper Preservation Act of 1970 not only failed to preserve newspapers but prevented would-be competitors from arising in the twenty-eight cities affected by the legislation. As evidenced by the 2010 rule making by the Federal Communications Commission on "Net neutrality"—a vague carte blanche for federal regulators to decide when Internet-infrastructure companies are behaving badly—McChesney and his ilk have considerable pull with the current White House. The dinosaurs may be buckling under their own deadweight, but they want to rig the rules to forestall their extinction.

The good news is that it won't work. Consumers will never again allow themselves to be nothing more than passive receptacles of the authoritative voice. What's happened to America over the past twenty years mirrors what happened to Andie MacDowell's character at the end of the predictive urtext of our age, Stephen Soderbergh's 1989 indie hit *Sex, Lies and Videotape*: After being subject to the flattering but voyeuristic attentions of the secretive and creepy man holding the media power, MacDowell seizes the camera, turns it back on James Spader, and watches with some amount of glee and uncertainty as his world proceeds to come unglued. At least since 1991, when George Holliday videotaped Los Angeles police beating Rodney King after a high-speed chase, we have collectively been shoving our cameras in the faces of cops, governments, and the media themselves, and the legacy journalism institutions in particular are reacting with panic. Meanwhile, with greater media and political sophistication come greater self-awareness and an understanding that the guy across the cubicle from you might harbor an exotic hybrid breed of politics you haven't seen before.

The forces of centralization in the media are outnumbered by the millions, and the potential reach of every new pamphleteer is limitless. There are Fred Eckhardts around every corner, grinning like imps at the way they're using media to alter our nonmedia lives. Owning the means of media production, they know well, is the first step in owning the means of political production. The ever more user-friendly World Wide Web has made not just media (and beer) but politics a much more fluid and unpredictable place. Now is the time to use that force to confront the grave problems that politicians were busy foisting on us while we were getting our drink on.

PART III

OPERATIONALIZE IT, BABY!

CHAPTER 9

WE ARE SO OUT OF MONEY

The previous section of the book is shot through with a common theme: In virtually all ways in the United States, things have been getting better and better over the past thirty, forty, or fifty years (ask your older siblings, your parents, your grandparents). This isn't a blind hymn to inevitable Progress with a capital *P*, an unironic hopping aboard Nathaniel Hawthorne's ironic Celestial Railroad, a come-on for Epcot Center, or a failed General Electric slogan. It's a simple observation free of the ideological cant that covers right- and left-wing ideologues like so much flop sweat during open mike night at a school board meeting. In order to secure their futures, politicians and their enablers must romanticize the past as somehow superior to whatever ruinous contemporary moment the other party has gotten us into. Things were always brighter, cleaner, fresher, better back in the day, when we were young and the world lay in front of us, ours for the taking. For the political class, a fabled past is always calling, especially when you're trying to cadge enough votes to grab a fleeting majority.

But the typical individual, male or female, black or white, human or cyborg, for that matter, has exponentially more options and opportunities than those who came earlier. The rich may indeed be getting richer, but the poor no longer only get children, as the 1920s hit song "Ain't We Got Fun" put it. When it comes to ownership of or access to basic consumer goods such as TVs, cell phones, houses, washing machines, and the like, more and more of us get a reasonable facsimile of what it's like to be Bill Gates. The vastly expanded middle class, comprising anywhere from 20 percent of the population (the middle-income quintile) to upwards of 90 percent (depending on whom you ask), is doing so well comparatively, even during these lean economic times, that they suffer from class and status anxiety—until recently the preserve only of the truly wealthy. Imagine that, Kennedy ulcers on a shanty-Irish income!

In 2010, "middle-class tax cuts" were reserved for the lowest 97 percent of income earners (that is, households making under $250,000). These days, it matters less who your parents are, what your skin color is, or where you come from. This is no small thing in a country founded on tragically clouded visions of opportunity and equality. It is, as we have argued, no coincidence that those areas seeing the most progress—sometimes incremental and almost imperceptible, sometimes radical and obviously transformational—are those farthest afield from the grim thunderdome of politics, where garnering fifty-one votes out of one hundred gives you the right to tell others how to live.

For all those advances, three large areas—three great blots on the X-ray of the American Dream—buck the broad trend toward increased democratization and decentralization, toward increased opportunity and dispersed power. Unsurprisingly, in all three areas, the state, at various levels, still calls all or most of the shots, either through straight-up racketeering or by rigging the rules of the game in a way that makes it nearly impossible for people to escape. Long after liberation day should have come, a figurative Berlin Wall still hems in K–12 education, health care, and retirement. The specific paths to improving each area are different (and will be examined in Chapter 10), but the problems stem from a single dynamic: A tightly controlled, politically operated system created to address the issues of the past is now increasingly at odds with current and future needs and demographics. Similarly, the fixes to each area will be different (and multiple), but to achieve anything they must embrace choice and innovation as experienced and directed at the individual level. We are tailoring everything else in our lives to our different needs, desires, and wants. Yet, despite their centrality to our lives, education, health care, and retirement offer us considerably less choice than we have at the soda fountain of our local 7-Eleven.

But change is a-coming for two main reasons. First, as documented so far in the book, folks are sick and tired of the two main parties and ideological perspectives that don't deliver anything and don't represent how they feel and think. If our only choices are between the "leadership" offered up by John Boehner and Nancy Pelosi, is it any wonder that Americans increasingly refuse to identify as Republicans or Democrats?

Second, and far more importantly, the simple fact is that we are out of money. A decade into the twenty-first century and in the long throes of an unprecedented spending binge, the public sector at every level has maxed out our credit cards and taxed our grandchildren. As of this writing, aggregated federal debt equals 62 percent of the nation's economic activity, up from 37 percent in 2007. (For reference, member states of the European Union are forbidden by charter from crossing the 60 percent threshold.) And the situation will almost certainly have deteriorated by the time this book reaches stores. If all goes according to the president's sunniest scenarios, the debt-to-GDP ratio will reach 77 percent by 2021. At least forty-eight out of fifty states face long-term structural deficits that have bond markets shaking. Cities all over the country are openly contemplating bankruptcy. The end of the era of big government will not come because libertarians have won a political argument. It is coming—and soon—because politicians spent their way to the brink of a massive fiscal shock.

This is not to say that the political class is acknowledging this reality. Look to the top of the pyramid for the clearest example. President Barack Obama presides over a government whose own analysts in the Congressional Budget Office (CBO) assume that interest payments on the national debt will more than triple over the next decade, shooting past combined discretionary nondefense spending in total outlays. Think of it: We'll be spending three times as much just on the vig for today's spending! And yet, Obama, who could not even be bothered to muscle through a budget for fiscal year 2011 despite his party's controlling both houses of Congress back then, has for fiscal 2012 proposed doubling public debt over the next decade.

In light of the dismal finances of the nation he governs, what is one of Obama's top priorities? In two State of the Union addresses and many other speeches, the president has pledged tens of billions of dollars to his (and Joe Biden's) dream of high-speed rail, a dream transportation system that is still trying to approach speeds commonly attained by cars on highways.

There is something tragic about a train—tragic not in the sense of Anna Karenina, who tosses herself in front of a locomotive rather than live a life she deems insufficiently melodramatic, or in terms of murderous intrigue being hatched between cars, à la Patricia Highsmith's and Alfred Hitchcock's *Strangers on a Train*. No, the tragedy of trains, whether "heavy" or "light," regular or high-speed, is that they drive politicians and otherwise sensible citizens totally off the rails when it comes to reality. Dreams of mythical 300-mph super-engines cause fiscal train wrecks time and time again. These monetary catastrophes may be the only things that trains reliably accomplish on schedule—in addition to clarifying just how slow to action the political world is when it comes to relinquishing nineteenth-century modes of control and power.

Pie-in-the-sky visions of bullet lines, monorails, light rail, and streetcars manage to totally obscure while deeply exacerbating the most basic and urgent fact of contemporary American public policy—which is simply that we are out of money at the federal, state, and local levels. Taking a detailed look at politicians' obsession with publicly financed rail tells you most of why they can't be trusted to lead us into the future.

Consider the characteristic case of Cincinnati, Ohio. Like a lot of American cities, Cincinnati peaked population-wise in the decades just after World War II, when the metropolis that bills itself as "Porkopolis" (a legacy of pig farms and the sausage love of the large German American population) and the "Queen City" (lady regent of the Ohio River) was home to half a million residents. Starting in 1960, the populace lit out for the adjacent suburbs or fled the southwestern corner of Ohio altogether for greener pastures elsewhere. Cincinnati is now home to just 330,000 or so residents, a couple of generally awful big-league sports teams (football's Bengals and baseball's Reds), mediocre public schools and some well-regarded but dwindling Catholic ones, and the slow-fading memories of a Who concert gone horribly wrong in 1979 and a 1990 obscenity case over a local museum's displaying photographs by Robert Mapplethorpe. In 2001, the city was wracked by several days of race riots when the police shot and killed a nineteen-year-old black kid named Timothy Thomas after chasing him and mistakenly assuming he was carrying a gun.

In 2010, Cincinnati faced a $50 million budget deficit as federal stimulus money was running out and a tightwad Republican, John

Kasich, was revving up his ultimately successful campaign for governor. The incumbent state chief executive, Democrat Ted Strickland, had been relatively kind to the residents of Cincinnati and every other part of the Buckeye State, too, which was one of the reasons why he was broadly unpopular. Strickland had spent a lot of money—all he could put his hands on, in fact, plus billions more in borrowed cash—but all he had to show for it was the nation's seventh-highest state-and-local-combined tax burden and the second-worst job-loss numbers in the country (the only place more miserable in the 2000s was that sad sack to the north, Michigan).

Given this shrinking pool of other people's money, what were Cincinnati's leaders up to? Were they ushering in a bold plan to lure taxpaying families back into the city by crafting compelling school-choice programs to shore up public education? Were they figuring out how to cut the sorts of taxes and red tape that might, at least on the margins, make their burg a slightly more attractive place to live and do business? Were they finding a way to extract some money, even just spare change, from the Bengals and the Reds, for whose filthy-rich owners they'd financed sweetheart deals for new stadiums in which the tenants got all the revenue and none of the bills? Were they hatching a plan to fake their own deaths and abscond with whatever petty cash they could find around city hall?

Of course not. They were talking about going even deeper into debt to finance a train. Or more precisely, they were willing to break the bank (again!) for a desire named streetcar. This streetcar line, supporters insisted, wasn't a gimmick or a tourist attraction ("though tourists will love to ride them," supporters said). No, it was a bargain at a planned $128 million because it would link the rough-hewn Over the Rhine neighborhood (epicenter of the decade's race riots) to downtown Cincinnati in a way that cars and buses just can't quite manage. It would stimulate not millions but billions in economic development, just as streetcars had in Tampa, Florida, and Portland, Oregon, and even Kenosha, Wisconsin, named the ninety-fourth best place to live in the United States by *Money* magazine in 2005! Maybe best of all, the city only had to put up half the dough, a measly $64 million, because the feds and the state would cover all or most of the difference.

Cincinnati's hometown paper, the *Enquirer*, reported on the May 2010 meeting in which the city council—men and women of action, mind you—bravely pushed the Queen City into the future. "The question isn't whether we can afford to build the streetcar," one visionary explained. "The question is whether we can afford not to." But don't mistake the backers of this plan for head-in-the-clouds dreamers. "Yes, there are some risks here," another granted. "But we have to be bold enough to take those risks if we're going to grow this city and region." As the *Enquirer* put it in an admirably evenhanded account, "'This is a major first step,' said Mayor Mark Mallory, who minutes before the meeting began was still meeting privately with council members to allay concerns that the bonds potentially could commit the city to a project it might not be able to complete or afford to operate."

Precisely this sort of thinking helps explain two dismal and related facts about virtually all local governments in the United States: They spend ever increasing amounts of money and still seem to be broker than a sailor on the second day of shore leave. In 1970, aggregate local-level spending came to about $1,859 per person across the country in 2005 dollars. In 2008, cities were spending $4,793 per person in 2005 dollars. As with per-pupil costs at public schools, costs had more than doubled. And yet, cities all over the place are on the brink of insolvency. The math isn't difficult to plow through. In 1970, local revenues per capita in constant 2005 dollars came to $1,205. By 2008, local governments were pulling in $3,058 per capita—or more than twice as much but still $1,700 less than they were spending. To put it somewhat differently, we are out of money.

There's not a lot of mystery here. You strip away the speechifying, the long and boring municipal meetings, the endless tributes to the honor and integrity of everyone involved in the political process, and this is why cities—as well as states and whole countries—go broke: They spend more than they take in, and twice as much as a few decades ago, without delivering noticeably better services. In fact, they spend more than they could *ever* take in, even if they won the lottery every day of the week. This happens to cities and towns run by Democrats and Republicans alike. Like James Joyce's snow, the lowered bond ratings and the increased debt payments fall evenly on the living and the dead—but only the living have to pay higher taxes or move elsewhere. Yet, even when cities get a second chance, a do-over, an act of God, a snow day on the very day of the big exam on which their entire future is riding and for which they haven't cracked a book all year, they still can't admit the one basic truth that is staring them—and us—right in the face: We are out of money.

Take a look at Vallejo, California, founded in 1851, not too far from San Francisco and best known at various points for its sulfur springs, unfortunate involvement with the Zodiac killer, and a Six Flags amusement park. In 2008, just barely into the Great Recession, the 120,000-population city became the biggest municipality in California ever to file for bankruptcy. Imagine that, the brokest city in the brokest state in the greatest country ever! Top of the world, Ma! Vallejo was done in by a lot things, but the press accounts always make a point of fingering "declining revenues" due to the rotten economy, especially the implosion of the housing market—which is a funny way of putting it, since revenues only matter in the context of expenditures. And the expenditures were stunning. As investigative reporter Steven Greenhut put it in the

Wall Street Journal, Vallejo's outlays, especially on its public-sector workforce, were the "root cause" of the city's money woes. "Compensation packages for police captains top $300,000 a year and average $171,000 a year for firefighters," Greenhut wrote. "Regular public employees in the city can retire at age 55 with 81% of their final year's pay guaranteed. Police and fire officials can retire at age 50 with a pension that pays them 90% of their final year's salary every year for life and the lives of their spouses." A typical California city spends about 60 percent of its budget on salaries, benefits, and overtime for cops and firemen. In Vallejo, a Cato Institute study reported, that figure was 74 percent. Declining revenue may have been the match that lit up Vallejo's finances, but the powder keg itself was city employees treating the annual budget like an ATM. It was a bankruptcy waiting to happen.

Vallejo had its fiscal sins wiped away not by the Lamb of God but by U.S. bankruptcy judge Michael McManus, who said that the city had "the authority to void its existing union contracts in its effort to reorganize." This was it, the second chance that city leaders and beleaguered taxpayers had been dreaming of. So what did the city do? Bureaucrats proposed a three-year moratorium on all interest and principal payments on $53 million of municipal debt, thereby screwing the investors dumb enough to keep lending them money, and they agreed to hire new firefighters on more prudent terms than the guys lucky enough to have joined the force earlier. They cut police by more than fifty officers (and suffered higher-than-average rates of crime for a city of Vallejo's size). They put the screws to senior centers and parks, and asked residents to use the 911 system "judiciously" rather than as a party line. However regrettable some of these choices may have been, something had to change to right this listing ship. But what's more interesting is what didn't happen. After running through the various nips and tucks made by city leaders, the business magazine *Barron's* noted wryly, "The only thing that will be left untouched? The very thing that tipped the California city into Chapter 9—its $84 billion in future pension obligations." And why weren't these addressed? The vice mayor of Vallejo told Greenhut that council members, including some who were elected on a platform of pension reform, "did not have the political will to touch the pink elephant in the room—public safety influence, benefits and pay."

So what part of "we are out of money" doesn't the city of Vallejo understand? The same part that states across the country can't quite wrap their minds around either. In 2009, the states of Montana and North Dakota were not clearly in the budgetary red. Between them they've got a population around the size of Phoenix, so it's not immediately clear what larger lessons can be drawn. According to the Center on Budget and Policy Priorities, the combined shortfalls of all states in 2009 rolled in at around $166 billion. The state with the single biggest shortfall as a share of its budget was California, whose man-made lake of red ink comprised a whopping 58 percent of its annual expenditures.

How had the states come to this? It's tempting to blame their rotten balance sheets on a recession that officially started in December 2007. There's no question that the past few years have been tougher than a $2 steak. The feds can print money, while many of the states are legally bound to deliver balanced budgets. We all know the drill: As the economy tanks, tax and other receipts go down just as states need to beef up social welfare programs of all kinds. It's the classic double squeeze. But such an accounting fails to account for how states acted during boom times. Take a gander at how the states spent during the flush years of the twenty-first century, from 2002 (when the economy picked up after the high-tech bust) through 2007 (the start of the current woes). Here's how analysts from the Reason Foundation, the Los Angeles–based nonprofit that publishes *Reason* magazine, wrote up that half-decade period of sky-is-the-limit growth:

In the five years between 2002 and 2007, combined state general-fund revenue increased twice as fast as the rate of inflation, producing an excess $600 billion. If legislatures had chosen to be responsible, they could have maintained all current state services, increased spending to compensate for inflation and population growth, and still enacted a $500 billion tax cut.

Instead, lawmakers spent the windfall. From 2002 to 2007, overall spending rose 50 percent faster than inflation. Education spending increased almost 70 percent faster than inflation, even though the relative school-age population was falling. Medicaid and salaries for state workers rose almost twice as fast as inflation. . . .

In 2002 total combined state revenue was $1.097 trillion. In 2007 this figure had risen to almost $2 trillion. That's an 81 percent increase, at a time when prices plus population increased 19 percent.

Worse still is the reality that as soon as a state has a couple of nickels to rub together, it does two things, one in the short run and the other in the long. First, it hires more people. Second, it sweetens the retirement benefits for those workers down the road, often in closed-door sessions that attract little or no attention at the time. Between 1996 and 2009, for instance, California added 1 state worker per 1,000 residents, to reach a total of 9.3 per 1,000 residents and more than 350,000 overall. In 1999, before the high-tech bubble burst, the California Public Employees Retirement System told credulous state legislators that a major increase in retirement benefits wouldn't cost taxpayers much, if anything, because stock market increases would do all the work. As Steven Greenhut reported, the law was incredibly generous, creating, among other monstrosities, something called the "3 percent at 50 retirement plan." How did that work? "At age 50 many categories of public employees are eligible for 3 percent of their final year's pay multiplied by the number of years they've worked. So if a police officer starts working at age 20, he can retire at 50 with 90 percent of his final salary until he dies, and then his spouse receives that money for the rest of her life." And if, for that last year, that worker could wheedle a higher-paying job or—better yet!—work-related disability, her pension could spike far beyond the base salary ever merited. The result? Between 2001 and 2008, the state's annual pension fund liability increased by a factor of twenty-three: from $321 million to $7.3 billion. This sort of major swing—which has been replicated everywhere from Washington State to Florida, from Arizona to Maine—has a clear and devastating effect on state finances and the provision of public services. Every government dollar borrowed crowds out loans that the private sector might take out to expand business. Every dollar spent gilding a pension is a dollar not spent funding an orphanage. Most estimates peg the total unfunded part of state- and local-level pension liabilities at somewhere between $1 trillion and $3 trillion. The mind boggles.

This sort of buildup has been taking place for the entirety of the twenty-first century, where all net job growth in the country has been in the public sector. Say what you will about George W. Bush, but the public sector never had a greater patron. Under Bush, the Bureau of Labor Statistics reports, net employment increased by just 1.08 million jobs. But in the breakdown, the numbers are truly stunning: The federal government gained 50,000 jobs, state and local governments added 1.8 million positions, and the private sector shed a total of 673,000. Persistent weak levels of private-sector job creation were ultimately done in by the recession that kicked into high gear at the end of Bush's two terms. Looking at Bureau of Labor Statistics data from January 2008, the first full month of recession, through the end of 2010, economist Veronique de Rugy of the Mercatus Center came up with the following net figures for that time frame:

Private sector: –7.2 million jobs (6 percent of the January 2008
   workforce)

Total government: –118,000 jobs (0.5 percent of its January
   2008 workforce)

Federal government: +98,000 jobs (a 3.5 percent growth since
   January 2008)

State government: +42,000 jobs (less than 1 percent growth
   since January 2008)

Local government: –258,000 jobs (1.7 percent of the January
   2008 workforce)

That sort of showing is unhealthy for a long list of reasons and
helps explain why we're out of money at every level. Driving down
the number of private-sector jobs doesn't just kick people off the tax
rolls; it also puts them on other sorts of social welfare plans that cost
money too. But if the past is any indication, the private-sector number will come up again when the economy eventually recovers. The
real tale, not simply of the recession but of the twenty-first century
to date, is in the other numbers. Here we are, living through the
worst downturn since the Great Depression, and the one place you
can find safe harbor is in the public sector, where it's still damn
tough to get canned. The feds have added workers during this time
frame (and note that the nearly 100,000 jobs figure above is net
after temporary Census Bureau workers were given the heave-ho).
State government employment is basically flat, as is local government work—and this during what is supposed to be the worst economy in anyone's memory. Go back and look at the number of state
and local employees in 1970. It was fewer than 5 per 1,000 residents.
Now it's 6.5. At the federal level, things have actually gone in a different direction, with one worker for every 155 residents, or half as
many as in the early 1950s—which isn't to say that issues don't exist
with current levels of staffing. The federal government remains the

single largest civilian employer in the country, with more than 2 million full-time workers on its payrolls (not including employees of the U.S. Postal Service, which employs another 770,000).

Public-sector workers at any level of government don't come cheap. Time was that people who went into government work sacrificed salary up front for job security, better-than-average health and retirement benefits, and a generally lighter workload. This used to be called the "grand bargain." At some point during the past couple of decades, not long after public-sector workers got the legal right to unionize, this stopped being the case. Public employees now often make more in straight salary than their private-sector counterparts—and lots more when health-care and retirement benefits are counted.

How much more is a matter of some legitimate debate. Meaningful straight-up comparisons are difficult, though not always impossible, to make. For the 2007–2008 school year (the latest figures available from the National Center for Education Statistics), the nation's more than three million full-time public school teachers made an average of $53,230 in "total school-year and summer earned income." That compared to just $39,690 for private-school teachers. Groups such as the Center for State and Local Government Excellence and the National Institute on Retirement Security (whose agendas are built right into their titles) argue in the April 2010 study "Out of Balance?: Comparing Public and Private Compensation Over 20 Years" that public-sector workers have more education and advanced degrees than private-sector drones; when you account for that and control for age and years on the job, the study says public-sector workers make about 7 percent less in total compensation. Such studies, however, fail to control for a very important factor—namely, whether such jobs actually require advanced education. Put more bluntly, the fact that more public-sector workers have higher levels of education doesn't mean they need it to execute their duties. As with any workforce, the question isn't whether the employees are worth it; it's whether you can get the job done better for less.

The "Out of Balance?" study is in any case an outlier among most analyses. In a recent attempt to match workers with similar backgrounds and job qualifications, Jason Richwine of the Heritage Foundation and Andrew Biggs of the American Enterprise Institute concluded that federal workers receive a salary premium of about 12 percent. Biggs did a further search of the literature and found six studies between 1987 and 1991 that consistently found salary premiums for federal workers ranging between 6 and 25 percent. Indeed, a mountain of evidence suggests that public-sector workers at all levels are doing exceptionally well. Willie Brown, the longtime Democratic Speaker of the California State Assembly who later served as mayor of San Francisco, recently put it this way: "The deal used to be that civil servants were paid less than private sector workers in exchange for an understanding that they had job security for life. But we politicians—pushed by our friends in labor— gradually expanded pay and benefits . . . while keeping the job protections and layering on incredibly generous retirement packages." Brown told political blogger John Fleischman what led to his awakening: "When I was Speaker I was in charge of passing spending. When I became mayor I was in charge of paying for that spending. It was a wake-up call."

USA Today's Dennis Cauchon provides the data to back up Brown's observations when it comes to federal employees. Using Bureau of Labor Statistics data, Cauchon compared average salaries in occupations that exist in both the public and private sectors. In 2008, federal workers pulled down an average of almost $68,000 in salary versus about $60,000 for private-sector workers. In eight out of ten occupations, federal workers earned a higher salary than their private-sector counterparts. For instance, federal chemists averaged

$98,000 versus $72,000 for private-sector chemists. Federal exterminators made $49,000 while private-sector ones averaged $34,000; federal office clerks averaged $5,000 more and federal nurses $11,000 more. The occupations for which the private sector proved more remunerative included airline pilot, train engineer, and surgeon. But overall, federal pay was better than private-sector pay. And when average benefits get added to the pile, the differential grows even more. Health-care, pension, and other benefits averaged $41,000 per federal worker as opposed to about $10,000 per private worker, according to Bureau of Economic Analysis figures. Cauchon's study seconded the conclusions of an earlier look-see done by New Jersey's *Asbury Park Press*, which found that in three out of four occupations, federal workers outpaced their private-sector counterparts.

At the state and local levels, the same trend holds, albeit with lesser orders of magnitude. For September 2010, the Bureau of Labor Statistics estimated that state and local workers received $40 per hour in total compensation. The comparable figure for private-sector workers was $26.25. The Buckeye Institute, an Ohio free market think tank, looked at state-worker compensation in the Buckeye State and found that in eighty-five of eighty-eight counties, public-sector employees were paid more than their private-sector counterparts. All told, total compensation was about 34 percent greater for state workers (in Michigan, the differential was 45 percent).

Assume for a minute that the comparisons are all wrong, that they don't control well enough for the complexity of job tasks or years of experience or whatever else you want to say is in play. There's still the issue of government workers getting more and more expensive without reference to the private sector. The Buckeye Institute notes that since 1986, state-employee annual raises have averaged 3.5 percent. And that doesn't include yearly "step" increases of 1 to 3 percent and longevity increases of 2 to 10 percent for folks working five to twenty years. The Buckeye Institute calculates that bringing Ohio's state pay in line with the private sector would cover more than 25 percent of the state's $8 billion deficit. Ohio bills itself as the "Heart of It All," the very essence of mainstream America. If this is what's happening all over the country, the only question is why we didn't run out of money sooner.

It's not as if the federal government hasn't been trying, both under George W. Bush and Barack Obama. On Bush's watch, federal outlays increased an eye-popping 60 percent in real 2010 dollars. Where did that money go? To wars in Afghanistan and Iraq, obviously, but also to funding a seemingly endless stream of domestic programs that accomplished little more than driving the nation a few bipartisan clicks closer to the poorhouse. There was No Child Left Behind (championed by Democrat Ted Kennedy and Republican John Boehner alike), the creation of the Department of Homeland Security and the Transportation Security Administration, and Medicare Part D (the prescription drug benefit), just for starters. Later came a failed $100 billion stimulus package in 2008 and then the really big-ticket items at the close of Bush's presidency: the Troubled Asset Relief Program and the first wave of auto-company bailouts. At the same time, there was zero reform of the long-run problems related to entitlement spending and compounding debt levels.

For his part, Obama hit the ground running, immediately passing his own Godzilla-sized stimulus package that manifestly failed even at disbursing funds quickly and efficiently. Give him this much: He continually moved the chains on what he sought to accomplish. Like Yossarian in *Catch-22*, Obama almost daily redrew the lines of what constituted "mission accomplished." The originally promised "millions" of jobs created, 90 percent of them in the private sector, became "created or saved," all in the public sector. When unemployment busted through the 8.5 percent level that the stimulus was supposed to save us from, the argument became that things would have been still worse if we hadn't spent money on "shovel-ready projects" (which themselves failed to materialize as promised). When it comes to overall spending, Obama is looking to beat Bush's record. During fiscal year 2010, which ended on September 30, the government spent around $3.6 trillion, or 25 percent of GDP, while collecting $2.1 trillion in tax revenue, or 14.5 percent of GDP. The resulting deficit was $1.5 trillion. The total debt held by the public—the sum of all accumulated annual deficits and interest payments—reached 63 percent of GDP.

You have to go back to 1946, in the immediate aftermath of World War II, to find spending that equaled as large a percentage of GDP. You need to return to 1945 to find a deficit that big on a percentage basis as well. Just a few years ago, in 2007, the debt was 36.2 percent of GDP, which was plenty bad enough. If current trends continue, the CBO projects, the number will reach 87 percent in 2020. Most economists talk about a debt equal to 60 percent of GDP as a trigger point at which investors become very nervous about a country's ability to pay its obligations and start jacking up the price of government debt. Because the U.S. economy is more than twice as large as anybody else's, we've got more wiggle room than Greece, say, or even China when it comes to negotiating with creditors. But clearly, at some point even the most optimistic buyer of U.S. debt will close his wallet.

At the heart of the federal deficit is the same simple message that confounds state and local budget officers: The federal government spends more than it takes in. It's not complicated really, but the message never quite seems to sink in with the folks of the Republican and Democratic persuasion who reside in Washington, DC. It took St. Reagan, the would-be apostle of cutting government, just eight years to triple the federal debt, all while saying he was kicking welfare "bucks" off the dole and repossessing the Cadillacs that welfare queens were allegedly buying with their food stamps. The annual deficits Reagan ran up in the 1980s averaged out to 4.2 percent of GDP, high enough to give even the most free-spending Democrat the vapors. Under his sunniest budget assumptions (and they are sunny enough to cause melanoma even in John Boehner), President Obama assumes deficits greater than any racked up by George W. Bush in his first seven years in office.

What part of "we are out of money" don't the feds understand? They can't seem to grasp this simple fact of history: Since 1950, total federal revenue from all sources has averaged right around 18 percent of GDP. In some years, government receipts have been bigger—even reaching a bit over 20 percent of GDP once under Bill Clinton—and many years they've been a bit lower. But the variance hasn't been all that great; it's pretty tight at around 18 to 19 percent. If history is any guide and if the federal government wants to balance its books, it's got to spend no more than around 19 percent of GDP, which is what the CBO, in its realistic "alternative-scenario" projections, estimates that federal revenues will be in 2020 if the Bush tax rates remain basically in force. At various points, different leaders have tried to push that number higher—by increasing taxes, by lowering taxes, by monkeying with capital gains taxes, by jacking payroll taxes, or by broadening the base—while others have tried to lighten the load. But it's all come to naught. If the number gets bigger for any length of time—as it did at the end of the Clinton years as a result of increases in some tax rates (and decreases in others)—especially during a booming economy, the pressure builds to return the windfall to taxpayers in one way or another. In 2000, both Bush and Al Gore campaigned on tax cuts.

What would it take for the federal government to restrain spending to just 19 percent of GDP in 2020? Again, according to the CBO's alternative-scenario projections, it would mean coming up with a budget equal to $3.7 trillion in today's dollars, rather than an anticipated $5 trillion if spending stays on autopilot. How do you disappear $1.3 trillion in projected government spending over a decade or so? The most straightforward way is by cutting $130 billion out of projected spending (including projected increases) every year for the next decade. This will require a budget based on reality rather than fantasy.

That may be a bridge too far for politicians, but it's the only one that can actually keep the federal government solvent until we get around to fully revising outdated entitlement programs that are set to beggar us more than any stock market collapse ever did. And to put that 19 percent figure in perspective, spending under Bill Clinton's final budget amounted to just a hair over 18 percent of GDP. Nobody back then was surviving on cat food. If anything, the future looked wonderfully, if a bit naively, bright.

The 19 percent solution, or some variation thereof, is not a matter of choice. We are out of money, and if we don't adopt the "austerity" of pruning government back to Clintonian spending levels on our own terms, then the bond market and/or resurgent inflation will impose a reality considerably harsher. And still Washington can't have a serious discussion about this reality. Even the president's own National Commission on Fiscal Responsibility and Reform, which made many hard-nosed (and thus ignored) recommendations about spending cuts, ahistorically assumed federal revenue that equals 21 percent of GDP.

Here we are, a decade into the twenty-first century, in what used to be known as the future, and we're as mired as ever in leaden debates between two parties that have about as much governing difference between them as Fidel and Raul Castro. In Washington, DC, and most state capitals, you can't swing a dead cat without hitting a pol or a lobbyist or a newspaperman nattering on about the need for "bipartisanship," for an end to the poisonous atmosphere that has pervaded politics for so long.

If the only partisans in town are Republicans and Democrats, conservatives and liberals, with all that red ink on their hands, then the time has come not for bipartisanship but postpartisanship. These tribes have each had enough swings at the piñata to bust it wide open and grab all the candy and coins for their friends. Where did it all go? What do *you* have to show for the 60-percent-plus increase in federal spending over the past decade other than higher blood pressure and lower savings? Has politics become democratized and decentralized like the rest of the world you live in, the world where you shop and eat and create and work and live and die? It hasn't. The time has come to try something very different.

Men and women of Obama's age reached political puberty around the time that the great fiend Richard Nixon was darkening the United States with wage and price controls and a short-lived experiment called double-daylight-saving time, in which the Colossus of Yorba Linda attempted to hold back the sun for an extra hour or two a day to conserve energy. Weren't we supposed to run screaming from Nixon's legacy of paranoid centralization of power and disenfranchisement of democratic government? Weren't we going to move on from the alphabet soup of oppressive, top-down agencies and organizations he created, from EPA to ATF to OSHA to DOE to CREEP? Instead, for the ruling class in our country, Nixon provides not a negative example but a goddamned role model.

In 1971, Nixon created Amtrak to provide "intercity" passenger train service in a country designed by God for other forms of transportation. Ever since, Amtrak has been a surer bet than the Detroit Lions to lose big. In many ways, it is the archetypal government program that, like a virus, is designed only to replicate itself indefinitely into the future. So many congressional districts have an Amtrak line running through them that even the most penny-pinching cost cutters will get up on appropriations day to swear before Jesus,

Chevrolet, and Sam Waterston that the 76,000 riders who choose Amtrak every day (out of 140 million Americans who commute daily) must continue to be served along subsidized routes that lose as much as $200 per individual rider. The alternative is just too terrifying to contemplate.

In the great age of "we are out of money," Obama has updated Nixon's passenger-rail fantasy with shiny new coats of paint and extra zeroes on the price tag, then rolled out his own supertrain fantasy, a national high-speed rail system that will be better than China's, Japan's, and France's put together and end up costing (according to CNN) north of $500 billion. "Building for the future" is how Obama put it to a Tampa, Florida, audience in 2009, while unveiling blueprints that will, at long last, make it possible to travel from Indianapolis to Louisville in only slightly less time than it takes to drive. "I'm excited," the president told the throng in Tampa. "I'm gonna come back down here and ride it."

Yes, there is something tragic about a train, something that captures the imaginations of politicians and the most gullible of partisans, shielding them from the simple, brute facts of their unsustainable economic program. And, perhaps more importantly, it keeps them from looking beyond government as the engine of what makes America and the world a better and better place to spend our longer and longer lives.

Such tunnel vision (and what good is a train boondoggle that doesn't include a big, long tunnel?) is blinding us indeed. But the compelling alternative is to declare independence not simply from Democrats and Republicans but from politics itself, that awful playground zero-sum game where they win and we lose, and instead walk in a different direction along a path also familiar to us. It's the path that brought us the Internet and Amazon.com, the Velvet Underground and Václav Havel, cheap airline flights and delicious American beer and everything else that is worth a tinker's ding-dong.

We've already routed around the government in so many other areas of our lives. The next chapter discusses how to take those same liberating forces of decentralization and democratization and use them to tear down the sclerotic cartels in education, health care, and retirement. Those are the last and most expensive refuges to which political scoundrels still cling, so it's time to storm the castle through the front door.

CHAPTER 10

YOUR MIND, YOUR HEALTH, AND YOUR RETIREMENT ARE TERRIBLE THINGS TO WASTE

Donate money to the United Negro College Fund, the old public service advertisement used to encourage us, "because a mind is a terrible thing to waste." Sadly, the status quo is not only wasting our minds through its underperforming public schools but wasting our health-care dollars and gobbling up our retirement savings as well. Americans, ever inventive, keep constructing elaborate work-arounds to circumvent the petrified forest of rules, regulations, and taxes that support these three vast empires of concentrated political power. But it's time to stop sneaking out windows and creeping through back doors. Forget "winning the future"—if America has any hope of winning the present, then it's time to confront head-on our profound problems with education, health care, and retirement.

K–12 education in the United States is so hugely expensive and thoroughly mediocre for two main reasons: (1) it's mandatory, and

(2) unlike in higher education, there is virtually no consumer choice between competing alternatives. If you want to go to college, law school, or graduate school, there are more than 4,000 institutions of higher learning to sample. If you want to switch from one grammar school, middle school, or high school to another, even within the same district, unless you can afford private school, good luck.

About 73 percent of K–12 students attend "assigned" public schools based solely on home address. Only 16 percent attend public schools of their choice—magnet, charter, or competitive-entrance schools. The remaining students either attend private schools (church related or secular) or get their schooling at home, the latter comprising a rapidly growing minority of 1.5 million children (or about 3 percent of K–12 kids), mostly of elementary school age. The first charter school—charter schools are publicly funded institutions that are freed from most of the bureaucratic dictates of traditional schools but also receive less in per-pupil funding—did not open its doors until 1992, back when the number of "assigned" students was at 80 percent.

It would be inaccurate to say that American education is worse than in the past. In terms of the most basic output—the achievement level of graduating high school seniors—the results have been almost exactly the same over the past forty years. The basic measurement of student performance is the National Assessment of Educational Progress (NAEP), which bills itself as "the nation's report card." Since 1969, NAEP has compiled national test-score data at the fourth- and eighth-grade levels. For twelfth graders, NAEP uses data from eleven states to compile an ongoing index of achievement in reading and math. This continuing data series provides the basic benchmark for how American students are either improving or declining and the long-term trends are terrifyingly flat for seventeen-year-olds. When it comes to math, "There was no significant change in the scores of 17-year-olds in comparison to either 2004 or 1973." When it comes to reading, the average score in 1971 was 285; in 2008, the latest year for which data are available, the average score was 286. In neither test area was there any variation throughout the decades, any significant spikes up or down. Just same old, same old. To get your head around that, think for a moment back to 1970. What else in your life hasn't gotten better since then, only more expensive? Nearly everything else has moved on from the Nixon-Agnew era.

Only when it comes to schooling, there's one big difference: Education is considerably more expensive. Since the 1970–1971 school year, per-pupil spending in real, inflation-adjusted terms, has more than doubled, from about $4,500 to over $10,000 (since 1961–1962, the amount has more than tripled in real dollars). Indeed, across every possible metric, the number of inputs has been jacked through the roof. The number of students per teacher in public schools has declined from about 22.3 in the early 1970s to around 15.5 nowadays (the figure for private schools is 13). In the decade between school years 1998–1999 and 2008–2009, outlays increased 32 percent beyond the rate of inflation. There is simply no question that we are spending significantly more on education to achieve exactly the same results.

But why would we expect much in the way of change? More money is getting poured down the educational drain, but the system is staying true to the course set on autopilot decades, if not more than a century, ago. No other industry still adheres to a calendar based on nineteenth-century agricultural cycles—even agriculture has given up that schedule. The system is the problem; no amount of extra money dumped onto a broken assembly line is going to produce more or better widgets.

For the most part, the powers that retain the upper hand in elementary and secondary education remain mired in a postwar romance of bigger equals better. Pyramids, after all, look great from the pharaoh's perspective, and it's always easier to add some bricks around the bottom than to rebuild the whole project. Like the great "too-big-to-fail" conglomerates of the 1950s and 1960s, most of which have either vanished completely or are shells of their former shelves, educational fiefdoms continue to grow in individual size while shrinking in composite numbers. In 1940, there were almost 120,000 school districts in the country. That number was down to 40,000 by the early 1960s, and to just 18,000 by the 1970s. Today, the figure continues to shrink, albeit more slowly, with the current number at about 14,000.

Power has concentrated in other ways too. State governments now account for a higher percentage of school funding than they did before, and the federal government's spending on K–12 education grew 30 percent after inflation between 2000 and 2008 alone. With the extra layers of lucre come extra layers of distant control, such as the magnificently ineffective and unpopular No Child Left Behind law pushed through Congress with backing from the likes of George W. Bush, Ted Kennedy, and John Boehner. As one education expert who had supported the legislation and its main goal of reducing the achievement gap between minorities and white students told the *New York Times*, "Trends after the law took effect mimic trends we were seeing before"—which is to say, we are seeing flat results and throwing increased amounts of money at the problem. Expect more control—and more useless dollars—as the Department of Education explicitly begins to push "national standards" as a way forward.

Can this system be saved? The short answer is no. The longer answer is only slightly more complicated: No, and the only thing that should matter is the timing of the exit plan. Whose child will be the last to live a frustrated life for this dreadful mistake?

Without making any sort of fundamental change in funding levels, structure, or school taxes, we can accomplish significant ed-

ucational improvement virtually overnight through widespread implementation of what's known as the "weighted-student formula," a
concept developed in the 1970s in Alberta, Canada. Public schools
in the United States traditionally follow a "staffing-ratio model," in
which personnel and funds are calculated based on how many students are expected to enroll in a given year. You build the school,
basically, and order kids to attend. Under the weighted-student
formula, schools receive a discrete amount of money per child actually enrolled, with supplemental per-student funds added for conditions that require extra care or attention, such as physical handicaps
and English as a second language. In a weighted-student-formula
model, the money follows the students, who are free to choose
among whatever public schools will enroll them (a more ambitious
but constitutionally dicey version would allow kids to attend private religious schools on the same dime, as is permitted in Canada
and France). The formula inherently pushes budget and curricular
decisions out of a central office and into a particular school, which
will flourish or falter based on its ability to attract and retain students. With a minimum of fuss from the outside, weighted-student-
formula funding creates a market in education. Long-problematic
school districts such as San Francisco and Oakland, California,
which have adopted versions of the formula, have seen sharp increases in parental satisfaction and test scores with the reversal of
the traditional education power dynamic.

The weighted-student formula is just one way to give power to
the consumer of K–12 education, as a means of mimicking the
consumer revolutions that have improved our lives in so many ways
outside the cafeteria line. Many other reforms vary in their level of
direct challenge to the status quo. Since their creation in Minnesota
in the early 1990s, charter schools have proven a relatively noncon-
troversial and popular method for empowering individual students
and creating a market for education. Somewhere around 1.5 million

students currently attend charters in the District of Columbia and the more than three dozen states that allow them. They are typically run by nonprofit groups and receive a fraction of the average per-pupil funds that a traditional public school does (across the country, charters receive an average of about $6,600 per student, or 40 percent less than traditional public schools). Different rules govern charters depending on the state, but most are given a far longer leash than conventional public schools to set curricula, hire and fire teachers, and otherwise tailor their offerings to the needs of the student body and the pedagogical vision of the educators themselves. In the public school district serving New Orleans, long one of the worst in the nation, a majority of children after Hurricane Katrina now attend charter schools. While there remain questions about the long-term effectiveness of charters, there are no such open questions about the long-term ineffectiveness of the conventional public school system. Tellingly, parents of children attending schools of choice routinely report satisfaction rates between 20 percent higher for public schools and 40 percent higher for private ones, be they religious or secular.

The more reforms step outside traditional public school models, the more controversial they naturally become. Several states, such as Arizona, allow educational tax-credit programs in which corporations can donate money to philanthropies that fund schools and vouchers in return for a lower tax bill; the Supreme Court is weighing the constitutionality of that system. Publicly funded voucher programs that allow students to attend private schools, including religious ones, date back to the 1990s and have so far survived Supreme Court challenges (in the end, vouchers that go to individuals are no different from Pell Grants going to religious colleges). Since the nineteenth century, Vermont and Maine have operated quasi-voucher programs in which towns that don't have elementary or secondary schools pay children's tuition to attend public or private schools in other towns. The list of potential reforms goes on, including homeschooling, online learning, and a thousand flowers yet to bloom. All are worth trying to the extent that they place power in the hands of students and parents and take it away from the powers that be. K–12 education is a $600-billion-plus industry. That essentially one model dominates the delivery of education is a sign that something is very wrong, that a monopoly impervious to its customers' needs is calling the shots.

The delivery of health care in the United States presents a variation on the education dilemma: Like education, health care has indeed gotten vastly more expensive, but unlike schooling, it is also delivering measurably better results. In 1970, spending for health care came to about 7.5 percent of GDP. That figure is now closer to 17 percent and is expected to climb to nearly 20 percent over the coming years, even if Barack Obama's health-care plan is enacted exactly as he dreams it should be. Part of the rise comes from an increase in the number of treatments available and their efficacy. Nobody was undergoing in vitro fertilization, for instance, in 1970, and dentistry has been almost completely revolutionized from a reactive to a proactive discipline. Anyone who wears glasses or contact lenses or has had LASIK surgery immediately understands that things have generally changed for the better when it comes to the quality of health-care treatments. Pills are more effective for what ails you—and more widely prescribed. With the exception of some troubling applications—such as the doping of children deemed to have attention-deficit disorder on often flimsy evidence—this is a trend for the good, as it allows us to more fully control our own minds and body chemistries. We are living longer lives (life expectancy at birth in 1970 was seventy-one years; it's now seventy-nine). Cancer incidence rates continue to decline in the United States, and survival rates continue to climb. Acid blockers have made ulcers a relic of 1960s-era sitcoms. While the United States spends a higher percentage of its income on health care than Europe or Canada, it also delivers a better product when it comes to life-threatening diseases. Over 99 percent of U.S. men with prostate cancer survive, compared to 78 percent of Europeans. Over 90 percent of American women survive breast cancer, compared to 79 percent of European women. Whatever you read about seniors driving north to buy cheaper prescription drugs, when it comes to life-extending and quality-of-life-enhancing procedures such as cancer treatments and hip replacements, the patient traffic between Canada and the United States flows decidedly north to south.

Of course, health care and health coverage are two very different beasts. Recall that the recent health-care reform aimed less to increase health outcomes and more to increase the number of people with health insurance. Too much of "health-care reform" proceeds from the questionable assumption that if more people are covered by insurance, everything will be okay. A 1993 study by the RAND Corporation—called the "only" methodologically rigorous study by a harsh critic of its conclusions—separated people into five randomly assigned treatment plans. The cheaper the health care, the more of it people consumed. But the most stunning finding was that "for the average person, there were no substantial benefits from free care." Most studies of the topic will at least grudgingly admit that no "definitive" or "universal" findings link having insurance or even receiving free care with better health.

For most people, especially the poor, who are most at risk for shortened lives, general lifestyle issues trump medical interventions. Not smoking, eating moderately, not overindulging in alcohol, and avoiding a sedentary lifestyle together provide far greater health benefits than a low-deductible, low-co-pay insurance plan. Indeed, a number of studies have found that recipients of Medicaid, the federal health insurance program for the poor, actually fare worse than the uninsured. Researchers at the University of Pennsylvania found that Medicaid patients with colon cancer had a 2.8 percent mortality rate, while the uninsured had a 2.2 percent rate. Studies by researchers at the University of Virginia, Columbia University, and Cornell University, as well as another of Florida Medicaid patients, found similar outcomes with melanoma and prostate cancers.

If Medicaid insurance is not necessarily producing better outcomes, it does point to the main driver of rising health-care costs: the government's increasing role in health care and health insurance. Prior to the introduction in the late 1960s of Medicare (health insurance for the elderly) and Medicaid, state and federal spending made up about 25 percent of total health-care spending. That percentage jumped to almost 40 percent with the introduction of those two programs, and it now stands at 48 percent. Insurance covers a larger percentage of health-care costs as well, as programs are covering more treatments. At the same time, out-of-pocket costs—money actually paid by patients at the point of delivery— have been declining. So even if employers are paying higher premiums (and they are), the net result is that health care feels less expensive to the individual user, who is thus likely to consume more of it. This is no way to run any sort of system; indeed, to the extent that the very people consuming a product or service are further removed from understanding its value and price, you're guaranteeing a dysfunctional flow of information, power, and results.

As with education, the answer is to place more power—both economic and informational—in the hands of the consumer. A basic starting point is to clarify terms. Though routinely described as insurance, health-care packages in the United States are better understood as prepayment plans. As homeowners and car owners can tell you, insurance typically guards against statistically rare, catastrophic events: lightning strikes, fires, accidents. They do not cover routine maintenance. Health insurance has evolved in a completely contrary direction, mostly as a way of avoiding governmental wage controls imposed during World War II. Employers back then used generous health-insurance plans as a means of increasing employee compensation. No one expects auto or homeowners insurance to cover oil changes or gutter cleanings; yet, we expect our health plans to cover a virtually unlimited number of checkups and office visits. Despite the importance we place on health care, few patients and, truth be told, few doctors or nurses could tell you what a typical office visit costs beyond their co-pay. Prices are vital to any sort of functioning economic exchange, yet we are systematically shielded from such information (try asking a hospital its basic charges for delivering a baby).

On top of that, medical care is heavily regulated by a series of rules that are either directly written or immediately co-opted by politically connected players. There's a reason why insurance providers are prevented from selling policies across state lines: In any given region, a few major companies have carved up the territory and are happy to cartelize their market positions. In over three dozen states, the major insurer has at least 33 percent of the market, and in sixteen states, it has over half. In some thirty-four states, when providers want to build new or expand existing hospitals, they need to obtain a "certificate of need," which is granted only after a state agency consults with existing competitors to determine if the new capacity is really needed (this rule, smacking of the pre-deregulation airline industry, dates back to a Nixon-era directive that mistakenly assumed surplus hospital beds drove prices up). Insurers are forced to offer minimum coverage guarantees that vary from state to state and push prices upward while being unresponsive to customer demand. Why should a nonsmoker, for instance, be forced to buy a plan that is required to offer smoking-cessation coverage? The supply of doctors, pharmacists, nurses, and other practitioners is tightly controlled, not in the best interest of the patient but in the narrow interests of the medical industry.

If "health insurance" is a misleading phrase, the cult of the doctor, of "saints in surgical garb" who are wiser and smarter than you, needs to be thoroughly demythologized and recognized for the centuries-old propaganda campaign it is. Good doctors are valuable and should be rewarded, but as the recent cost-cutting turn toward nurse practitioners suggests, much of basic medical care can be delivered just fine by less credentialed professionals. As patients become more empowered and as knowledge and information become more widely dispersed, doctors will be treated less like gods and more like auto mechanics.

To put it prosaically, there is virtually no free market in health care. To the extent that there is, innovation and improvement are rewarded, which explains the increase in treatment options and outcomes. But to the far larger extent that the market is contorted, stifled, or totally absent due to a nearly impenetrable fog of rules, regulations, third-party payments and reimbursements, subsidies, and more, the price and quality of care are vastly inflated and always inscrutable. A report by President Obama's Council of Economic Advisers suggests that "nearly 30 percent of Medicare's costs could be saved without adverse health consequences." Admission of this level of useless spending is stunning by any measure, particularly in a study arguing for even more government control of health care. It is far easier to gather information about a potential car you want to buy than about a general practitioner, surgeon, or other medical specialist in whose hands you might place your life. Even as doctors push back against online ratings and new forms of information sharing, they have offered up no systematic way for consumers to gain independent information about their skills, prices, and quality of service to patients. Why should they? In a 1974 interview with *Reason*, Milton Friedman suggested that the genius of a market system is that it protects customers by forcing providers into a fight for their money. "There's the old saying," he explained, "'if you want to catch a thief, set a thief to catch him.' The virtue of free enterprise capitalism is that it sets one businessman against another and it's a most effective device for control." Until doctors and insurers are recognized as businessmen first and foremost and forced to compete with one another for patients' dollars, little meaningful change will happen aside from the ever forward march of prices.

Our *Reason* colleague Ronald Bailey has written persuasively about the most basic, necessary health-care reform—the use of markets rather than the avoidance of them:

> One of the chief problems is that consumers haven't a clue about what their insurance and medical services cost. Hospital charge-masters (essentially comprehensive lists of all charges) typically contain prices for over 20,000 items and services. Sorting through those lists for the best prices would be impossible for consumers. But why should they have to? In markets, the proper dictum is that "nobody has to know everything." Markets are superb at gathering widely dispersed information and resources from millions of people and firms and then distilling that information into prices.
>
> When someone buys a car, they are not confronted with a bill listing separate prices for pistons, radiators, assembly line screw tightening, seats, gas tanks, windows, and so forth. Nor when they buy a hamburger are the prices for the beef, bun, wrapping paper, and special sauce listed and charged for individually. The market has bundled those separate items together into a single price. Competition sparked by consumer demand could unleash a similar simplifying dynamic in which prices for health insurance and medical services become bundled and more transparent.

Bailey suggests a series of obvious reforms, including repealing the 1945 McCarran-Ferguson Act, which allows state insurance commissions to regulate health insurance without running afoul of constitutional guarantees of freedom of commerce between the states. Repealing that law would allow insurers to compete across state lines, thus opening up medical insurance and care to competition. Breaking the decades-old link between health insurance and employment, too, would put consumers in charge of their own portable health insurance plans, a key precondition to both price awareness and post–organization man mobility. Essential to this enterprise is a core truth that doctors, insurers, and government regulators want you to ignore: Competition in markets tends to lower prices and improve quality over time. It can do so in health-care markets as well. But first it must be tried.

Assume that you make it through the public school system, avoid major health problems, and actually reach your retirement age. If you spend your life in the public sector, odds are that you will draw a defined-benefit pension, that whatever you contributed to your retirement was generously matched (or overmatched) by your employer, and that your basic benefits are guaranteed by law. By most accountings, your retirement pension and free or heavily subsidized old-age health-care plans will be double what your counterpart in the private sector will enjoy. But if, like 90 percent of the population, you will have spent all or most of your career in the private sector, odds are that you are expecting to finance your retirement through a mix of Social Security payouts and mostly self-funded savings stemming from defined-contribution plans, most commonly 401(k) plans (so named for the tax-code revision that allowed for pretax retirement savings). For the past eighty years, Social Security has been an integral part of Americans' retirement plans, and it is the core around which most private-sector pensions are built (many state pension systems have been granted waivers from Social Security on the grounds that the state's benefits would be far more generous).

Enacted in 1935, during the midst of the Great Depression, Social Security is often regarded as one of the high points of twentieth-century government. Its architect, Franklin Roosevelt, talked about the program in unrestrained terms: "The civilization of the past 100 years, with its startling industrial changes, has tended more and more to make life insecure. . . . We can never insure 100 percent of the population against 100 percent of the hazards and vicissitudes of life, but we have tried to frame a law which will give some measure of protection to the average citizen and to his family against the loss of a job and against poverty-ridden old age." As the Social Security Administration is quick to point out, its monthly payments to retirees have become a huge part of most people's retirement income. In 2010, some 37 million retired workers and their dependents received an average monthly payment of $1,170, and a majority of retirees received most of their income from Social Security.

Far from representing the largess of the state, however, Social Security represents a spectacularly awful way to fund old age, especially for anyone currently under the age of fifty. Leave aside for the moment the enormous burden the system places on the workers who are funding it for current retirees, and think instead about just what a rotten product Social Security is for the perceived beneficiary. Social Security is funded by Federal Insurance Contributions Act (FICA) payroll taxes of 12.4 percent, split between employee and employer on the first $107,000 of earned income. To use a basic hypothetical example, a worker making just $20,000 a year for forty years—or much less than the average full-time employee—has $2,480 in annual FICA taxes taken from his pay. If he had control over that money and invested it in a mutual fund earning an annual 8 percent return (adjusting for 3.1 percent annual inflation), he would, upon retirement, have available around the same payout as Social Security: $1,200 or so per month. That means the average worker is getting a worse return than if he had had control over his own money. What's more, if his retirement savings had been invested in a 401(k) or annuity account, he might also be able to pass on some of the proceeds in the event of an early death.

Far from being a retirement investment instrument, Social Security is a simple guaranteed income payment based on an inscrutable formula. There is little to no transfer ability (other than to spouses and then at reduced rates). Writing in 2003, Michael Tanner of the Cato Institute calculated that "workers retiring today receive a rate of return [on their contributions to Social Security] of 2 percent," and "future retirees will receive even lower rates of return." Using a market-rate comparison of 4.6 percent annual return on investment of the same amount of FICA taxes, Tanner argues that "a worker earning $30,000 per year will pay $120,000 in Social Security taxes over a 40-year working lifetime. A 2 percent return on that money yields Social Security benefits equivalent to $185,000. But a 4.6 percent return would yield $344,000, nearly twice as much." And, Tanner notes, estimating a 4.6 percent return is conservative based on historic rates of return dating back to the 1920s.

A move toward allowing future retirees to place some small portion of their payroll taxes into "private" accounts was briefly floated by George W. Bush shortly after his reelection in 2004, when he bragged that he had amassed significant "political capital." The proposal was strangled in the crib, partly because Bush oddly attempted to sell it by saying it was a way of preserving the current system rather than a means to let future retirees prosper by their own lights. That is, he pushed the plan on uninspiring actuarial grounds rather than as a path toward self-empowerment.

Two immediate objections were raised against Bush's privatization plan in the mid-2000s. First, the transition costs out of the existing system were too huge; there was simply no way to pony up the money necessary to keep paying current retirees and people just a few years away from collecting benefits. In essence, the future must be held hostage to a system that, by design, cannot sustain itself. Because current Social Security benefits are paid by future retirees, this argument implies, there is effectively never a time when the system can be changed. This is at best a weak argument, one holding that no change can take place because, well, it would require that things be done differently. The federal government has shown no hesitation in spending money it does not have in a million other ways; surely, it could find a way to draw down contributions to a system that is incapable of keeping pace with its own needs. By 2014, the trustees of Social Security project, it will be red ink from that point forward, as the collection of FICA taxes falls short of the amount paid out in benefits. Allowing, say, those under fifty or forty-five to opt out of paying into the system (or drawing anything out) would begin a process and create an endpoint for a program whose moment has come and gone. If the government must continue to pay for the retirements of those in the system, let it sacrifice money that would have gone instead to inefficient health-care programs, ineffective education programs, and monstrously bloated military appropriations, many of which have no effect on actually defending the nation's citizens and borders.

The second objection made in the previous Social Security privatization debate was that market returns are not guaranteed or certain. That's true, for sure, but neither are government returns, which have been declining since the program cut its first check in 1940. The federal government will always have the option of making welfare payments to impoverished retirees. It need not hijack 12.4 percent of virtually every dollar earned by workers in every decade of their careers to guarantee that the elderly will not have to live on cat food.

Whatever the outcome of this debate, there's no question that Social Security remains a weak salve for retirees (especially African

Americans, who tend to die younger and hence receive fewer retirement benefits). It's a system that discriminates against single people, increases the difficulty of passing wealth from one generation to the next, guarantees submarket rates of return, and ultimately precludes beneficiaries from having any say in how or where their own money is invested. It is not even clear that the government must pay retirees anything. In the 1960 case *Fleming v. Nestor*, the Supreme Court ruled that workers don't have enforceable rights to benefits and that the government can cut payments if it wants to. That is no way to face the future. Sadly, along with Medicare, a system that all agree is on the fast track to beggaring our nation while wasting enormous amounts of dollars and resources, Social Security has managed to shoulder its way next to the flag, apple pie, and mom in the hearts of Democratic and Republican politicians alike.

Government-dominated retirement, K–12 education, and health care are all so spectacularly inefficient and expensive that politicians have effectively removed them from our control, as if we the people are too stupid, too shortsighted, and too undisciplined to make decisions about our schooling, our health, and our future. To the extent that any of that is true, our incompetence can only be magnified when filtered through the local, state, and federal bureaucracies that have been erected over time to save us from ourselves. And to the considerable extent that all of it is plainly false—look at all the parts of our world in which government control is minimal and progress is maximal—it is time to sweep away the rusted-out, rotting hulks of the past. Over the past forty years, Americans have turned on to what interests them, tuned in to their vision of happiness, and dropped out of a stultifying world of grim alternatives when it comes to work, sex, entertainment, and so much more. The idea that we would be incapable of doing the same with education, health care, and retirement is not simply offensive on a basic level but patently wrong.

We have effectively declared our independence in politics over the past forty years by refusing to subordinate our individuality any longer to the chimeras that are the Republican and Democratic parties; fewer of us see ourselves as either liberals or conservatives as well. We have spent the past decades creating new universes of meaning for ourselves in our love and work, in cyberspace and meatspace. We do this as far away from politics as possible. Now, though, we have the means, motive, and opportunity to kick the props out from under the last vestiges of a one-size-fits-all world of top-down control and mainstream straitjacketing of difference. We are out of money, and we have workable strategies for breaching the remaining strongholds of central power. All that remains is to move the same forces that have transformed most of our lives for the better into the specifically political arena. Partisan dead-enders in the major parties fall asleep dreaming of ever elusive permanent governing majorities, insuperable electoral advantages that will allow them to do whatever they want at other people's expense. Unfortunately for the power-mongers, we are entering a very different age, one made up of permanent nongoverning minorities that will help us all declare not just independence in politics but independence from politics.

CHAPTER 11

THE PERMANENT
NONGOVERNING MINORITY

Republican Mitch McConnell has only been in the Senate for twenty-six years, though in fairness it feels like a century. He's been minority leader since 2006, chaired the Republican Party's Senatorial Committee in 1998 and 2000, and is "widely considered a kingmaker in Kentucky Republican politics," according to the hive mind of Wikipedia. So it must have come as quite a shock when Trey Grayson, Kentucky's secretary of state and McConnell's handpicked candidate to replace the retiring senator and undeserving Baseball Hall of Famer Jim Bunning, got trounced by twenty-three percentage points in the 2010 Republican primary. Worse still, the victor was a weird-haired outsider and known turtleneck wearer who had never even held political office. Adding insult to injury, the upstart politician pledged his primary loyalty not to McConnell's GOP but to an independent, decentralized organization that arose partly out of disgust for Mitch McConnell–style politics: the Tea Party.

If you believe either Republican applause lines or Democratic scare stories, Rand Paul should have been the ideal GOP candidate rather than a reviled "kook" drawing unusual primary-campaign rebukes from Dick Cheney, John McCain, and commentator David Frum. The son of onetime Libertarian Party presidential candidate and eleven-term congressman Ron Paul (R-TX), Rand Paul ran chiefly in opposition to runaway government spending, federal meddling in private enterprise, and prime-the-pump policies from the Federal Reserve. On these issues, which comprised the bulk of his campaign emphasis, Rand Paul couldn't have been more in line with the patron saint of the modern Republican Party, Ronald Reagan.

But for well over a decade now, Republicanism in practice has borne little, if any, resemblance to Republicanism in theory, and in the process a venerable tradition in American politics—the Thomas Jefferson/Henry David Thoreau/Barry Goldwater insistence that government works best when it governs least—has been nearly driven to extinction. The bad news is that marginalization of this worldview has opened the door to such expensive mistakes as the Troubled Asset Relief Program (TARP), Medicare Part D, No Child Left Behind, and the Iraq War. The good news—and this goes for people who don't share Rand Paul's limited-government philosophy—is that the disintermediating technology of the Internet, coupled with the rise of political independents, has created a built-in corrective mechanism. Thanks to major shifts in attitudes and major developments in technology, it is no longer possible for the two parties to snuff out important strains of American politics. In just the past decade, Team Red and Team Blue have faced a radically different ballgame whose rules they can no longer dictate.

Every two years, the political establishment gets rocked anew by the sight of alienated citizens banding together in a decentralized manner to bring their shoved-aside concerns back to the adults' table. *New York Times* columnist David Brooks may have been crow-ing about a "permanent governing majority" of big-government con-servatives and Republicans before the 2004 election, but in fact we have seen since then the emergence of something closer to the oppo-site: a permanent, though highly fluid, nongoverning minority of in-dependents and disaffected party members who come together in swarms to push or block legislation and punish those pols who would keep them down. Rightist or leftist, statist or libertarian, these moti-vated mavericks are upending status quo bias, provoking purple-faced rebukes from the political establishment, and pushing politicians in directions they had no intention of going. These smart mobs are the future of American public policy and elections, whether pushing single issues such as education or drug policy or altering the very du-opoly that has served them so poorly for so long. And the more inde-pendent they have been, the greater their potency.

In the 2004 election cycle, the main tech-driven protest bloc was the Howard Dean movement, which used the Internet in revo-lutionary ways to organize and vent about the Left's sizable but long-marginalized antiwar tendency. Though Dean won only a handful of delegates, he and his supporters gained prominence and power within the party, helping galvanize the 2006 wave of "net-roots" enthusiasm for Democrats, who were more confrontational toward Republicans—particularly on issues of war, trade, and Social Security—than the accommodationist and viscerally apologetic "New Democrats" who had held sway within the party for nearly two decades.

In 2008, the Left's antiwar sentiment and guerilla-organizing skills found a willing vessel in inexperienced underdog candidate Barack Obama, while the Right's long-buried anti-interventionist tradition in both foreign policy and domestic spending coalesced around the you-gotta-be-kidding-me "REVOLUTION" of Ron Paul. Nobody would have predicted that an uncharismatic seventy-something obstetrician with a bug up his ass about the Federal

Reserve would become the darling of Internet hipsters and popularize the fund-raising term *moneybomb* into the political lexicon. But Paul did both things, while scoring more than twenty times the number of Meetup followers as Obama. (During the heat of the primaries, "Dr. No" had more than 60,000 followers.) It's a simple truth: Wherever in America a political tradition is being disrespected, you are certain to find motivated backlashers deploying technology much better than their top-down betters. We all know that the Internet has been the greatest preserver of weird old music and TV clips; it does the same job for political movements too.

The main 2010 election swarm was the Tea Party movement, which shows all signs of maintaining its strength well into the coming presidential election cycle. It was set into motion on September 24, 2008, when an ashen-looking President George W. Bush stood in front of the American people and waved a white flag for all to see:

> I'm a strong believer in free enterprise. So my natural instinct is to oppose government intervention. I believe companies that make bad decisions should be allowed to go out of business. Under normal circumstances, I would have followed this course. But these are not normal circumstances. The market is not functioning properly. There's been a widespread loss of confidence. And major sectors of America's financial system are at risk of shutting down.
>
> The government's top economic experts warn that without immediate action by Congress, America could slip into a financial panic, and a distressing scenario would unfold:
>
> More banks could fail, including some in your community. The stock market would drop even more, which would reduce the value of your retirement account. The value of your home could plummet. Foreclosures would rise dramatically. And if you own a business or a farm, you would find it harder and more expensive to get

credit. More businesses would close their doors, and millions of Americans could lose their jobs. Even if you have good credit history, it would be more difficult for you to get the loans you need to buy a car or send your children to college. And ultimately, our country could experience a long and painful recession.

Fellow citizens: We must not let this happen.

It was a final, unconditional surrender from an administration that lost its last remaining vestige of free market nerve when the housing market at last went south. A country with capitalism embedded in its DNA like no other was now being instructed by its political class that capitalism's great corrective mechanism—bankruptcy—was just too risky to consider this time, because it might lead to a long and painful recession (how that differs from what we ended up with, we're not sure). Instead, the moment required an urgent transfer of money from Main Street to Wall Street, from the majority of people who paid their mortgages on time to a wealthy and politically connected minority who gambled on their real estate investments and lost.

Then something peculiar happened: Americans declined their leaders' invitation to panic. Five days after Bush got the vapors on live TV, the House of Representatives set out to vote on a piece of legislation every bit as rushed and ill considered as the September 14, 2001, authorization of "all necessary and appropriate force" against anyone either connected to the 9/11 attacks or potentially connected to future terrorist violence, a congressional blank check that to this day remains the legal justification for holding suspected terrorists indefinitely or even killing them outright without anything resembling due process. The $700 billion Emergency Economic Stabilization Act of 2008 (whose humongous price tag was "not based on any particular data point," a Treasury Department spokeswoman told *Forbes*. "We just wanted to choose a really large number") was similarly expected to sail through Congress, and its passage was cheered on at every step by establishment media that knew *something* had to be done. As the *Washington Post* editorial board put it on September 25, "The fine points of financial reform can wait. For Congress, the immediate task is to avert economic disaster." (That details-schmetails sentiment was widespread: On the adjacent page, columnist David Broder wrote that Congress "can tinker with the details, but inaction is not an option," and Ruth Marcus averred, "A good weekend's work at Andrews [Air Force Base] ought to be enough to hammer out the complicated parts.")

With the president, his economic team, the Democratic congressional leadership, the *Wall Street Journal* and *New York Times* editorial boards, most DC think tanks, and the two major-party presidential candidates foursquare behind the bailout, passage of the act was all but a formality. So Americans got informal. With no real organized opposition, citizens erupted in revulsion at the bill and the speed of its creation, flooding talk shows, blogs, and (most effectively of all) the phone lines of their elected representatives, who reported that calls were coming in ten to one against any sort of financial-sector bailout. Just as polls had been showing for more than a year that Americans were virulently opposed to bailing out homeowners who were underwater when the housing bubble burst, every indicator of popular opinion about the 2008 law was—and continues to be—overwhelmingly negative. To almost everyone's surprise, the Emergency Economic Stabilization Act failed in the people's chamber by a vote of 228 to 205.

Just as the bailout itself would be the first great rehearsal for our modern political era of bailout economics, the reaction to this temporary populist blip foreshadowed what would flower into a full-blown antigrassroots panic by the government and media elite during the Obama presidency. "Among the 133 Republicans and 95 Democrats who voted no yesterday, there are certainly some who know better, and their lack of political courage is stunning," the *Washington Post* fumed. "The usual partisan splits gave way to two new coalitions: pragmatists and wing nuts," clucked *Post* columnist Dana Milbank. "If we fail to act, the gears of our economy will grind to a halt," warned GOP presidential candidate John McCain. But some of the most spittle-flecked anger of all came from the influential big-government conservative David Brooks, whose representative rage is worth reading at length:

> Let us recognize above all the 228 who voted no—the authors of this revolt of the nihilists. They showed the world how much they detest their own leaders and the collected expertise of the Treasury and Fed. They did the momentarily popular thing, and if the country slides into a deep recession, they will have the time and leisure to watch public opinion shift against them.
>
> House Republicans led the way and will get most of the blame. It has been interesting to watch them on their single-minded mission to destroy the Republican Party. . . .
>
> Now they have once again confused talk radio with reality. If this economy slides, they will go down in history as the Smoot-Hawleys of the 21st century. With this vote, they've taken responsibility for this economy, and they will be held accountable. . . .
>
> What we need in this situation is authority. Not heavy-handed government regulation, but the steady and powerful hand of some public institutions that can guard against the corrupting influences of sloppy money and then prevent destructive contagions when the credit dries up.
>
> The Congressional plan was nobody's darling, but it was an effort to assert some authority.

Here you have the modern, Goldwater-repudiating Republican Party in all its glory: naked appeals to authority, vague hand waving about policy details, reflexive contempt for popular opinion and the party's grassroots, apocalyptic warnings about the certain horrors to come if the panic button isn't pushed, and some grossly inaccurate predictions about both economics and politics. At this, the hinge point of our modern era, the majority of Americans who had different ideas about how best to respond to the financial crisis were treated like lunatics. Forget disrespecting a minority tradition in U.S. politics; the two parties were now colluding to treat most Americans—on the left as well as the right—as if they were a danger to themselves. It was inevitable that, at a time of online political work-arounds, usable swarms, smart mobs, and all the rest, the backlash against bipartisan bailout economics would be larger than your average union protest.

Boy, has it ever been. It took just five days of the legislative bribery known as "sweeteners" ($470 million for Hollywood! More school construction in rural Republican districts!) to whip the House back into line, and the Senate's approval of the bailout—led by Mitch McConnell, John McCain, and Barack Obama—was never in doubt. Bush's initial $100 billion stimulus and $700 billion bailout were soon matched by President Obama's opening gambit of an $800 billion stimulus in February 2009. That month CNBC trading-floor shouter Rick Santelli went on an instantly famous rant against bailing out homeowners, in which he called for a new "Tea Party" to protest government policies that promoted moral hazard. The meme went viral, attaching itself to an already growing movement of citizen protests against unchecked government economic intervention (including some self-styled "Tea Party" fund-raising events for Ron Paul as far back as 2007), and within weeks there was a brand-new force to be reckoned with in American politics.

Like most people, we have our differences with the men, women, and Patrick Henry impersonators who attend Tea Party rallies (many of which we've covered), just as we have our differences with the people who attend Democratic and Republican conventions (ditto) or Star Trek conventions (don't get us started). In our view, Tea Party loyalists are far too likely to prefer military intervention, immigration restrictions, and constitutional amendments to prohibit activities they do not favor. But the movement remains so potent, in large part, because—to the extent that a headless, bottom-up, regionally varied affiliation of Meetup groups can be reduced to any one description—the Tea Party has almost totally refused to take the bait on divisive social issues, focusing instead with admirable single-mindedness on the one crisis that matters most right now: We are out of money. Check out the message discipline contained in the Tea Party's 2010 "Contract from America":

1. Protect the Constitution
2. Reject Cap & Trade
3. Demand a Balanced Budget
4. Enact Fundamental Tax Reform
5. Restore Fiscal Responsibility & Constitutionally Limited Government
6. End Runaway Government Spending
7. Defund, Repeal, & Replace Government-run Health Care
8. Pass an "All-of-the-Above" Energy Policy
9. Stop the Pork
10. Stop the Tax Hikes

You can and probably do see some items to object to there (we get creeped out when the phrase "all-of-the-above" is mentioned anywhere near "policy" or "government"). But there is no doubt as to the overall philosophy: It's the spending (and the Constitution), stupid.

Yet, that's not the impression you would get about the Tea Party movement from reading the newspaper or watching the television.

From the moment that the first TARP vote failed—which, according to a *New York Times* news analysis, somehow "captured just how much the Republican Party has changed from its 19th-century roots as the party of business and economic stewardship"—the easily understandable, clearly enunciated focus of the Tea Party movement and the stirrings behind it have been portrayed as everything but. The Tea Party, don't you know, wasn't what its leaders and legions told every reporter who interviewed them. No, it was engaged in political skullduggery that would make nineteenth-century Freemasons and Know-Nothings proud.

Tea Partiers (waggishly called "teabaggers" after an obscure, if impressively calisthenic, sexual practice) were not participating in a grand tradition of political dissent. They were angry racists deeply disturbed by a black man becoming president. "Violence" is "in the air," warned Woodrow Wilson International Center scholar Jamie Stiehm in a *Philadelphia Inquirer* op-ed that revisited the 1830s torching of an abolitionist hall in the City of Brotherly Love. "If it could happen there and then, it could happen here and now." The American Right's "recurrent" and "deep-seated problem with political violence," warned popular liberal blogger Josh Marshall, "endangers the country." The "election of Barack Obama," wrote *Mother Jones*'s James Ridgeway, "adds even more fuel to nativist rage." Lefty historian of the Right Rick Perlstein, in a *Washington Post* chat to discuss his theory that "the crazy tree blooms in every moment of liberal ascendancy," analogized anti-Obama protesters to "brownshirts" and "Nazi street thugs" in Germany's Weimar Republic, warning that "authoritarian takeovers of nations happen, they happen slowly, and it's a process." *Washington Post* columnist and regular public broadcast commentator E. J. Dionne went even further with the Nazi comparisons, describing Tea Party activism as "the politics of the jackboot." And all of those dire warnings about impending (and never arriving) Tea Party violence came within the span of just one month, August 2009.

This spasm of panicky derision, echoed nationally by such prominent voices as Jimmy Carter, Frank Rich, Bill Maher, Paul Krugman, Joan Walsh, Maureen Dowd, Michael Wolff, and David Frum (among hundreds of lesser-known lights), was just an extreme version of the same sneering condescension directed at every unauthorized political swarm over the past decade. Howard Dean's admittedly insane scream after coming up way short in the 2004 Iowa Caucus became the shorthand to describe and dismiss all of his supporters. The most recent antecedent to the Deaniac phenomenon—the largely forgotten 2000 Green Party campaign of Ralph Nader, which not only polled 2.7 percent and tipped the election to George W. Bush but also featured such hard-to-believe sights as sold-out audiences in Madison Square Garden for campaign rallies—was met with daily mockery by the political press. In 2006 the netroots kids were treated like green-eared hotheads, intemperately punishing the likes of Senator Joe Lieberman because of his patriotic support for the Iraq War. In 2008, supporters of Ron Paul were given the nickname "Paultards," and in 2010, the first stirrings of a non–Tea Party, mostly left-of-center push to make marijuana legal not just for California yuppies with a doctor's recommendation but for all adults through state referenda were greeted with scores of hoary "reefer madness" and "What were they smoking?" jokes by the Golden State political establishment. In the ossified, multibillion-dollar world of professional politics, coloring outside the lines is at best unintentionally hilarious and at worst downright dangerous to the important business of state.

The anti–Tea Party dynamic began to change in January 2010, after national Tea Party organizers flooded money and enthusiasm into Massachusetts to help elect long-shot Republican Scott Brown to Teddy Kennedy's just-gone-cold seat. Outside of the Keith Olbermanns of the world (you should go on YouTube to watch some of Olbermann's throbbing rants against the man he calls "irresponsible, homophobic, racist, reactionary, ex–nude model, teabagging supporter of violence against women"), it became kind of hard to sustain the white racist backlash narrative in a state that less than fifteen months before had a elected a black guy named Barack Hussein Obama by twenty-six percentage points.

By that time, the teabaggers had begun backing primary challengers to incumbent Republicans seen as insufficiently dedicated to the core value of limiting the size of government. Despite some way-off-kilter choices (such as Joe Miller in Alaska and Christine O'Donnell in Delaware), characters such as Rand Paul in Kentucky and Mike Lee in Utah won not only their party primaries against Establishment candidates but general elections too (Lee even unseated a long-serving senator, Robert Bennett). Most terrifyingly for the Republican Party, Tea Party activists demonstrated early on—in a special House election in upstate New York—a willingness to back a third-party candidate even at the cost of giving the election to a Democrat. Nothing shakes a major party to its core more than when the dog whistle of "Yeah, but the other team might win" no longer works.

That is in many senses how the Dean/netroots movement was reassimilated back into the Democratic Party. After successfully backing peacenik businessman Ned Lamont in a primary election versus Joe Lieberman, then losing the general election when Lieberman ran as an independent, the netroots, especially its antiwar wing, allowed itself to become totally subsumed within the Democratic Party. Howard Dean was chair of the Democratic National Committee from 2005 through 2009. Antiwar voters flocked to Barack Obama on the hope that he would govern differently than he campaigned. While he railed against "stupid wars" on the campaign trail, Obama was careful never to promise a quick and honorable withdrawal from the Middle East or Central Asia. Those hopes were projected onto him by antiwar supporters, and he did nothing to spoil the illusion. Thus domesticated, the left-wing anti-interventionist movement has been predictably ignored, as President Obama fulfilled Candidate Obama's little-noticed promise to triple down on military efforts in Afghanistan and made the case for military intervention even while accepting the Nobel Peace Prize. Shamefully, the antiwar movement is effectively dead. And all that enthusiasm and youthful innovation have been either channeled into sad-sack arguments denying that Obama has actually expanded the Bush administration's already overblown definition of executive power or misspent on regulating the Internet in the name of "Net neutrality." About the only grassroots energy and independent-bent backbone on the left is coming in libertarian-flavored efforts such as the pro-drug-legalization Just Say Now campaign by the cussedly independent progressives at Firedoglake, and in the civil liberties activism of commentators such as *Salon's* Glenn Greenwald.

By the time Rand Paul decisively won the Republican primary in Kentucky in May 2010, you'd have thought that the political elite would have been able to recognize the moment as the first great reemergence of a time-honored political tradition brought out of retirement by an interesting new political movement. Instead (or in addition), it produced mostly hoots of derision. "Rand Paul's victory in the Kentucky Republican primary is obviously a depressing event for those who support strong national defense and rational conservative politics," former Bush speechwriter David Frum wrote. "How is it that the GOP has lost its antibodies against a candidate like Rand Paul?" There it is: the insurgent candidate as a deadly virus in the body politic. Over at the Center for American Politics, a newish Washington think tank with close ties to the Obama administration, the popular liberal blogger Matthew Yglesias wrote, "By nominating a lunatic, Republicans have suddenly taken what should be a hopeless Senate race and turned it into something Democrats can win. At the same time, by nominating a lunatic, Republicans have suddenly raised the odds that a lunatic will represent Kentucky in the United States Senate."

Six months later, after surviving fierce press scrutiny and accusations by his Democratic opponent of "mocking Christianity and Christ" as a college student, Paul won the general election by a fat twelve percentage points. What did the lunatic have to say for himself? "Tonight there's a Tea Party tidal wave," the senator-elect said at the outset of a seven-minute speech that didn't once mention the word "Republican." "It's a message that I will carry with me on day one. It's a message of fiscal sanity. It's a message of limited—*limited*—constitutional government and balanced budgets. . . . America is exceptional, but it is not inherently so. . . . America will remain great if and when we understand . . . that government cannot create prosperity. . . . Do we wish to live free, or be enslaved by debt? Do we believe in the individual, or do we believe in the state? Thomas Jefferson wrote that government is best that governs least. Likewise freedom is best when enjoyed by the most." Terrifying stuff.

Within days, Senator-elect Paul was uttering words not heard from a prominent Republican in decades: The Defense budget needs to be cut. When the new Republican majority in the ostensibly more radical House of Representatives proposed $100 billion in budget cuts for 2011, Paul called for $500 billion. When his GOP colleagues talked compromise about raising the debt limit, Paul delivered a fascinating denunciation of the compromises made by his Kentucky predecessor, the legendary Henry Clay. And as Congress prepared reauthorization of the PATRIOT Act, Paul put on his turtleneck, stared into a camera, and delivered one of the most stirring defenses of the Fourth Amendment and indictments of liberty-for-security trades you'll ever lay eyes on (check it out at www.youtube.com/watch?v=ZSDBswx90Cs).

In the process, something interesting happened. Some of the same corners of American politics that painted Paul as a beyond-the-pale extremist started singing his praises. Lefties everywhere who recoiled from his criticisms of the 1964 Civil Rights Act during a cable TV interview began comparing him to the civil liberties–focused former senator Russell Feingold (who had been sent packing in the midterms by a Tea Party Republican). Even people who didn't agree with his philosophy admired the fact that he *had* one, that it was based on principle and ultimately tethered more to the independent Tea Party than a GOP full of tired hacks like Mitch McConnell, who actually walked out of the World's Greatest Deliberative Body when Paul denounced Clay. Writing at *The Nation*, John Nichols—a man who supports, among other things, a massive government bailout of media companies—argued at length that Democrats need to start taking their cue from the Paul family.

Those who would like to see the Democratic Party stand for something other than a soft variation on Republicanism might want to take a few cues—no, not all their cues, just a few—from Ron Paul.

In his [Conservative Political Action Conference] speech, Paul hailed the failure of the US House to renew the Patriot Act. But he did not stop there. He declared: "The Patriot Act, as we know, has nothing to do with patriotism—they always name it opposite of what it is. The Patriot Act is the destruction of the Fourth Amendment. That's what it's all about!"

Paul celebrated the overthrow of Egyptian President Hosni Mubarak. But he did not stop there. He declared: "How much did we invest in that dictator of the past thirty years?" he asked. "Seventy billion dollars we invested in Egypt, and guess what, the government is crumbling, the people are upset, not only with their government, but they're upset with us for propping up that public dictator for all those years." . . .

Paul decried the folly of the US occupation of Afghanistan. But he did not stop there. He declared: "It makes no sense for us to think that we can keep troops in 135 countries, 900 bases, and think that we can do it forever. . . . It's time to reassess that foreign policy. It's time for us to bring troops home." . . .

Paul criticized bloated Pentagon spending. But he did not stop there. He declared: "I'm sure half the people in this room won't cut one penny out of the military. And the military is not equated to defense. Defense spending is one thing, military spending is what Eisenhower called the military industrial complex, and we have to go after that!"

Paul condemned bailouts of big banks and corporations. But he did not stop there. He declared: "Guess who does the bailing out? The Federal Reserve used $4 billion to pass out without Congressional approval. Most people say: 'That's the Federal Reserve's job to do that.' No, it is our job to check up and find what the Federal Reserve has done, audit them and find who their buddies are that they're taking care of."

Paul's willingness to defend civil liberties without apology, to criticize dictators and the US policies that support them, to call for bringing troops home, to attack the military-industrial complex and to condemn bank bailouts and crony capitalism is not just on target. It's compelling.

If Democrats are interested in identifying themselves as anything more potent than a kinder, gentler variation on mainstream Republicanism, if they recognize that drab managerialism does not excite the American people, if they want not only to win elections but to make those wins mean something, they should borrow the best lines from Rand Paul's text.

You don't have to be a member of the Rand Paul fan club to recognize that we live in a fluid, unsettled time alive with rich political possibility. Never before has a major entitlement such as President Obama's health-care legislation been pushed through Congress with public support levels at consistently below 50 percent. Rarely has a bipartisan economic policy survived multiple years and administrations despite being reviled by solid majorities. The question isn't just about the current swarm of Tea Party activism; it's about the coming swarms of Americans who will no longer accept having their views mocked by a political class drowning in red ink.

The cultural and political moment that we live in is robustly libertarian: Most parts of our lives are based on the notion that individuals will and should have always-increasing power and autonomy over the things that matter most to them. Current politics simply don't allow for that; indeed, they are premised on the exact opposite. But independence day is upon us. Americans are now finally taking the same tools and insights that have liberated their personal lives and are applying them to their public ones. The results won't always be perfectly aligned with our own particular ideas about public policy, and that's as it should be. But only by insisting on the same kind of control over our tax dollars that we insist on having over every other bit and byte of the rest of our lives will we ensure that our own children can pursue happiness the old-fashioned way—far the hell away from politics.

THE FUTURE'S SO BRIGHT . . .

We write as sons, as grateful heirs to an America that did pretty damn well by our parents and by us too. We also write as parents of school-age kids, as worried stewards of a country whose political class is doing almost everything it can to screw our children's future more fully than Marilyn Chambers in *Behind the Green Door* or Brad Davis in *Midnight Express*.

Nick Gillespie was born in Brooklyn in 1963 to parents who were themselves born in the 1920s to off-the-boat immigrants from Ireland and Italy. They were thus charter members of the Greatest Generation, meaning that they had the privilege to live through the Great Depression and, in the case of his father, hit the beaches in Normandy during World War II and fight his way across Europe, taking German bullets in the gut along the way. Then came the postwar boom, when even uneducated folks with a decent work ethic could bump a few notches up the pecking order just by showing up and doing what they were told. Like everyone else, they fled New York in the 1960s for New Jersey (the Garden State!) and managed to buy a house with a green lawn every bit as unbelievable to them as Gatsby's far larger one on the Long Island Sound was to that tragic figure.

Matt Welch was born in 1968 and grew up in the Southern California Levittown of Lakewood Village and Long Beach, home to aerospace, baseball, and the punk band TSOL (True Sounds of Liberty), not necessarily in that order. His parents, both born in 1939, were members of the Silent Generation, producing four kids and a classic suburban tract home before most Baby Boomers had graduated from (or dropped out of) college. They, too, exceeded the scope and quality of life of their hardworking parents, laboring primarily not with their hands but with their minds, moving on from a sleepy Pacific Northwest childhood with sporadic indoor plumbing to young adult life in Cuban Missile Crisis Manhattan before finally living the California dream (including, to be sure, its periodic nightmares).

Our parents' America had an infinite number of failings. Organization men paid for their relative standing with ulcers and subservience; smart women found far too many of their dreams thwarted by a world not yet ready for anything approaching gender equality. Racial, ethnic, and sexual minorities were not merely harassed but blocked from full citizenship, sometimes by law, sometimes by custom. But for the most part, to quote from one of the worst Beatles songs ever recorded, things were getting better all the time.

Coming of age in the 1970s and 1980s amid oil shocks, inflation, divorce, killer bees, the slim but real threat of thermonuclear annihilation, tricolored baseball uniforms, religious revivals, and record levels of drug use by everyone but Welch, we developed a sense of the apocalyptic and the ironic (they go together better than Cheech & Chong). Sure, the world was going off the rails, but to an undersupervised adolescent, that's a feature, not a bug. Freed from what the great Cardinals outfielder Curt Flood rightly likened to slavery, athletes, musicians, and actors alike could not only earn something approaching what they were worth but speak their minds on subjects they knew nothing about and grow afros the size of small planets. Women could start talking back to men, infiltrating old boys' clubs, and kicking ass like Billie Jean King mopping up the court with a wheezing Bobby Riggs. Hollywood was paranoid, mean, and great. Punk rock was bubbling up like poison from the suburbs, *Saturday Night Live* was still unfriendly to Democrats, and *Sesame Street* was even interesting for a couple of episodes there. How did it ever take so long for America to loosen up and undo those top three buttons?

Latchkey kids in a latchkey world, we learned early on the value of independence and autonomy, based on the realization that even those who loved you first and foremost wouldn't, couldn't, or shouldn't always be there to bail you out and clean your wounds, let alone prevent injury in the first place. Authority rightly took a beating in our most formative years. The accumulated evidence of Vietnam, Watergate, the Church Commission, *Who's Next* (featuring the anthemic "Won't Get Fooled Again" and a cover image of millionaire rock stars urinating in public), movies as different as *The Godfather* and *The Bad News Bears*, Jimmy Carter's cardigan-clad incompetence, and Ronald Reagan's dress rehearsal for Alzheimer's during the Iran-Contra charade all taught us that politics was not the answer; politics was the problem. That last point was nailed into our consciousness by the epic events of the year 1989, when in China and Eastern Europe regular people rose up not so they could participate even more in mandatory neighborhood watch meetings but so such things would disappear forever.

We were not natural libertarians, nursed on the wizened breast of Ayn Rand or fed formula from Milton Friedman and F. A. Hayek. We went to public schools for all or part of our educations (as do/will our kids), walked without a second's hesitation on public sidewalks, and are still not averse to calling tax-funded fire departments (though we will defend your right to pay for supplemental fire insurance in hazardous brushfire areas!). We consumed more modernist literature than Austrian economics and thrilled especially to the countercultural derring-do of the Beats and protohippies. We were jingoistic enough to be outraged when the East German women's swim team cheated its way to gold in the 1976 Olympics and dug it when Bruce Jenner dethroned Nikolai Avilov as the world's greatest athlete in that Summer Games decathlon. We were both glued to the boob tube in anticipation of Gerald Ford's utterly anticlimactic *Bicentennial Minutes* segment (which, true to the minimized expectations of the era, clocked in at a mere forty-two seconds) and generally prefer mid-1970s Elton John to any-era Rush.

But at key early moments for both of us, we also encountered *Reason* magazine, the publication that we would end up working for, which gave the alluring promise from its inaugural issue of "logic, not legends"—truth, not the usual bullshit. Along with it came the futuretastic optimism of creating what the philosopher Robert Nozick called a "utopia of utopias," a framework encompassing all different visions of how the good life could be tried. Gillespie's older brother went to college and started sending the magazine back home. Welch's stepfather had the publication around the house, along with some alluring Robert Heinlein sci-fi and some less appealing doorstops by the most original writer since Aristotle (her description), Ayn Rand.

Our early adulthood coincided with freedom in Central Europe, where Welch lived for most of the 1990s, and the rise of the Internet as a mass phenomenon, which let Gillespie telecommute to the coasts from a Texas prison town. Margaret Mead once said that all children grow up in a different country than their parents, and we're more than living proof of that. Gillespie's father didn't ride in a car until he was ten years old, and his mother didn't speak English until she entered a grammar school that told her all dagos were dumb. Welch's father "fought Sputnik" in a long aerospace career anchored in the Cold War, and his mother became a director of nursing back when that was as far up as a female hospital administrator could expect to go.

We know that our kids are growing up in a very different and for the most part a much better world than we did. Gillespie has two sons, ages seventeen and ten. Welch has a daughter, soon to turn three. What kind of nation will they inherit? What kind of future will they face? Will they—and possibly their children too—be paying for unpopular, ill-conceived, and incompetently prosecuted wars in Iraq and Afghanistan that will (hopefully) end before they can vote? Will they be paying for free and reduced-price prescription drugs for grandparents who died before they were born? Will they be taxed so that zombie versions of *Time* and *Newsweek* and the *San Francisco Chronicle* can be preserved in the name of some quaint mid-twentieth-century vision of "civic journalism"? Will they be taxed more and more to pay for lower and lower levels of state-run health care? Will the Internet still be an autonomous zone when they make it to college, or will it have been straitjacketed by government regulators seeking to prove their own relevance? Will the federal debt have finally reached 100 percent or more of GDP, and will they be living in a world where the single biggest budget item their skyrocketing taxes pay for is vigorish on money that never should have been borrowed in 2011?

The good news for them is that the existential threat of communism and the Cold War that underwrote our childhoods is dead and buried, and despite the abject horror of the 9/11 attacks, radical Islamic terrorism is no serious threat to our way of life or even the future of the globe. Terrorism of whatever origin is the herpes of international conflict, more a chronic and occasionally painful breakout, not a twilight struggle, thanks be to Allah. Who knows—with each passing day of early 2011, the unthinkable prospect of a semidemocratic Middle East gets tantalizingly closer in our headlights.

The bad news is that we are facing yet another hinge point in history, this one almost entirely of our own damn making. The first decade of the twenty-first century—God, that seemed so far in the future only thirty years ago—was a bigger bust than the final Fátima revelation, the second *Star Wars* trilogy, and the presidency of George W. Bush put together. The government is broke in literal, figurative, and even spiritual terms. The programs and mentality that still darken too many aspects of our daily lives are relics born of prehistoric fears that people really can't be trusted to live their own lives according to their own desires. Power, goes this line of thinking that still patrols Washington's corridors, statehouses across the country, and city halls in every zip code, must be centralized and titrated into small but immensely influential concentrations that can dictate how the rest of us should live, think, feel, and love. Around the globe, currents of history are moving in the opposite direction, whether it's the end of state capitalism in Europe (which had slashed public spending as a percentage of GDP over the past few decades before the global recession) and autocracy in the Middle East (where even the "most docile" of Arab countries such as Egypt are tossing off tyrants such as Hosni Mubarak like so many bugs). And as we have documented in the previous pages, Americans have spent the past forty or so years routing around the government and its top-down controls to found flourishing ecosystems in what John Stuart Mill called "experiments in living."

There was a song that was briefly but hugely popular in the second half of the 1980s, as we stumbled toward adulthood. It was called "The Future's So Bright I Gotta Wear Shades":

> *Things are going great, and they're only getting better*
> *I'm doing all right, getting good grades*
> *The future's so bright, I gotta wear shades*

Dripping in irony, the song still captures the instinctive American belief that whatever comes next, despite the worst efforts of every bad guy out there, people will somehow figure out a way to improve things. That is the ultimate appeal of libertarian thought, policy, and prepolitical comportment to us: Unlike sour nostalgia for a golden age that never was or obsession with a restrictive vision of the one and only heaven, libertarianism always places a confident, all-chips-on-black wager on the ability of free individuals to invent more and more interesting choices for how we can live our hyphenated lives. Our kids, we most fervently believe, will get to do stuff we cannot imagine—not watching old TV shows on iPads or spending workdays sifting through cross-tabulated statistics of the 1979 Angels, but maybe vacationing in a different solar system or building a house without having to apply for a zoning variance.

Yes, the future will be so bright, we'll have to wear shades or, preferably, money-back-guaranteed optical implants with complimentary lifetime upgrades. But the course of human events has come knocking, so if we want to purchase our children's freedom from the dreary slog and atavistic zero-sum scrum of politics and cronyism, we're going to have to work right now so they can declare their own independence later. That, above all, is the inheritance we hope to give them: the freedom to flourish or fail, on their own terms, pursuing happiness as they define it.

ACKNOWLEDGMENTS

This book would not have been possible without the long-term intellectual and institutional support of our boss, Reason Foundation president David Nott. Of our predecessors at Reason magazine, special thanks go to Virginia Postrel, for finding (and developing) value in us that others didn't see; Bob Poole, for creating and sustaining our organization; and Lanny Friedlander (1947–2011), who was just crazy and inspired enough to lift this ship off the ground back in 1968.

Everybody at the magazine, foundation, and Reason.tv has a little of their DNA in this book, for which we offer gratitude and the hope we haven't embarrassed them too much. Extra thanks to Mike Alissi, a war-time and peacetime consigliere, and to Jesse Walker, Katherine Mangu-Ward, Damon Root, Ted Balaker, and Chris Mitchell for helping make sure our day jobs continued getting done.

Our agent Kate Lee at ICM offered encouragement and ideas. Lisa Kaufman of PublicAffairs helped clarify our argument and wrestle it into print. Over the years, we bounced many, if not most, of our ideas off a long list of people. All errors and mistakes are our own, but we were made smarter by conversations with folks including Ronald Bailey, Peter Bagge, Radley Balko, Greg Beato, Bill Beaman, David Boaz, Meredith Bragg, Drew Carey, Tim Cavanaugh, Veronique de Rugy, Brian Doherty,

ACKNOWLEDGMENTS

Charles Paul Freund, John Gillespie, Katharine Gillespie, Maureen Gillespie, Kristi Kendall, Matt Kibbe, Terry Kibbe, David Kirby, John Mackey, Deirdre McCloskey, Voros McCracken, Michael C. Moynihan, Andrew Napolitano, Gerry Ohrstrom, Glenn Reynolds, Matt Ridley, Scott Ross, Louis Rossetto, Jack Shafer, John Stagliano, John Stossel, Peter Suderman, Jacob Sullum, and Harry Teasley.

On a personal level, Nick Gillespie wishes to thank Veronique de Rugy, whose collaboration has not only improved his life tremendously but made his future far more likely to happen. Matt Welch wishes to thank the entire Richard family, and Emmanuelle Richard in particular, for the kind of time-saving TLC and complaint-free burden-sharing that this Amerloque neither deserves nor takes for granted. Merci!

NOTES AND SOURCES

For a more detailed, hyperlinked, and up-to-the-minute list of sourcing for the material in this book, please consult gillespie-welch.com. The following provides some additional chapter notes.

FOREWORD TO THE PAPERBACK EDITION

USA Today's December 2011 story about large number of voters leaving the Democratic and Republican parties is available online at http://www.usatoday.com/NEWS/usaedition/2011-12-23-independents 22_ST_U.htm and remains bracing reading for anyone hopeful that change is coming to the same-old, same-old of electoral politics. Gallup's archive is online at gallup.com and provides a user-friendly guide to changing attitudes over the past seven decades. The Reason-Rupe Poll, a new quarterly opinion poll that's administered by the non-profit that publishes *Reason* magazine and Reason.com, is building a database of results as well and is online at reason.com/poll.

Many of the trends described in the paperback edition of this book will fluctuate as the 2012 election approaches and recedes, but we remain confident that the long-term trends toward loss of faith in partisan labels and the government's ability to effect positive change will continue.

Data and analysis of government revenue and outlays is available online at whitehouse.gov and cbo.gov, among other sites.

PROLOGUE: PURSUING HAPPINESS, NOT POLITICS

Regarding our current "bizarre snapshot in time," it's useful to compare the relevant politicians' own dire fiscal warnings—start with President Barack Obama's National Commission on Fiscal Responsibility and Reform (www.fiscalcommission.gov)—with their stunningly impotent proposals to do anything about them. That goes for Republican "fiscal hawks" as well. The only reality checks on that front are happening at the state and local levels, and even there, 2011 is basically the first year since the housing market began tanking in 2008 that states have had to absorb the costs of their own fiscal recklessness.

CHAPTER 1: BEYOND DUOPOLY

Perhaps the best example of existence-bias punditry in 2011 came in January, when controversial Foreign Policy analyst Stephen M. Walt wrote a piece titled "Why the Tunisian Revolution Won't Spread." Though Walt was correct in noting, "In fact, the history of world revolution suggests that this sort of revolutionary cascade is quite rare," he let the rare become the enemy of the possible.

Every journalism school should—but doesn't—present the hysterical reaction to the AOL Time Warner merger as Example A of why journalists are often the very worst analysts of their own industry. As the deal was unfolding in 2000, the still-ubiquitous media-ethics scold Tom Rosenstiel warned about "a new era in American communications that sees the end of an independent press." The even more influential Robert McChesney, who is one of the key people in the push to have the Federal Communications Commission regulate the Internet, predicted confidently that "the eventual course of the Internet—the central nervous system of our era—will be determined by where the most money can be made, regardless of the social and political implications." We were two of the only media commentators to laugh off the fear and cast doubt on the conglomerate's future in real time. In April 2000, Nick Gillespie noted that large mergers more often fail than succeed and argued, "The moment [the new company] stops doing whatever its customers want, it will join the ranks of Sears Roebuck, A&P, IBM, and other once-dominant companies that have either disappeared altogether or linger on as mere shadows of their former selves." Matt Welch wrote that "very few market-leading companies in entertainment or media stay on top for long; most go bankrupt;" that "very few mega-mergers between two companies in different businesses ever work, especially when the companies involved are in media and entertainment;" and that "the Internet is more tumultuous than any business sector in generations. The mighty are frequently chastened within 24 months." As it turned out, it took about thirty months for AOL Time to begin to dissolve.

Turn-of-the-1990s Nipponophobia—contemporaneously debunked in *Reason* (see Oren Grad's "Blinded by the Sun," www.reason.com /archives/1994/11/01/blinded-by-the-sun)—was another cultural spasm that can't be mocked enough. Longtime liberal columnist Richard Reeves, as one of a thousand examples, took to the pages of the *Los Angeles Times* to denounce a planned $150 million subway construction contract awarded to Sumitomo as national "hara-kari."

Larry F. Darby's fascinating work on duopolies and other economic matters can be found at www.theamericanconsumer.org/author/larry.

The average newspaper-company profit margin in the annus horribilus of 2009 (the last year for which data have been crunched) was still 8 percent, according to the Project for Excellence in Journalism.

CHAPTER 2: THE PIT AND THE PENDULUM

For instances of Republican triumphalism during George W. Bush's presidency, search out pieces such as David Brooks's February 2, 2002, Weekly Standard article, "The Reemerging Republican Majority," and his August 29, 2004, *New York Times Magazine* feature, "How to Reinvent the G.O.P."; Grover Norquist's "The Democratic Party Is Toast" in the September 2004 issue of *Washington Monthly*; and Hugh Hewitt's 2006 book, *Painting the Map Red: The Fight to Create a Permanent Republican Majority*. In 2008, it was time for Democrats to crow. See, for example, the November 7, 2008, POLITICO story "Dems Talk of 'Permanent Progressive Majority.'" In March 2009, Center for American Progress demographer Ruy Teixeira released a study titled "New Progressive America," which charted ironclad rises in Democratic voting blocs and led to headlines such as "Permanent Democratic Majority: New Study Says Yes" at the *Huffington Post*.

The *Washington Post*'s 2001 compendium *Deadlocked: The Inside Story of America's Closest Election* and Larry Sabato's *Overtime! The Election 2000 Thriller* provide copious details on the ins and outs of George W. Bush's eventual victory in the contested 2000 election.

Graydon Carter's 2004 *What We've Lost: How the Bush Administration Has Curtailed Our Freedoms, Mortgaged Our Economy, Ravaged Our Environment, and Damaged Our Standing in the World* catalogs the *Vanity Fair* editor's case against Bush in even greater detail than the book's subtitle.

David Boaz and David Kirby's "The Libertarian Vote in the Age of Obama" (www.cato.org/pub_display.php?pub_id=11152) and earlier voter studies are available on the Cato Institute's website (www.cato.org).

Mark Tushnet's *A Court Divided: The Rehnquist Court and the Future of Constitutional Law* (2005) is a fair and engrossing account of the Supreme Court from a left-liberal perspective. Chris Anderson's 2006 *The Long Tail: Why the Future of Business Is Selling More of Less* is a guide to much more than online commerce; see also *Reason*'s November 2006 interview with Anderson, "Welcome to Niche Nation," www.reason.com/archives/2006/09/22/welcome-to-niche-nation1), which explores many of the cultural and political implications of proliferating consumer choice.

CHAPTER 3: THE LIBERTARIAN MOMENT

This chapter expands and updates an essay that appeared in the December 2008 issue of *Reason* celebrating the magazine's fortieth anniversary. We also wrote about similar trends in a March 2008 cover story for *Politics* magazine and in pieces for the *Washington Post* and *Los Angeles Times*.

All discussions of the 1970s should begin (and probably end) with Tom Wolfe's "The 'Me' Decade and the Third Great Awakening," published in 1976, which remains one of the most illuminating analyses not simply of its time but of the current moment too. David Frum's *How We Got Here* (2000) is a great read and gestures toward evenhandedness ("The '70s: The Decade That Brought You Modern Life—for Better or Worse") before condemning the period for its high divorce rates and proliferation of gay bars and glory holes. Bruce Shulman's *The Seventies: The Great Shift in American Culture, Politics, and Society* (2001) goes easier on the period and also provides an excellent catalog of all sorts of weirdness long since forgotten or repressed.

Milton and Rose Friedman's *Free to Choose: A Personal Statement*, a 1980 PBS series and bestselling book, is a primer on libertarian public policy in areas ranging from school choice to free trade; David Boaz's *Libertarianism* (1997) and Charles Murray's *What It Means to Be a Libertarian* (1996) are rich in historical and philosophical details, and Albert O. Hirshman's 1970 treatise on political economy, *Exit, Voice, and Loyalty*, has heavily influenced our thinking. Former *Reason* editor Virginia Postrel's *The Future and Its Enemies* is a profound reconfiguring of the ideological spectrum that remains as relevant now as when it was first published in 1998.

Freedom House's country rankings are online at freedomhouse.org, and the *St. Petersburg Times'* Pulitzer Prize–winning site PolitiFact (politifact.com) is an invaluable source for journalists and citizens alike—even when it's wrong, which it is from time to time.

University of Alabama historian David Beito's *From Mutual Aid to the Welfare State: Fraternal Societies and Social Services, 1890–1967*

(2000) documents the world of charity organizations before the government took over more and more of such operations, ranging from providing food to health care to pensions to insurance and legal services.

CHAPTER 4: KEEP ON ROCKIN' IN THE FREE WORLD

Though the 2000 Democratic National Convention image most people can't erase from their heads is the extended smash-mouth kiss between Al Gore and his then wife, those inside the convention hall were also subjected to a bongo-playing revue called "Drums for Tipper," which tried to prove that the would-be First Lady and former drummer could indeed dance. For more on the comical "Filthy Fifteen" songs denounced by Mrs. Gore's Parents Music Resource Center, see www .reason.com/blog/2007/07/11/remembering-the-gores-and-the.

The Velvet Revival Band—featuring the late Milan Hlavsa on bass and objectively a much better live band than the Velvet Underground (VU) had ever been—was the go-to party/event band in Prague after the Velvet Revolution. Lead singer Jan Macháček, in addition to being a cosignatory of Charter 77 and a main artistic force behind the respected Czech band Garáž ("Garage"), is one of the best economic journalists in the country. He was disappointed upon meeting Lou Reed in 1990 that the man he'd been mimicking for years was pretty "stupid."

Velvet Underground drummer Moe Tucker made a thousand aging VU fans shudder in horror after news spread in late 2010 that she had attended—gasp!—a Tea Party rally. "Must admit I'm very shaken," *Slate*'s Jacob Weisberg tweeted, in sadness more than anger.

Václav Havel's rock fandom was such that he took just about every graybeard Western rock band that made it through Prague during the 1990s—the Rolling Stones several times, Paul Simon, the remains of Pink Floyd—out for beers at one of his favorite local pubs. Then again, he did the same with many heads of state, including Bill Clinton.

For more on Havel, see *Reason*'s "Velvet President" (www.reason
.com/archives/2003/05/01/velvet-president) and read his *Open Letters: Selected Writings, 1965–1990*, *Disturbing the Peace*, and *Summer
Meditations*.

CHAPTER 5: YOU ARE NOW FREE TO MOVE ABOUT THE COUNTRY

For more on the notorious Consumer Product Safety Improvement Act,
which protected Mattel at the expense of do-it-yourself craft toymakers,
see *Reason*'s "Dangerous Toys, Strange Bedfellows" (www.reason.com
/archives/2009/05/18/dangerous-toys-strange-bedfell/singlepage).

In 2010, former vice president Al Gore belatedly concluded that
ethanol subsidies were a policy and environmental "mistake" and
pointed out that "it's hard once such a program is put in place to deal
with the lobbies that keep it going." Yet, the next month, the annual
$6 billion in destructive, inflation-spiking corporate welfare was ex-
tended for another year.

If you don't know about the inextricable link between ObamaCare
and the Pharmaceutical Researchers and Manufacturers of America—
"whose $26.1 million lobbying effort in 2009 was the most expensive
by any industry lobby in history"—Google the astounding work of
D.C. *Examiner* lobbying columnist Timothy P. Carney.

For more on the late, great Alfred Kahn, see Welch's *Reason* blog
post titled "On the Passing of a Liberal Deregulator" (www.reason
.com/blog/2011/01/03/on-the-passing-of-a-liberal-de), which links to a
Financial Times obituary by economist Thomas Hazlett, plus some past
Reason interviews and links to Jimmy Carter's views on deregulation.

Robert Poole's retrospective comments about deregulation come from
a December 2008 oral history of *Reason* (www.reason.com/archives
/2008/11/17/40-years-of-free-minds-and-fre), assembled from interviews
by Senior Editor Brian Doherty, also author of the must-read history
*Radicals for Capitalism: A Freewheeling History of the Modern American
Libertarian Movement*.

For more on the European low-cost air revolution, see *Reason*'s "Fly the Frugal Skies" (www.reason.com/archives/2005/01/01/fly-the-frugal -skies).

CHAPTER 6: THE DISORGANIZATION MAN (AND WOMAN)

Time magazine's annual "Time 100" lists are available online at time .com.

Bill James started publishing his annual baseball abstracts in 1977. In 1985, Villard published his *Historical Baseball Abstract*, a multi-authored volume that included endlessly readable disquisitions on everything from how racial segregation affected baseball statistics to Shoeless Joe Jackson's culpability in throwing the 1919 World Series to the decline of mean nicknames such as "Dummy" and "Three-Finger." The book was revised in 1988 and again in 2001. His books are not simply joys to read for baseball obsessives; they are excellent examples of persuasive writing in that James always explains in detail how he reaches a particular conclusion.

A 2009 Pew Economic Mobility Project study (available online) concludes the "American economy promotes upward mobility over two-and ten-year periods just as well as it has in the past." Paul Krugman's *The Conscience of a Liberal* (2007) and *The Return of Depression Economics and the Crisis of 2008* (2009), along with his *Times* columns and blogging, are best read in conjunction with Brink Lindsey's *The Age of Abundance: How Prosperity Transformed America's Politics and Culture* (2007) and Lindsey's June 2009 essay in *Reason*, "Nostalgianomics."

CHAPTER 7: RISE OF THE MUTANTS

Grant McCracken's Plenitude 2.0 is available for download from www.cultureby.com/site/wp-content/uploads/2010/05/Plenitude2.0 -for-pdf-may-2010.pdf. His most recent book, *Chief Culture Office* (2010), continues to build on related insights, and his blog at www

.cultureby.com is a lively read. For a distilled version of his thoughts on plenitude, read "The Politics of Plenitude," in the August/September 2008 issue of *Reason*.

MIT media studies professor Henry Jenkins's 1992 *Textual Poaching: Television Fans and Participatory Culture* is an early and influential attempt to adapt ideas of *détournement* to the digital age. Though the examples discussed in the book are now dated—they include such pre-Internet phenomena as *Star Trek* fan fiction and VCR tape dubbing of shows such as *Magnum, P.I.*—Jenkins articulates the rules by which new technologies enable individuals to alter themselves and their cultural identities.

CHAPTER 8: WE THE MEDIA

The American craft beer revolution, which as people who went to college in the 1980s or before can testify is almost impossible to even *believe*, is documented and celebrated in the *Reason* archives at www .reason.com/archives/2009/02/24/draft-dodgers and www.reason.tv /video/show/683.html.

Rich Lederer grew up on the same street as Welch. For more about his role in Bert Blyleven's election, see *Reason*'s "How a Part-Time Blogger Changed the Face of Baseball's Hall of Fame" (www.reason .com/blog/2011/01/05/how-a-part-time-blogger-change).

For more on bottom-up media and its implications for modern life, read Glenn Reynolds's *Army of Davids*, Chris Anderson's *The Long Tail*, and the continuing media analyses of Jack Shafer, Jay Rosen, William Powers, and Jeff Jarvis. Other *Reason* texts include Gillespie's "Culture Boom" (www.reason.com/archives/1999/04/01/all-culture-all-the-time), Welch's "Woe Is Media" (www.reason.com/archives /2002/12/01/woe-is-media), and Ben Compaine's "Domination Fantasies" (www.reason.com/archives/2004/01/01/domination-fantasies).

The anti–Proposition 19 editorials by California's daily newspapers must be read to be believed. Start with *Reason*'s "Anti–Prop. 19 Editorials

Update; Lord's Burning Rain Edition" (www.reason.com/blog/2010 /10/19/anti-prop-19-editorials-update) and work your way back through the links.

New York University journalism professor Jay Rosen, mentioned above, is a must-read source on modern media. His "View from Nowhere" writings are collected at www.pressthink.org/2010/11/the -view-from-nowhere-questions-and-answers. We also highly recommend his lecture titled "The Journalists Formerly Known as the Media: My Advice to the Next Generation" (www.jayrosen.posterous .com/the-journalists-formerly-known-as-the-media-m).

For more on the ideology of post-ideology, see *Reason's* "No Labels, and the Ideology of Post-Ideology" (www.reason.com/archives/2010 /12/20/no-labels-and-the-ideology-of).

Robert McChesney and John Nichols expanded their 2009 *Nation* essay into a book titled *The Death and Life of American Journalism: The Media Revolution That Will Begin the World Again*, which Welch reviews in "Bailing Out Big Brother" (www.reason.com/archives/2010 /03/22/bailing-out-big-brother).

The definitive piece on how Barack Obama has worked to foist "Net Neutrality" onto a blasé nation is Peter Suderman's "Internet Cop" (www.reason.com/archives/2011/02/08/internet-cop).

CHAPTER 9: WE ARE SO OUT OF MONEY

W. Michael Cox and Richard Alm's *Myths of Rich and Poor: Why We're Better Off Than We Think* (1999) and the series of annual essays they wrote for the Dallas Federal Reserve from 1990 to 2007 are among the best discussions of income distribution, economic churn, and growth in living standards for the period covered by this book.

Gillespie lives part-time in Oxford, Ohio, not far from Cincinnati, whose city politics he takes grim pleasure in following. Rail boondoggles have long been a topic of interest at *Reason*, since they combine eminent domain, lavish subsidies, edifice-complex-obsessed politicians, and other awful elements of government overreach. Peter Bagge's cartoon essay, "Amtrak Sucks," in *Reason*'s December 2005 issue and the March 2010 Reason.tv video "3 Reasons Why Obama's High-Speed Rail Will Go Nowhere Fast" are representative critiques.

Reason's cover stories from May 2009, "Failed States," and February 2010, "Class War," are detailed accounts of how state spending has grown far beyond most voters' and taxpayers' understanding. Discussion of public-sector compensation is a regular topic at Reason.com; "What's Round on the Ends and High in the Middle? Ohio's Public Sector Salaries, That's What" (www.reason.com/blog/2010/07/07 /whats-round-on-the-ends-and-hi) is a good starting point for our coverage. The March 2011 *Reason* story "The 19 Percent Solution," written by Gillespie and Mercatus Center economist Veronique de Rugy, is the source for many of our budget recommendations for federal spending.

CHAPTER 10: YOUR MIND, YOUR HEALTH, AND YOUR RETIREMENT ARE TERRIBLE THINGS TO WASTE

The National Center for Education Statistics provides an enormous amount of data online at nces.ed.gov. The National Assessment for Educational Progress is available at www.nces.ed.gov/nationsreport-card. For a discussion of the weighted-student formula and an interview with Arlene Ackerman, the woman who brought the concept to San Francisco's schools, read "The Agony of American Education" in the March 2006 issue of *Reason* (www.reason.com/issues/april-2006). *Reason*'s archive on education can be found at www.reason.com/topics /education.

Ronald Bailey's October 20, 2009, column, "In Health Care, Nobody Knows Anything" (www.reason.com/archives/2009/10/20/health -care-nihilism), is a depressing but essential starting point for understanding just how screwed up the insurance markets are in the United States. In 2006's *The Cure: How Capitalism Can Save American Health*

Care, David Gratzer, a Canadian-trained doctor who works with the Manhattan Institute, brings a rare international perspective to improving treatments.

Social Security is a topic of continuing debate at *Reason*, and our constantly updated archive is online at www.reason.com/topics/social -security. A particularly interesting debate took place in 2005 between James K. Glassman and Tyler Cowen during President Bush's quickly abandoned bid to allow individuals to invest some portion of their payroll taxes in personal accounts. That exchange, titled "The Death of Social Security," can be read at www.reason.com/archives/2005 /04/01/the-death-of-social-security. Michael Tanner's 2003 study for the Cato Institute, "The Better Deal: Estimating Rates of Return Under a System of Individual Accounts," is online at www.cato.org/pubs /ssps/ssp31.pdf.

CHAPTER 11: THE PERMANENT NONGOVERNING MINORITY

There's plenty more about the Republican Party's explicit rejection of libertarianism between 1998 and 2008 in Welch's *McCain: The Myth of a Maverick.*

Just before the November 2010 election, former Howard Dean campaign manager and all-around netroots guru Joe Trippi told a skeptical audience at a taping of Fox Business Network's libertarian show *Stossel* that Tea Partiers shared much in common with 2004 Deaniacs. Though the crowd protested, Trippi was right.

If you're interested in knowing more about libertarians' general (and generally split) take on the Tea Party, read the 2009 *Reason* debate among Brink Lindsey, Jonah Goldberg, and Matt Kibbe titled "Where Do Libertarians Belong" (www.reason.com/archives/2010 /07/12/where-do-libertarians-belong).

Ralph Nader's 2000 campaign, like Dean's in 2004 and Barack Obama's in 2008, promised to galvanize "the Democratic wing of the Democratic Party." Though Nader himself is often baffled by technology, the impressive (if short-lived) movement that sprang up around him was incredibly tech-savvy.

In February 2011, news outlets like Reuters were already calling Rand Paul "Captain America of the U.S. Senate" (http://blogs.reuters .com/frontrow/2011/02/08/is-rand-paul-a-u-s-senate-action-hero).

EPILOGUE: THE FUTURE'S SO BRIGHT . . .

Gillespie joined the staff of *Reason* in October 1993, after applying for an assistant editor position advertised in the magazine. He became editor in chief of the print edition in 2000 and moved on to Reason.com and Reason.tv in 2008. Welch joined the staff in 2003, moved to the *Los Angeles Times* opinion page in 2005, and returned to helm the magazine in 2008.

"The Future's So Bright, I Gotta Wear Shades" was released in 1986 by Timbuk3, a band out of Madison, Wisconsin. It was the group's only chart success; the members threw in the towel in 1995.

INDEX

KENNY MORRISON

CRAIG WADLIN

Nick Gillespie is the editor-in-chief of the websites Reason.tv and Reason.com and **Matt Welch** heads up the print edition of *Reason*, which since 1968 has been "a kick-ass, no-holds-barred political magazine" (*New York Post*) whose "refusal to carry water for the Republicans or Democrats is deeply refreshing in this age of partisan bickering" (*Folio*). Follow the authors on Twitter (@nickgillespie, @mleewelch, @reason), Facebook, and online at gillespie-welch.com.

PublicAffairs is a publishing house founded in 1997. It is a tribute to the standards, values, and flair of three persons who have served as mentors to countless reporters, writers, editors, and book people of all kinds, including me.

I. F. Stone, proprietor of *I. F. Stone's Weekly*, combined a commitment to the First Amendment with entrepreneurial zeal and reporting skill and became one of the great independent journalists in American history. At the age of eighty, Izzy published *The Trial of Socrates*, which was a national bestseller. He wrote the book after he taught himself ancient Greek.

Benjamin C. Bradlee was for nearly thirty years the charismatic editorial leader of *The Washington Post*. It was Ben who gave the *Post* the range and courage to pursue such historic issues as Watergate. He supported his reporters with a tenacity that made them fearless and it is no accident that so many became authors of influential, best-selling books.

Robert L. Bernstein, the chief executive of Random House for more than a quarter century, guided one of the nation's premier publishing houses. Bob was personally responsible for many books of political dissent and argument that challenged tyranny around the globe. He is also the founder and longtime chair of Human Rights Watch, one of the most respected human rights organizations in the world.

•   •   •

For fifty years, the banner of Public Affairs Press was carried by its owner Morris B. Schnapper, who published Gandhi, Nasser, Toynbee, Truman, and about 1,500 other authors. In 1983, Schnapper was described by *The Washington Post* as "a redoubtable gadfly." His legacy will endure in the books to come.

Peter Osnos, *Founder and Editor-at-Large*

Printed in the USA
CPSIA information can be obtained
at www.ICGtesting.com
LVHW041228011123
762292LV00004B/113